D1562781

A Bold Return
to Giving a Damn

A Bold Return to Giving a Damn

One Farm, Six Generations,
and the Future of Food

Will Harris III

with Amely Greeven

VIKING

VIKING
An imprint of Penguin Random House LLC
penguinrandomhouse.com

LIBRARY OF CONGRESS CATALOGING-IN-PUBLICATION DATA
Names: Harris, Will, III, author.
Title: A bold return to giving a damn : one farm, six generations, and
the future of food / Will Harris III and Amely Greeven.
Description: New York : Viking, [2023]
Identifiers: LCCN 2023003675 | ISBN 9780593300473 (hardcover) |
ISBN 9780593300480 (ebook)
Subjects: LCSH: Farms. | Agriculture. | Animal welfare.
Classification: LCC HD1393 .H33 2023 | DDC 338.1068—dc23/eng/20230626
LC record available at https://lccn.loc.gov/2023003675

Printed in the United States of America
1st Printing

Designed by Nicole Laroche

I dedicate this book to the generations of my family that came before me, who took the risks and made the sacrifices that allowed me to do the same for the generations who will come after me.

There is nothing more difficult to take in hand, more perilous to conduct, or more uncertain in its success, than to take the lead in the introduction of a new order of things.

—Niccolo Machiavelli, political theorist

||||||||||||||||||||||||||||||||||

We pray for plenty of good hard work to do and the strength to do it.

—*Harris family prayer*

Contents

Introduction

I have a story to tell. It's about the way that farming and food production oughta be—a different kind of farming from what most people today think is normal. A better way of raising food. What I've got to share is not a scientific white paper stacked full of technical knowledge. It reads closer to a fable—except that it's verifiably rooted in real events. It's one that my family, the Harrises of Bluffton, Georgia—sometimes referred to as the Damn Harrises—has lived over the last hundred-and-sixty-odd years.

It's a story about farming done the old ways, in harmony with nature, and the rapid takeover of those ways by profit-driven industrial methods, and the terrible effects of those new methods on the land, the animals, and rural America. There was too much money involved to get these damaging methods outlawed by legislators—too much greed, stupidity, excess, and corporate malfeasance—but a few farmers figured out how to farm in ways that could mitigate the damage that the misapplied technology had wrought. So they did them, returning to a kinder, gentler type of agriculture that emulated nature. They circled back to those older methods practiced in their family lines.

Since the farmers weren't using products purchased from corporations, no agricultural researchers wrote papers about them, and no advertising campaigns told the public what kind of good food they were raising. No deep pockets funded slews of eager salespeople in new pickups to spread the knowledge to other farmers. Which meant it was up to the farmers to tell what they had learned.

I am one of those farmers. And I want to share with you what I did on my family's farm, White Oak Pastures, to take farming and food production back from the extremes it's gotten horribly stuck in—extremes of excess, and resource use, and animal cruelty, and of profit for everyone in the food chain but the farmer him- or herself—and bring it back to what some call pioneering or renegade but we call the sensible middle. A way that treats every part of the whole—the land, the animals, and the humans doing the work—the way they should be treated.

You and I might not see eye to eye on everything we do here. Maybe you don't especially enjoy eating meat, and I do. I'm committed to my rural lifestyle and perhaps you'd be lost without the city. But reasonable people can probably agree that the way our food system has evolved—into one based on mass-produced industrial inputs, monocultures of foods that nobody, not even animals, should gorge on, unspeakable conditions for animals and undignified conditions for humans, and corporate monopolies controlling almost every link in the chain—ain't working too good. After three generations of us having put this system in play, the results are clear. It has been brutal on the land and the environment at large. It has created misery for billions of animals and turned once bustling rural economies into ghost towns. It has made several generations of people hopelessly addicted to obscenely cheap food, much of it unhealthy. Now it's starting to show its weak spots, the rents in the fabric, in a plethora of ways I never thought we'd have to face. You might not know it from the way some media spins it, though. Technology makes some sexy-ass promises about solving the very problems it brought us, with meat-like products mulched out of waste-like commodity grains and beans, and salad that's unnaturally grown, without soil, in giant artificially lit warehouses that are funded by global investment firms and delivered to your door by drones.

If you like the sound of where we are going with all that, there's nothing to do. Consider it a great direction. But if you don't like the sound of it, or if you've even felt a hint of skepticism that the solution to our looming food problems is gonna come from the offices of Silicon Valley and the corridors of Wall Street, then we better do something else.

This is the something else.

The basis of what we do at my farm is broadly called "regenerative agriculture." I tend to put it simpler than that. I call it "regenerative grazing." Whichever words you use, the definition of this approach, as I see it, is restarting the cycles of nature that the industrial, monocultural, input-heavy methods of modern land management broke, so that land naturally produces the abundance that a farmer can turn into products they can sell, that helps to finance the good farming practices they follow, that ensure the cycles keep spinning. Though there seem to be more experts on regenerative agriculture by the day (according to their online bios, at least), White Oak Pastures is one of the very few farms that has spent almost three decades hammering regenerative food production into a working, operating, scalable, and replicable model. Which makes this a tale of not what *could* happen but what *has* happened. And it's been done by a guy who's limited in both intellect and finance.

I don't have to just tell you about what we have done, I can show it to you. But if you think what I'm about to share is a guidebook to starting your own regenerative farm, it's not. (Though if you want to do that, I welcome you to the fight, and I have some words of wisdom for you.) Nor is this another exposé of factory farms, though I'm going to tell you the truth about how they work. My message is broader than that. It's about how to think about the food you eat in a new light; and about the people who grow and raise it and the places they live; and about what happens when food raised badly, cruelly, and unfairly is so pervasive and cheap and easy to get, while food raised right is more of a stretch to find and to purchase—the opposite of how it used to be, by the way. There are veils between you and the sources of your food today, layers of them, artfully placed by Big Food in order to obscure the actual conditions in the field or factory so that your attention gets fixed on the surface, never going past it. I want to inspire you to start pulling back the veils and looking deeper.

At our farm, where we raise and process meat along with other food products, thousands of people come to visit us every year. And we show them *everything*, start to finish, inside and out. They are getting to know their farmer—or at least *a* farmer—working in an alternative system, and discovering there is a better way. They're restoring that connection between the person with the fork and the person with the farm. And it's making them take a more critical look at what they always accepted as the status quo. That's what this book aims to help you do as well.

I don't want to just help you get excited to source beef, pork, poultry, and lamb that you can actually stomach—food raised with kinder methods. Nor simply encourage you to look outside the discount grocery chain for your food, or even to buy directly from a holistic and regenerative farm like ours (though if you do that, thank you). I want you to start understanding why it matters to build resilience into the production of our food and fiber, which is the very foundation of who we are as humans. Survival. Shelter. Our food supply. Most of us eat food three times every day. It provides the energy that fuels our activities, and determines much of the health of this vessel that we live in. After air and water, it is the most essential component of our life and the lives of our loved ones. Is there anything more important to get right? What I want to show you is that even while the current industrial methods of producing our food are getting wobbly—stressed to the max and prone to systems failure—I think that at my farm, and others like mine, we've got a good solution. Not the whole answer to this big and unfathomable problem of how we procure our food—but one solid piece of it at least.

As I write this, the perils of fucking up this earth are coming into laser-sharp focus. Experts opine how there are only sixty harvests left on planet earth—probably a good few less than that by the time you read this—because soil has been eroded and stripped of life. Bird flus threaten to take down our poultry supply, grain crops may fail due to drought, and nut crops may tank due to pollinator collapse. Let me say this: all of it may be true, when you're looking from the perspective of modern industrial farming and the food system as we know it. It's been built on extracting resources and separating land from livestock and siloing nature's complex system into neat little technological boxes. It's not surprising that the chickens are metaphorically coming home to roost. But here's the rub: that system only got started about eighty years ago. It crashed quickly. The system I advocate, which is about putting back into the natural cycles we pull food from, and healing the split between land and livestock, and working with the complexity of nature in all its mystery, is millions of years old. It still works beautifully. And it offers a pathway to reversing the downhill plummet.

A caution for the faint of heart. The theme song for the real-life fable you're about to read is not "Old MacDonald." The theme song for this story is "Born to Be Wild." There will be some socially unacceptable expletives used. Some feathers may get ruffled, some eyebrows raised. This is not your average American farm story, and it might not read like you expect. I'm not a Republican or a Democrat. I'm a Second Amendment guy who's a fiscal conservative; I'm also a screaming environmentalist with a gay daughter. And one of my highest values is gumption—a word that, I've come to learn, not many people know how to use today. If you are of delicate inclinations or somehow committed to commodity food production, please do not take offense. No urgent change ever came wrapped in tissue paper. At White Oak Pastures, what fuels us is an attitude we call "a bold return to giving a damn." Everyone who works with us has to have that mindset. We scout for people who've got it and quickly filter out those who don't. I hope this book helps you make the bold return to giving a damn, too. I really do.

Children of my generation were taught to obey the Ten Commandments. I'm not sure how much emphasis there is on this today. (It was a big deal in that earlier era.) I was a very average student academically, and I was probably a below-average student spiritually—I never fully got the commandments, because it troubled me that they were mostly focused on telling me what I should not do. I don't believe that a person's goodness is wholly based on what they *don't* do, so while I don't contest these biblical instructions, I made myself a set of commandments about what I *will* do.

‖‖‖

I will treat the animals that I husband with respect and dignity, providing them with an environment that allows them to express their instinctive behavior.

I will study the cycles of nature and learn how to not obstruct them.

I will implement practices that leave the soil, water, and air better than I found it.

I will heal the damage that my family's previous farming practices have inflicted on the land that I tend.

I will provide a comfortable and wholesome life for my family. (This includes my biological family and the many at White Oak Pastures that I have come to accept as family.)

I will provide the abundance that our land and herds produce to nourish those who need and appreciate it.

I will nurture the village that we live in.

I will get off my ass, seven days a week, and work as hard as I can, and invest all that I have to make all of this happen.

I will openly teach what I have learned about these things to those who want to know.

‖‖‖

I can only come up with nine commandments, but I can achieve 100 percent of those nine. That might be better than achieving 70 percent of the original ten. And while I know they sound like plain common sense—and they are, rooted in the traditions of American agriculture—they are also a departure from what has become the norm of modern farming and food production. Which makes it a radical act to return to them. We call the model of food production we've pioneered at White Oak Pastures "radically traditional." Radical in that it is an alternative to a very-well-established reality. Traditional in that it returns to something our ancestors did: farming in a way that's good for the whole, not just for a corporate bottom line.

Regenerative agriculture and resilient food production are finally getting the attention they're due. I'm watching these things pick up momentum, to where people forty years my junior think that what I started doing before they were born is relevant and interesting and they want to know how it works. For a constellation of reasons, halfway through my life I thought it was my job to figure out what was wrong with the way I was farming, and fix it. So I did that. Now, down here in far rural Georgia, my family and I are way out in front of this farming movement that needs doing badly. For close to three decades, I've literally bet the farm on this way of raising food working out. It's been a white-knuckle ride for most of that time. Now that the bet is paying off, I know this is a story whose time has come. And I'm the only sumbitch who can tell it.

Part One

||||||||||||||||||||||||||||||||||||||||||||||||

The Damn Harrises
of Bluffton, Georgia

Chapter One

A Different Kind of Eden

Come on out with me to my pastures in Southwest Georgia one evening and let me show you what I see. Dusk is the best time to look at animals; it's when they are out in the open after a day of sheltering from the sun, moving around and showing you what they got. My summer calving herd grazes before us, a massive congregation of mama cows and heifers and their babies, with a few bulls still peacefully mingled in, causing no kind of trouble. The cattle's coats, lustrous from good grass eaten all year, have gotten extra shiny from a good rain the night before. In the glint of the sunset, these cows look like new money, freshly minted.

There's a particular kind of cacophony that happens out here as the sun sets on the horizon: the lowing of over a thousand cows, reverberating into twilight air. From their point of view, they're saying they've picked off all the good stuff from their current paddock—tall, fresh grass so high in chlorophyll it's almost its own Pantone shade; black green grass, my daddy used to call it. They're ready for the next stash and itching to get after it. From my point of view, they can wait. They'll get that good stuff when we move them tomorrow morning, as we do every day.

Just past the cattle, a drove of heritage hogs grunt merrily as they nudge their noses into oak roots, digging for acorns after hours of wallowing in ochre-colored mud. And in the distance, hundreds-strong flocks of clucking chickens and churring guinea hens and gobbling turkeys peck the earth for grubs, the shaggy white guardian dogs that live with them barking as they warm up for their nightly patrol. I take it all in with my ears as much as with my eyes.

This ritual is how I end every single day of the year at White Oak Pastures, my jeep crawling along the fence lines at five miles per hour so I can scan the herd from end to end; my seat belt unbuckled under me so I can open and close the gates; and a sizable serving of Yellow Tail Shiraz in a no-spill mug reliably set in the cupholder. I make no apologies for the wine; there are thousands of acres, tens of thousands of animals, and scores of employees under my watch. Without a little imbibing before bedtime, my brain wouldn't ever stop fussing over how to keep all of them, including the humans, well fed and watered.

If you come out here with a certain expectation of American ranching in mind—arid Marlboro Man rangelands sparsely dotted by cattle—you might be surprised by a few things. First, how primeval my place looks. Down here on the coastal plains of Southwest Georgia, only eighty miles from the Gulf of Mexico as the crow flies, it's hot, wet, and outrageously green. No sagebrush and dust devils on this landscape. Lush and riotously productive, thanks to the fifty-two inches of rain a year we get down here, we are a coastal savannah of expansive grasslands peppered with massive hardwood trees. Squint your eyes and you might mistake this for the Serengeti. There's no monotony of cattle grazing this terrain. At my farm, large ruminants like cattle, small ruminants like sheep and goats, and a variety of hogs and birds graze, root, and peck the land within spitting distance of each other. My flocks, herds, and droves regularly hopscotch around the farm's many paddocks, forests, and shrubland areas in a kind of agricultural chess game of strategic moves, working symbiotically to keep the terrain properly grazed.

You might also be momentarily stunned by how healthy these animals look. My livestock are athletes, robust and impressively conditioned, constantly walking across pastures from their first day until their last. They benefit from the choices we make around here daily to ensure they have as low stress an existence as animals can have. This is what it's like to raise food in cooperation with nature, not against it. If you're gonna be a cow—or a sheep, hog, chicken, or goat for that matter—this is a good place to be one.

And what I hope will impress itself upon you, if you are open to looking just a little deeper still, is the abundance that emanates no matter which way you look. This place is the definition of fertile. Some have joked that with its super-size flora and packs of impressive fauna, it's a Jurassic kind of farm. Others, more reverently, have dubbed it a Garden of Eden. I call it a biome that is teeming with life. And I don't mean teeming with just the species we raise for food. *Teeming with life* includes a plethora of other ones, too: the pleasant kind of creatures you wouldn't mind getting close to—deer, bunnies, and butterflies—and the less Disney ones like alligators, bobcats, snakes, and eagles that you'd be wise not to mess with. Everything flourishes on my farm now that we haven't used pesticides for twenty-five years and we manage the landscape so that it expresses its natural potential.

This abundance has not appeared as a result of me being brilliant or much smarter than anybody else. I'm not sure I've ever had an original thought in my life. But what I *am* good at is making decisions and not shying away from risk. And twenty-five years ago, I made the decision to stop following agricultural conventions and to raise food a different way.

This change of heart changed a lot of things around here. My bottom line included. But I wouldn't change *it* for anything. Because by persisting for over two decades with what I started, I've seen everything get better and better around me: the land, the animals, and the rural economy that this farm contributes to. It's become a place of bounty that ripples from plant to beast to woman and man, driven by the cycles and rhythms of nature.

Back in my prior chapter of life, when I was the quintessential industrial cattleman, things would have looked a helluva lot different out here. The farm's monoculture of cattle would have been scattered a little more widely across the landscape, moving only once a month or so, because most of us doing this job figured that was less damaging to the land. There'd have been a big feedlot on my property, too, where I'd finish a good percentage of them on cheap grain, fattening them up as fast as possible before they disappeared into the commodity beef system, never to be heard about again.

We'd have had a couple of guys out here doing the labor with me, just four employees on a thousand-acre farm instead of the close to two hundred employees on the four-times-bigger acreage we have now. It was certainly quieter as a result—less of the sparring and the ribbing that happens when dozens of passionate people work together. And, frankly, things might have looked a little neater, more pleasing to the eye from a conventional point of view: the fence lines stripped free of unwanted brush and weeds thanks to the hundreds of gallons of Roundup and other chemicals we sprayed regularly; the air populated with fewer biting, stinging—or pollinating—insects, because we killed those, too, as the manuals for the chemicals I purchased instructed. And there were fewer sloppy mud pits to get your truck stuck in, because we didn't raise hogs, or poultry, or anything but commodity cattle back then. Everything was a little more contained and boxed in. I'd wager a bet that I looked a little less harrowed, too, not just because of my age at the time but due to fewer furrows on my brow. Raising food industrially gives you a safety net of sorts, a reliable consistency with fewer risks.

But this surface-level niceness did not reflect the truth of what was occurring, that several decades of raising food this way had been hell on the land, hell on the animals, and though it took me longer to realize, hell on the local community, too. Sure, there was a reliable yield of product for my operation to sell; there was a satisfying income and a comfortable life for me. But it came at a terrible cost. My farm had lost the abundance that gets generated when nature is working as it should—in a vigorous cycling of many, many different life-forms all growing, dying, and decaying symbiotically and then feeding back in to start over again. I'd lost the abundance that ripples out from the ecosystem itself to a farmer's business and his family and to the local workforce. I even lost any hope that my kids would ever want to join me on the farm, or raise their kids anywhere near it. What I was doing, and what my daddy had been doing before me, was kind of a one-way street: take, take, take from nature, without much giving back. And you can only extract from nature for so long before you reach the end of the string.

I ran a good operation that was consistently profitable. I'd learned livestock ranching from my dad, and he'd learned it from his. I could have kept going that way, except that I started to find a lot of what it unintentionally created along the way to be displeasing. And at the very root of that displeasure was this: When you farm industrially, you don't create a Garden of Eden. You destroy one.

As the sun drops lower over the horizon and I continue the evening surveillance of my herds, here are a few of the things that my senses are taking in.

I notice how turbocharged the pasture's thick carpet of grasses, forbs, and foliage appears. It's a treasure trove of plant life constantly photosynthesizing sunlight then converting that energy into sugars and proteins that are the first step on the food chain leading all the way to your plate.

I take in the unmistakable freshness that only a big rain delivers, which tells me that the previous day's rainwater has infiltrated the healthy, microbe-rich soil, which is holding it tight like a giant-size sponge instead of letting it rush off into the watershed like poorer soil would do.

I observe the calves staying close to their mamas, a sign that my herd has good maternal instincts bred into it, and the humidity lightly clouding around the savannah's towering hardwoods—my farm's longest-living organisms help to create our farm's very moist microclimate—tells me that the water cycle on this land is working properly.

And I appreciate all the shit. The manure that my cattle and other livestock have deposited all over the pastures is what I call the currency of life; it started as plant matter, got fermented in their bellies, and is now food for microbes that will help it cycle back into the soil and promote more plant growth.

These are all the signs that things are going right out here. I've learned to look for them, after years of looking for what was wrong as a conventional cattleman, and when I see them, they soothe the human in me—the man who's seeking to know that the world is in order. They soothe the businessman in me, too. They tell me there's enough abundance to monetize so that I can keep the whole thing going, which after all is what every business must have. And because we are working with nature, not fighting it, I also feel the reassurance of a quality that at the end of the day may be most critical of all: resilience. There's a lot that feels fragile in the world at large. But I, and my land, my animals, and the little economy we've revived here, are going to be okay.

If you've never had the chance to visit the places your food comes from, you might think this scene I'm depicting is the status quo. After all, an unfathomable amount of the products we eat today spin an origin story much like this. A farmy sounding name, a bucolic-looking picture with florid prose on the container suggesting nothing less than natural environments or small family farms. But for the very most part, it's just a mirage. One that has been painstakingly crafted by Big Food—by which I mean the colossal industry of multinational corporations that control over 90 percent of the food we eat—to make you feel you're getting the beautifully sourced food that you want. I got a tip for you: you're not. Ever since the food production system started becoming industrialized, commoditized, and centralized in the mid-twentieth century, the bucolic and pastoral farming culture that used to be the norm has gotten harder to find and harder to sustain. The confinement animal feeding operation that is the source of 97 percent of the beef consumed in this country today, or the industrial chicken houses that are the source of 99 percent of the eggs and chicken we buy, are a complete universe away from the small operations that used to define American farming. Yet Big Food continues to describe this as the origin story of its products even while it has moved cruelly, destructively away from it.

This farm, White Oak Pastures, is an effort to circle back. The methods we use here to raise, process, and sell ten species of livestock—cattle, hogs, sheep, goats, rabbits, chickens, turkeys, guineas, geese, and ducks—are closer in many ways to those my great-granddaddy and granddaddy used on this land before me than to anything me and my father—both of us indoctrinated into industrial methods—knew to do. Today we feed our cattle and other livestock what they evolved to consume—mother's milk, grass, and hay—and feed it to them for their entire lives; we allow each species to express their instinctive behaviors instead of cutting that off through confinement. Letting the animals do this allows them to contribute to the vitality of the land and its proliferation of good, sweet grass and succulent forage. We process the animals that are born on this farm ourselves so that nobody ever owns them but us; and what leaves our farm is food that has been made from sunshine and rainwater and trillions of microorganisms creating profoundly healthy soil. Then we compost and return any part of the animal that can't be eaten, worn, or used in some other purposeful way into the land it came from, where it feeds into the fertility cycle to start things over again.

In essence, what we do here is a very simple business. In day-to-day reality, of course, it's way more complex than that. My friends and neighbors thought I was crazy when I set out on this path; most of them believe that's still the case. What we're doing here, pasture-raising livestock, processing it, and selling it ourselves, is more risky financially than the type of farming they do; it's far less convenient labor-wise, and if you're into the latest agricultural technology and cutting-edge machinery, it probably seems a lot less cool.

But in evolving away from the ruthless methods of the conventional agricultural system, we have created something different: a farm that refuses to be a cog in Big Food and Big Ag's machine, and instead is its own tiny food-producing machine. ("Big Ag" refers to the multinational corporations that make billions of dollars providing inputs for farmers to grow crops, and further billions of dollars buying the raw commodities back from farmers.) Our six-generation family farm, a good hundred and sixty years old and counting, paid its dues in the industrial system for fifty of these years, under my father and partly under me. But I rethought things and now have a farm that's a living system that follows nature's principles. This system, based on holistic land management and owning every step of the supply chain from field to fork, retains the value of everything it creates and regenerates rather than degenerates the land it occupies, and it has helped my farm become one of the largest pasture-raised livestock operations in the country. We've evolved *backward* in a way, going all-in on the *de*s: de-industrializing, de-commoditzing, and de-centralizing agriculture.

To find us, you've got to be prepared to drive a little. About three and a half hours south of Atlanta, skewing west enough to wave at the Alabama border, you'll have left behind fine dining restaurants, movie theaters, and even the Walmarts and Costcos. This place is rural—really rural. And just to make sure you have no rose-tinted visions of it, I'll add that it's poor. Of the two counties we straddle—Early County and Clay County—one is the poorest county in the country from a household income perspective, and the other is not far behind. The economy here has always been purely agrarian, and you can tell where that's got it when you pass through our nearest town of note, Blakely, about fifteen minutes away. Its formerly impressive town square, where farmers once loaded livestock onto trains and brought crops to market, is now fringed with empty storefronts, and a liquor store sits on the corner.

As you drive up Highway 27 toward our farm, you'll pass several indicators of modern industrial farming. Enormous monocultural fields of corn, cotton, and peanuts—the southern 'trifecta of commodity crops—may be in various stages of growth or, depending on the season, naked and exposed after harvesting. Great swaths of longleaf and loblolly pine trees, planted by farmers in exchange for government subsidies, fringe the fields, awaiting the year that they'll be cut and fed into the timber industry's supply chain. Speeding semitrucks might overtake your vehicle; the poultry inside have just been yanked out of their crowded, climate-controlled houses, and after seeing the sun for the very first time are hurtling toward slaughter. Many people outside this region are unaware that Georgia is a heavily agricultural state; in a few moments on the road, you can get a real glimpse into the activities that make it so.

Cattle and livestock ranching is only a niche player here, compared to the crops, including the peaches and pecans that get shipped around the country. So you might speed right on through our farm if you weren't looking for it, four miles long and about a mile across at its widest point. Until the colors shake you present: There's the green, of course, and then there's the red of our dirt roads—the terra-cotta colored clay that is the foundation of the American South and that will weigh down your boots after a big rain. Here and there you might glimpse the chocolate brown of soil rich in carbon, from all the biomass that's naturally fertilized it. And then there's the blue, a sky that on a good day is so saturated with color, it seems to pierce the most polarized sunglasses.

Before you even notice the animals, you probably take stock of the trees: The savannah uplands give way to hardwood bottoms where the canopies of oaks, sugarberries, poplar, and pecans create shady, cool refuge from the sun. Of all these, the most impressive is the tenac oak, though nobody from beyond a fifty-mile radius would know this name. More commonly known as the white oak, it's the king of the oak genus: slowest growing, oldest, and largest, with acorns sweet enough for people to eat. Now drop your speed, and you'll start to see our livestock: The sheep nibbling purple verbena along the fence lines, keeping them clear of weeds. The goats clustered in the shrubbery, browsing on the foliage. The mama cows and their calves from our breeding herds, nursing and feeding together in one paddock, with the not-yet mama heifers alongside them. The weaned bulls from our male herds, fattening up on the richest pasture we have, in another herd nearby. And if your eyes are really sharp, farrowing hogs under the wooden shelters we build them out in pasture, preparing to give birth to a litter.

Soon after you pass the oldest part of the farm, which boasts the richest soil we've got (it has been regeneratively managed the longest), you'll pass the 1920 house my granddaddy built, which I grew up in and is now the home of my daughter Jenni, her wife, Amber, and their two children. Farther ahead is the house my great-granddaddy James Edward Harris built in 1878, which is now occupied by my daughter Jodi, her husband, John, and their three kids. These two homes have housed six generations of Harris farmers between them so far, if you count my grandkids' early contributions in backyard chicken care. A ramshackle structure just off the highway may catch your eye; that's the old commissary and farm store where, in the early 1900s, my predecessors famously circulated their own home-minted coins to and from the community's workforce, until the Feds got wind of the activity and sent a man to shut it down.

You'll pass the entrance to one of the only recently built structures around: the USDA-inspected processing plant where we slaughter and butcher our livestock, and if you feel so inclined, you are welcome to come inside and see what happens at every step of the process. There are no secrets on this farm. Next to it, the fulfillment center, where we ship about a thousand orders a week around the country, and the grinding machines and dump trucks readying meatpacking waste for compost piles that eventually produce free, natural fertilizer for my pastures. One stop over, the commissary where bones get turned into broth, and fat into tallow, and the bounty from our organic garden becomes pickles and relishes and jellies we can sell. Then the capacious dehydrator where the scraps that used to get tossed—ears and tails and tracheas and penises and esophaguses from all kinds of livestock—are transformed into thirty different kinds of pet chews. These three facilities have made White Oak Pastures close to a zero-waste farm.

A quick drive from there past our farm-stay cabins and RV park takes you to the heart of the village of Bluffton. It wasn't long ago that almost nobody would make that turn, and you could walk down the two parallel main streets of this town without seeing a soul. This town had been rendered economically irrelevant by a postwar agricultural exodus that literally hollowed out its center. After generations of young people left, and opportunity caved, it had fallen to a greater level of decay than any little farm or community I know of. The only thing you could buy here until recently was a postage stamp. These days, however, our reclaimed General Store, a 175-year-old building, complete with groaning wooden floorboards and shelving stocked with provisions, supplies, and gifts, is a thriving hub of activity. Employees and customers congregate inside, visiting with each other; the sound of horses tied up in the barn next door mingles with the buzz of conversations. And the whole space is infused with the mouthwatering smell of lunch. Adjoining the store, our restaurant serves pulled pork and pickled beef tongue tacos and collards and grits, all raised on our farm, to a steady stream of visitors as well as locals from the area looking for a good meal. Outside, families gather on the lawn to eat and play; kids meet the softest and fuzziest of our animals, temporarily stationed in corrals in a kind of redneck petting zoo. We have a working theory about why folks from all kinds of unexpected places seek us out, arriving in greater numbers by the year. Fluorescent-lit, Formica-floored, climate-controlled lifestyles have gotten people so far removed from nature that they can't even tell how screwed up most of the food on offer actually is, because they don't know the way things are supposed to be. Some kind of homing instinct has brought them here to look and smell and listen and taste, to remember, maybe, what they've forgotten.

By the time you've seen the pieces of this place, something may start to click. All the things we do contribute to the synergistic phenomenon we've built here. If you don't have firsthand experience of how siloed and separated the modern agricultural and food system is, with each link of the food chain existing in its own separate world and huge gaps between consumers and the farms that feed them, this may not seem as revolutionary as it is. We've tied back together the pieces that have been split apart and, in so doing, created a unique kind of organism, populated by a hundred thousand beating hearts, that is more than the sum of its parts.

As the sun falls lower on the horizon, most rational people might be at their dinner table having supper with their spouse. I'm almost always still out in my pastures, making my rounds until it's too dark to see without headlights. It's my blessing and, as some of those closest to me might say in private, it's sometimes my curse. I'm a one-trick pony. And this is my trick. It's my livelihood, my vocation, my passion, and my legacy and my heritage. Raising food right, stewarding the land.

But there's something magical about being inside the cycles of nature like this, so I don't take a minute of it for granted. The closest my non-verbose cowboy self can get to describing what it's like is the feeling when all is right with the world. It's the same thing that draws you to sit by a fire, or by a body of water, or in the dappled light of a forest. You just want to sit there forever, hooked in to the very source of life. I think a lot of people long for this deeper connection to the rhythms of the days getting longer and shorter, and the springtime trees budding in succession, or to the knowledge that after you put the bulls out for breeding, the calves will come 283 days later.

That's the beauty that this place has—it's certainly not economic beauty, nor is it a scenic wonders-of-the-world type of beauty. The Ritz-Carlton isn't rushing to build a resort in Bluffton, Georgia, nor would you want your vacation villa here. It's not always comfortable; it gets too hot, then too wet and messy, and the bugs will eat your ass at one time of year, then in another it will be so cold it hurts to pee. But the beauty comes from being in a place where you are inside nature functioning at its zenith. It's not unlike how some people feel when they're in the remote wilderness. And there aren't a lot of opportunities for that these days.

My daddy, Will Harris II, used to say when somebody was doing something they shouldn't be doing, "Some sumbitches ought not to be allowed to own land." Just like some people shouldn't be allowed to own pets, or have children. I think he meant that there were only a few kinds of people who'd give land, and livestock on it, the caring it requires. I am one of those kinds. I am pretty much only about this. And I do it be-cause I love being part of the perpetual endlessness of the land and the herd; everything else that I know of comes and goes, but the land and the herd last forever. I love that while plants grow and die, and indi-vidual animals are born and perish, the land and the herd never end. I do it because owning land that you know what to do with, and produc-ing food that people will always need, is good business, the kind that you can leave to your children and grandchildren for them to take over and evolve further. And I do it because even though it's hard as hell to find the way back to the pastoral food system that got co-opted, and even though most will likely go broke trying, if you *do* figure out how to get back to it, it's absolutely worth the pain it took to get there.

As true night sets in, the white noise of the cattle gets punctuated by the calls of owls—barn, horned, and screech. The nocturnal ac-tivity begins to pick up. I reflect upon all the ways that things have gotten better. Remaking the farm the way I wanted it brought my daughters and their families to work it with me. Emulating natural principles and reducing dependencies on externalities let us build a resilient little food system for an increasingly uncertain world. What we're doing here is cooking on fires and building boats—shoring up one corner of food production to minimize the chances of severe ad-versity taking us down. And while this area is still economically chal-lenged, we have made a significant contribution to it becoming a little less so. I'm far from religious, but it strikes me that it is not a common occurrence for man's will and God's will to coincide; here, in this Eden that I oversee day in and day out, it damn sure has.

Whether this is *enough* is above my pay grade to determine. I'm too old and too hardened to be free of skepticism completely. Though supply chain disruptions and plant shutdowns, cyberattacks on Big Meat, and destructive weather events are happening more frequently by the year, pointing to something very wrong in the system we've got, many still "don't believe lard is greasy" as my momma liked to say. But I take some comfort in knowing that even if I can't fix everything in the world, I can fix this. I can fix the dire state of the farmed-to-death land that I acquire piece by piece; I can fix the way animals we rely on for food are treated, and make it easier for more people to support—or participate in—fully independent farming, by sharing how we do it here. That's a good fit for me, because I fear irrelevance more than I fear death.

Wendell Berry says something to the effect that there is no way to place a value on how much a farmer knows about his place. He's learned that this corner of the field can't do well after a big rain; and that corner of the field is gonna get droughty early when it stops raining; and an underground crop like peanuts doesn't do well on the other side of the farm. I've spent so long out here on evenings like this that I think I know exactly what he means. I've absorbed its rhythms so they are indistinguishable from my own. I know that a particular paddock of grass won't last this herd all day, or we have to move that herd before the afternoon. I call this deep connection to my land my Sense of Place. The older I get, the stronger my Sense of Place becomes. I don't really want to go far from this different kind of Eden, or travel much afield. I don't want to be anywhere but here.

The sky turns inky, and the shift change is complete. Predators like foxes and possums, and skunks and coyotes, get their time on the land, and mosquitoes take over from butterflies. It's a different place here entirely when darkness falls—not like a city where streetlights go on but the rest of it stays the same. Eyesight becomes less important, and smells and sounds fill my senses. It's time for humans to leave things to the creatures of the night. I get in my jeep and slowly drive home.

Chapter Two

An American
Family Farm Story

I never used to tell the story of White Oaks much. Not for lack of pride—I am inordinately proud of our heritage here. But I was raised cowboy, and cowboys don't gush about themselves to other people. I figure that since I don't give a damn about most of *their* stories, why would they give a damn about mine? Yet that has been changing as more people realize that the food system is not as fine as they thought and that almost all their food comes from factories—the processing plants that produce the final products *and* the animal factories and the "crop factories" of massive monoculture farms that raise the raw materials. It's human nature to be attracted to authenticity, and it gives people an urge to learn more about the opposite: the truly independent American family farm.

Maybe the interest has been stoked by the fact that farms like this, and farmers like me, are, quite literally, a rare breed. At the start of the twentieth century, farmers comprised 41 percent of the American workforce. Today, farmers make up about 1 percent, and I'd estimate less than 1 percent of this 1 percent are working outside the factory system entirely. An even smaller percentage have been farming the same land for over a century and a half, and probably an even smaller percentage of *them* are as outspoken as I am about how it got to be this way. Rarity breeds curiosity.

Maybe the story about how one family has stayed the course in agricultural America helps people feel like things aren't as completely upside down as they seem. Trying to make sense of how our food and agricultural system got so far from what is natural and normal, and became the many-headed, rapaciously money-hungry beast it is, will make your head spin. The pendulum has swung so far toward massive scale and multinational power that the roots of food feel very hard to find. Hearing about one bastion of normalcy still standing is, it seems, reassuring.

Or perhaps it's that listening to one of the last Good Ol' Boys who doesn't care what others think and isn't intimidated by a damn thing is refreshing. Country people—real country people, the kind raised in very sparsely populated areas—are different to begin with, and being an unapologetic meat producer at a time when meat is being villianized erroneously, in some circles, gives me extra bite. I'm sure that it is not my political correctness that draws people close. But I wonder if getting proximity to something they have in their own ancestral history, but can't quite locate or name, is what does. Today, the majority of Americans are generations away from the farms or homesteads and the agricultural way of life that their predecessors knew. It's there in their bloodline, but it's been lost somewhere in the mists of time. I have never been any generation away from farming; it's right up close to me, and you can't shake DNA. I guess it feels good to know that one corner of food production is in the right hands.

For all these reasons, and despite my initial discomfort, I started telling the story of my people and of this place more often. I noticed that people liked hearing it. And I started to enjoy telling it.

Our family farm, like many others tucked off country roads across the nation, contains within it a pretty good accounting of the history of American farming. My great-grandfather built a solid little operation on this land in the second half of the nineteenth century, feeding his immediate village with a variety of meats and other goods. My grandfather took it bigger, creating prosperity as a larger herdsman and landowner and building a store. My daddy started the industrialization of the farm on his watch, and I started the second generation of it on my watch, becoming pretty damn good at it, before abandoning that model for something better that I could pass on to my kids and theirs. And that led to the younger generation of Harrises returning to live alongside me on the farm and raise their own families here—something that, of all the successes I've achieved out here, gives me the most satisfaction.

The six generations of Harrises who have made this land our home and our livelihood are, I am quite proud to report, a little atypical. If we had a family crest, my daughters joke, it would read, "Talks too loud. Drinks too much. Plays to win." We also are blessed, for better or worse, with what I call the gift of fight—a mix of tenacity, courage, and strength that has caused some to call us the Damn Harrises, but without which I don't know if we would have survived the many phases of history we've seen, and would not have maintained our resilient, regenerative operation today. I'd also like to add, while we're on the subject of character, that we have an unwavering commitment to integrity—and a profound intolerance for assholes. But while we have our family idiosyncrasies, we also represent something common—universal, even—for some parts of America. Our family and our farm participated in creating the bedrock of rural America, then inadvertently helped to crack that foundation by participating in the industrialized, centralized, commoditized system that rendered rural America close to obsolete. We traded the total autonomy of the small farmer for the security that came by scaling up; then we began to risk degradation and disrepair to our land, animals, and community as a result. And we participated in a system that sold consumers a bucolic image of farming that wasn't actually true. I am not a nostalgic type of person; I don't dwell on the past. Even my jeep lacks a rearview mirror—that's how averse I am to looking back and how profoundly I am engineered to move forward. But I'm not sure you can fully understand what you are moving toward if you don't know the story of where you came from and keep that knowledge close, like a guiding light always slightly in your peripheral view.

We live *with* our history here. It is present in the buildings; it is in the people who stop by and see me during the day to discuss a matter that needs resolving or a job that needs doing, and end up reminiscing about stacking hay bales in Bluffton's former movie theater as a kid, or staying up late on the porch in the summertime, the men all chewing tobacco and talking about the war. When I'm working indoors, I'm sitting with history all around me in my office, which occupies the old one-room courthouse of Bluffton—fitting, I suppose, given how many tough decisions get made there every day. *Courthouse* sounds grander than it is—we're talking a small, shotgun-style building with a front porch boasting two well-worn rocking chairs and a heap of obsolete iron tools gathered from the woods and pastures over the years. It's mildly ramshackle but I sure like it. And though it is diminutive, it is the nerve center of our whole operation—it's smack in the middle of the town of Bluffton, and the town is right in the middle of the farm.

If you come in for a visit, you first have to step over my hundred-pound pit bull mix, Judge, eating raw meat scraps from an old stockpot on the floor, and ignore the fact that this room hasn't seen a good cleaning for a while. You'll notice a distinctive lack of business paraphernalia around the place—instead of whiteboards and planners, there are snakeskins and ram skulls, and framed hunting rifles and other dusty curios on the walls, plus a chunk of granite as big as two fists that says NEVER GIVE UP carved real deep. A bookshelf is crammed with tomes I've been gifted about the American farm—its historic past, its industrial apogee, its worrying decline. Their spines are not cracked and their pages are still clean because I don't need to read them; the whole story line has played out right here. At the head of the building, elevated a few feet off the floor, is my desk. It sits on the former Bluffton judge's bench; and when you walk up to it, you have to choose which side of the bar to stand on: plaintiff or defendant.

There are six framed images hanging over the courthouse door that face me as I work: six portraits that span from the first Harris to run this place, my great-grandfather, to his son, then his grandson, and to me, and then through to the ones who will one day take it over, my daughters Jenni and Jodi, and their children.

A visitor once laughingly said the men in our family look meaner by the generation—I laughed, too—but the pictures aren't there to scare anyone off. They tell the generational story of this place, of where it came from, where it is now, and where it is going. They are a constant reminder to me that this kind of farming, which repairs the land and uplifts communities, takes its view not in business quarters or growing seasons but in generations—in centuries, even. And seeing them daily from where I sit keeps me honest. They remind me that this place could have gone the way of many farms today: staying highly industrialized, losing more of the food dollar each year, and struggling to stay relevant under the command of an old man looking for an exit strategy. Instead, it tells a different narrative: four generations of tenacious, rough-around-the-edges southern patriarchs ceding control to a new generation of two gutsy, educated, and deeply competent matriarchs. That feels right to me. And what helped that to occur was a willingness to take risks, a stubbornness to go against the grain, and a fight every damn day to create what many thought was foolish.

To the left of my desk is a framed display of my most cherished family treasures: my great-grandfather's muzzle-loading shotgun, my grandfather's breech-action shotgun, my father's pump shotgun, my old semiautomatic shotgun, and my daughters' over-under shotguns. It represents my kind of technological progress.

This farm was established in 1866 by my father's grandfather. James Edward Harris was a student at Mercer University in Macon, Georgia, when the Civil War broke out. Like many of his generation, he enlisted in the Confederate Army, where he become a cavalry officer. Prior to the war, James had been setting up to farm a fairly sizable parcel of land he had inherited about forty miles away in Quitman County. But through some wartime dilemma never fully explained to me, James lost that land, which led to him starting over afresh in Early County. James had a relative here in Bluffton—an uncle, as I understand it—who was a medical doctor with some means. He helped finance the purchase of a property that is now what we consider the original five-hundred-acre farm or "Home Place" of White Oak Pastures.

Through sheer geographical good fortune, James found himself establishing his new farming operation on land with unusual attributes. Though few people notice this unless they are closely watching the elevation on their GPS, Highway 27 coming north into Bluffton takes you along a short section of ridgeline that stands a few hundred feet above sea level and that separates two watersheds—an east-facing one dropping to the Flint River and a west-facing one dropping to the Chatahoochee. It is sort of like the eastern version of the Great Divide, and it is a remarkable, sweet spot. The ridgeline, called the Kolomoki Ridge, is a twenty-five-mile-long strip, which, as I understand it, is the very tail end of the Appalachian mountain range where it has *almost* gone completely underground. Though its width is narrow, never over a mile wide and only a few yards across in some places, it offers something special to a farmer: it is an ancient mountain soil rich in minerals. It wouldn't knock your socks off if you were used to farming in, say, the profoundly deep and fertile prairie soil of the Great Plains, but it counts for a lot in the Southeast, where poor-quality sandy soils predominate. (The Gulf Coast and the coastal plains that surround my farm are, after all, an ancient seabed.) Combine this soil with a climate that is quite benevolent, with year-round rainfall, constant humidity, few extreme fluctuations in moisture, and only just enough of a freeze to take some of the insects out, and a Bluffton farmer wins a natural advantage in productivity that those only a county away would kill for.

My great-grandfather was by no means the first person to enjoy this fertile advantage. The short crest is called the Kolomoki Ridge in honor of the important Woodland Indian site named Kolomoki that formed there, long before any European set foot on this land. (The word *kolomoki* actually means "Land of the White Oak," in the language of that ancient Indigenous people.) I think the original peoples of the Mississippian cultures were so attuned to the very places where the soil was good, flora was abundant, and fauna existed in profusion that they chose them as the epicenters of gathering and ceremony. For about four hundred years, from 350 to 750 AD, large numbers of Swift Creek and Weeden Island people built, maintained, and used massive ceremonial mounds, grassy village plazas, and burial sites just three miles west of where our farm sits. (Kolomoki is famed as the oldest and largest Woodland Indian site in the southeastern United States.) They also did, from my understanding, one helluva of a better job managing the land than my people, the Europeans, did after we took it away from them. While my knowledge is perfunctory—my great-granddaddy got here about thirty years after the last native people had been forcibly removed to Oklahoma on the Trail of Tears—I know enough about the history of this land to know that they did not break nature's cycles. Under their watch, the ecosystem was perpetual.

James began raising livestock and poultry at the Home Place, slaughtering whatever was ready every morning before sunup except Sunday. He and his employees would butcher the animals with knives and haul the day's fare two miles into town on a two-horse wagon. There, the wagon would do a circuit, stopping at Bluffton's hotel, and the boardinghouse, and about four general stores that served the surrounding area. It was a very simple business: raise the food, process the food, and get it directly to the local market—all on man and mule power, because this was before the age of the internal combustion engine or anything as advanced as refrigeration or USDA Food Safety standards. If you couldn't store meat in a fridge, your business was by definition local; it had to be harvested and sold fresh daily, within a small radius. Either sell it or smell it was their attitude. (If a mule-drawn wagon could move at the speed of just a couple of miles per hour, traveling ten miles each way to the next town with unchilled meat wasn't an option.) My daddy used to tell me stories he'd heard from his grandfather of how the Bluffton townsfolk would meet the wagon on Saturday morning, write what they took on a piece of paper for the wagon driver, and then the next week, give the money directly to James when he did the rounds to collect it. Any part of the carcass that couldn't be sold—guts, feathers, beaks, and hooves—would be composted and eventually circle back to fertilize the land, turning into good grass for the livestock and rich soil for the vegetables and crops such as corn, wheat, potatoes, oats, and velvet beans.

During that era, many farms didn't raise livestock in isolation from crops and vegetables, because that is how the ecosystem worked. Most farms, no matter its size, integrated grazing animals with crops and vegetables. Most every home in the area would have had a vegetable garden and a cluster of fruit trees—peach, pear, pomegranate, plum, and fig—maybe a muscadine grape arbor, and a few pecan, walnut, and chestnut trees. The farmer who provided the meat and poultry, eggs and butter was an essential player, because not every farmer had the resources—the flocks and herds or the people to work them—to reliably provide the community with its protein needs. That's what my granddaddy and great-granddaddy did. They were able to sell all those things, plus anything else the bounty of nature provided. They were not gears in a huge food system like farmers are today; they served as their own tiny food system for the village of Bluffton.

For my great-granddaddy, the natural advantage of Bluffton's terrain endowed him with a little more prosperity than other farmers only a few miles away. Slightly more fertile land pays back in small ways that compound over time; land that is more productive means a few less acres are required to raise grains for the farm's work animals, which leaves more land available to raise crops or livestock to sell, and gradually the gains accumulate. His prestige and influence rose with his financial success, and toward the end of his life, he became a state senator. The privilege that afforded is not lost on me: I got the lesson quickly as a young man when, traveling down a dirt road one day, I saw an old farmer fishing in a creek. When I stopped to greet him, as is customary in the country, he made a disparaging comment about me being one of the rich boys. "That farm you got over there that you got from your father, your granddaddy and great-granddaddy—it'll produce ten to twenty percent more than my farm," he said. "Y'all had that farm for a hundred years—if you make twenty percent more than me every year for a hundred-something years, where do you think that puts *you*?" That frustrated old man was not being kind, but he was right. The early Harrises' hard work and tenacity—and luck—led them to accumulate wealth, which helped me get in the game and then build a better kind of business for my descendants to take over.

When James Edward's son, Will Carter Harris, took over running the operation at the end of the nineteenth century, his father's sweat equity and the farm's natural productivity gave him the means to expand the farm further. There wasn't a huge generational transition like there was when my daddy took over later; this handover was a continuation of farming methods, albeit one with growth. Will Carter grew the herd of cattle that James had established, to provide meat to over a hundred people a week. He became a well-respected cattleman in an area of the world where cattle ranching was a marginal activity, far overshadowed by growing corn, cotton, and peanuts. By the early twentieth century, my granddaddy had become a fairly large operator for his time, opening a store on the farm to sell the basic essentials of rural life—flour and cheese, dress fabric and shoes—to members of the local community. For a farmer, owning a store meant you got to another rank; you had become an entrepreneur. The store was also where the legendary Harris Dollar got traded in by employees. I've still got a few of these old coins—James had begun casting them himself because he didn't have any money, so why not produce his own? He made them out of a lead alloy called babbit that was used as bearings for watermill shafts and they were a primary currency around Bluffton until right after World War II, taken happily by the merchants in town for goods and services. It was an example of what today we'd call a hyperlocal economy (based, you could say, on the 1900 version of Bitcoin) and one that eventually got deleted by the federal authorities at the IRS who sent out a treasury agent to stop my ancestors from "counterfeiting."

Farming in the preindustrial era was not comfortable or easy. It took a lot of manpower hours to tend to animals and the land in every season, without a single mechanized convenience. But the recipe was not complicated; it just followed the food chain. The farmer grew grass; the cattle birthed calves on the grass; the calves grew on the grass; the cattle were harvested; their remains were composted back into the land; the new calves were born, and the cycle perpetuated. It was a naturally organic system (the term *organic*, with reference to food production, didn't even exist because there was no other way to farm back then). The business plan was simple, too. My grandfather took his own product to market, set the price, sold directly to the customer, and put the money toward his biggest expense—paying his employees—along with other operational needs. Anything extra he could use to build up his wealth in the form of more cattle or more land. And everything he needed to breed, raise, and finish the livestock before getting it to market came from what was there on the farm, inside his own system. My daddy, well schooled by his father, would relish sharing how this pastoral business model of the past worked. He'd say, "There are only three kinds of wealth you need in life: grass, cows, and money. You have to have grass"—in the form of land—"to feed the cows, you have to have cows to turn the grass into money, and you have to have money to buy more land to grow your grass. If you have too much grass, get more cows. If you have too much money, buy more grass and cows." Then he would wryly add the warning, "You cannot have too much grass or money, but you can damn sure have too many cows." That was about how complicated the supply chain got—and the farmer oversaw all of it. Which also meant that since there were no costly inputs being purchased to produce the food, and no middlemen or other entities processing it between farm and fork, the farmer kept all of the dollar that he made. I do not know if my granddaddy's customers thought his prices were fair or not; what I do know is that because he had to account for all his expenses—no subsidies from the government, no artificially cheap grains to feed the cows—they were much closer to the true cost of raising the food than is the norm today.

And what the customer got for *their* dollar—or nickel or dime, as the case would have been—was the real deal: nutritious meat, poultry, and eggs raised on grass, sunshine, clean water, and rich soil, unprocessed and uncontaminated by anything man-made. There was only one kind of beef to consume back then—it was fully grass-fed or nothing.

Perhaps most important of all, my predecessor Will Carter, like his father James Edward before him, worked in a system that inspired him to raise the very best product he could, and sell it in the most reputable manner. In those first decades of the twentieth century, just as in James Edward's time before that, the local market was the *only* market they had. There was no dumping their meat into a nationwide commodity market for a fixed price, no shipping it overseas. There was nowhere to hide if the food was poor quality, or unsafe, or cheated the buyers. Selling your product to some bigger company and retreating behind the cover of anonymity was not an option, because the people who consumed it knew how to find you. Out of sheer pride, farmers like my grandfather set high standards. And out of sheer self-preservation, they met them, because high production values had *monetary* value: if you raised the best wheat, the miller wanted to buy your wheat and would pay you extra for it; if you raised the best hogs or cattle, the butcher would pay you a premium. That's a far cry from what occurred in the generations that followed, when the commodity system, with its fixed prices no matter what quality of product got shipped out of the farm gate, created arbitrary minimum standards that completely changed where the goalposts stood. Back then, farmers shot for the maximum quality that they could.

When I think about my predecessors, it's not *what* they did that stirs me the most but *how* they did it—their core values. They took care of their land and took care of their herd, because they lived by the creed that when you take care of those things, they take care of you. After all, the land, which included the pastures for grazing, the forests where wild things lived, and the bodies of water that kept everything alive, was their only wealth. It was their savings account—they didn't have 401(k)s, or Social Security, or stock portfolios to fall back on. Their animals were the source of the cash flow they needed to stay afloat. And their customers in the village were their market. Being a good land steward, practicing good animal husbandry, and holding high standards of production for their customers were three nonnegotiables, because they ensured that the land thrived, a strong herd perpetuated itself year after year, and their market was stable and reliable, which meant that they and their families were taken care of, too. It would have been game over for them if they had ever let any of these three tenets get fucked up, even one time.

It also helped the local economy to live and breathe. James Edward's and Will Carter's success helped to build the town of Bluffton into something just a little more impressive than other towns nearby. It was already a flourishing agrarian trade center in the early twentieth century, when its population peaked with a whopping 380 residents. Bluffton didn't have anything *but* agriculture to trade in; there was no railroad track going through here, no factory or mill, save Harrison's grist mill, where local farmers could get their grain milled. I've done the math; assuming that small subsistence farms dotted the surrounding countryside at a typical rate of forty acres per farm, it made Bluffton a trade center for about five thousand people, which meant this humble village was more on the map than you might think. And while Bluffton was always a poor town, in a poor part of the nation, the success of the Harris family farm helped make it a little *less* poor. There was a two-story school for girls and boys here in the early twentieth century; two doctors and a drugstore; a movie theater and a professional baseball team my granddaddy played on. By the early

1920s, there was even a concrete swimming pool—though admittedly, it was a little rough around the edges. Down at the bottom of the jungle-like bluff—the geological namesake of the town where spring water poured out of the rock—a concrete basin was built for kids to swim in by day, and for adults to carouse around by night, thanks to a wooden dance pavilion that sat beside it. The town might not have been known much beyond its neighboring counties, but it definitely had a heartbeat.

While my forefathers' efforts strike me as special, there wasn't anything profoundly unusual in what they were doing. They just did it on a bit bigger scale than most. This highly local, producer-to-consumer food system, working with nature—not against it—was how most of the food in America was raised and grown in those times. Every populated county in the country had farms like ours, providing directly to their communities. I was already several years into running White Oak Pastures in a new, regenerative fashion when the similarities between what I was doing and what they had done before me fully hit me. I may have technologies they never had in order to cool, store, and ship our products directly to our customers, and our version has an inordinate number of USDA regulations to comply with that they could not have fathomed. But the foundations of what they were doing and what we are doing have a lot in common. That wasn't by design; I wasn't trying to harken back to history for the sake of history. We just did what we did, and later on, I remembered what I'd been told about the past. And I said, "Shit! Well ain't that something!" History does repeat itself sometimes. In our case, it was because we went so far down the wrong road that we had to double back.

When my daddy, Will Bell Harris, started industrializing the farm, it was a radical shift from what had come before. Born in 1920, he came of age during the Great Depression. In the rural South, most farm families lost everything they had, defaulting to the bank and losing their land. My dad's family was able to hold on to their farm by living frugally and working extremely hard, something he was proud of all his life, and was also profoundly shaped by. (As an adult, he loved the security of cash so much he carried a wallet bulging with hundred-dollar bills at all times, sticking out like a baseball in his pants pocket. But because he loved frugality even more, I bet he didn't spend but two dollars of it per week.) My daddy knew he was lucky to come from a family of "haves" when so many "had not," but still his childhood was tough in ways only farm childhoods can be: as the only child, he was forced to man up quickly when his father, Will Carter, lost his eyesight. My father was in seventh grade when it happened. By this time, Will Carter had grown his operation to something considerable; in an era of forty-acre subsistence farms, his operation was a five-hundred-acre-plus farm. But prosperity didn't protect my daddy's education; with his father unable to see, my grandmama Beulah—a little white-glove-and-hat-wearing southern matron—unceremoniously yanked my daddy out of school. I'll never know how he felt about it—but knowing how similar we turned out, and how much I hated school, I'd wager he was delighted to have a reason to skip. Every day, father and son would do the rounds on the farm in a two-horse buggy, with the younger Will reporting on what needed doing in the pastures and fields. He never went back to his studies. (Such is the tenacity of the Harris family that Beulah made sure my daddy got his school diploma anyway—family lore holds that she jumped in her Model T to drive to the school to harangue the principal and school board, who wanted to withhold it. That 1933 graduation diploma is displayed in our general store today, with "satisfactorily" completely marked out and "conditionally succeeded" written in.) My grandfather would later go on to be one of the first people to have cataract surgery at Emory University in Atlanta, at which point Will Bell and Beulah assumed all the farm duties until he recovered.

I think these experiences shaped my daddy into the dogged creature he was—obsessively focused on the farm, and having lived through the devastation of the Depression, almost ferocious in his single-mindedness to become financially successful. He was well positioned for it. For one thing, my father knew his strengths. Though we have also cultivated crops and other foods on this land over the years, the Harrises are cattle people, through and through. Cattle people are a certain kind of farmer; a little less predictable than the grain grower, and strong-willed to the core. We love the dynamic nature of the job, shepherding animals from birth to death; we relish the mess and the noise, and consider broken bones and suture scars to be signs of valor.

However, by the time my dad took over the farm as young man after the war, a new era in farming was starting around him, one that would become dominated by industrial methods of production. The framework for this change had been building for some time. By the 1920s, centralized meatpacking companies had started to take business away from small, local, and privately owned slaughterhouses; the first Confinement Animal Feeding Operation, a large chicken operation, had set up not far away, in Gainesville, Georgia. The US government had begun one of the most powerful interventions in agricultural history—crop subsidies, a measure that started with senators right here in the Southeast. (A note on that: committee chairmanships are assigned based on seniority. During that era, southern politicians generally had a lot of seniority, because southern politicians tended to be elected for life. The South had a very agrarian economy, so the senior southern politicians sought agricultural committees. They shaped the early farm bills and saw to it that the southern crops—cotton, sugar, peanuts, rice, and tobacco—were the most heavily subsidized. There are still remnants of this in the farm bill today, with all but tobacco receiving abnormal amounts of money, although the South does not elect their politicians for life so much any more.) Meanwhile, a whole suite of technologies were beginning to take the labor out of farming and reduce the farmer's role to that of just one link in the supply chain instead of all of it.

After World War II, this trend accelerated exponentially. Munitions plants, stocked with leftover ingredients for weapons, were converted into production plants that turned those ingredients into chemical fertilizers. By exploiting the properties of deadly nerve gas, pesticides were developed that could improve yields and increase production in agriculture by killing insects. Some of these products, like ammonium nitrate fertilizer, had been around since the late 1800s. But now it was cheaper and more widespread than ever before, and it meant that young, ambitious farmers like my father had the opportunity to move away from the fully pastoral system their predecessors had followed—and to do so surprisingly rapidly.

This opportunity showed up in Bluffton in the form of a visiting fertilizer salesman from an ammonium nitrate company. It was 1946, the war had recently ended, and farmers were hungry to get back to doing what they did best. The salesman called a farmer meeting at the Bluffton Peanut Company, right in the center of town next to the one-room courthouse. He threw a fish fry to break the ice, then he pulled out a hundred-pound bag of ammonium nitrate fertilizer. Touting its miraculous-seeming benefits, the salesman portioned out five or ten pounds of it into smaller brown paper bags, handed a bag to each farmer present, and said, "When you get home, spread it out there into your pasture or field, put some water on it and don't look at it for three days." My father did as he was instructed. Three days later, he came back to the pasture, and the grass had shot up several inches. No longer the pale green of early growth, it was deep in hue, with an almost blackish intensity to it. Immediately, he was hooked. "Damn!" he exclaimed. "I want the whole farm to look like that."

And so began a ritual that went on for over fifty years: putting ammonium nitrate on every acre of the farm, at least once, if not twice, every year. You see, as a typical cattleman saw it, the primary objective was to get the grass growing as fast, thick, and high as possible. Fast grass equaled faster-growing and fatter calves, which would make their way off the farm sooner, generating more revenue. The rush that my daddy felt, seeing his grass grow that much, was heady. Addicting even. Any fool could see what he saw: a quantifiable difference in growth from a Monday to a Thursday. Seeing the pastures around the Home Place springing into electrifying growth made him hungry for other industrial inputs like herbicides, pesticides, and fungicides to swiftly and easily kill weeds, pests, and fungi, and for plentiful corn, which he grew on this land or shipped in cheaply from outside, to feed to the cattle. The fertilizer was like a gateway drug: it made all the rest irresistible.

You can't fault farmers like my father for embracing these new tools. For one thing, they'd lived through the Great Depression and the Second World War; they had been close up to hunger, deprivation, and suffering in ways that most of us today have never been. And the industrial methods being offered were so much easier than the traditional methods for making nature produce in their favor; it was much less arduous than previous methods. From my perspective today, looking back, ammoniated chemical fertilizer was just about the most damaging thing a person could ever put on land, because of the way it nukes the microbial life in the soil. But from the perspective of the farmers of my father's generation, looking at their booming fields day in and day out, things were going exponentially better. And all it took was money.

Starting about the 1950s, the proliferation of cheap corn in the new commoditized market helped to create an entirely new kind of agriculture: confinement meat production. This didn't *start* as an industrial or corporate endeavor, mind you. Originally, it was a way for the corn-growing farmers of the Midwest to make more money from their corn harvest. By feeding the corn they grew to cows instead of selling it as a commodity, they could add a whole other layer of value to their farming and produce a much more profitable food—beef.

My father took note of the feedlots that started springing up in the Midwest to supply the growing market for grain-fed beef. These invited the farmer to sell off his cattle long before they reached slaughter weight, freeing him from the cost of raising them to several years of age. Now, after weaning from their mamas at about six or seven months of age, they were sent to massive facilities where they lived out the next two-thirds of their lives doing one thing only: consuming copious amounts of high-calorie corn instead of grass, and converting that corn into beef with the speed and efficiency of a machine. Holding the cattle in confinement instead of grazing them also reduced the farmer's or rancher's need for labor. My daddy started to sell his calves at auction to large feedlots that paid for them by the pound before shipping them off to their facilities in the Midwest. He was now a supplier to the new commodity beef system, one that took the cattle off his hands early and paid him a fixed price per head, offering him more stability and less risk. He also introduced a small feedlot onto his own land so that he could keep some of his calves until slaughter and sell beef to local stores. My daddy's feedlot was a mere speck compared to the ones in the Midwest, but it was the only one of its kind in our region. That, plus the size of his operation, made him an influential farmer, a worthy successor to the Harris family line. Will Harris II had officially left the old-fashioned methods behind.

It is hard to overestimate the significance of this shift to factory-style production. From grazing cattle to feeding them on intensively grown grains and from overseeing every step of the meat production himself to sending the live animal away in exchange for a check—that was liberating. For generations, farmers had raised a diversity of products they could sell or use on their farms. This not only was out of necessity—they needed to grow corn to feed the mule, and vegetables for consumption, and cash crops to sell—but it also buffered the risk of one species or crop failing. Now someone like my dad was rewarded for doing one thing: breeding mama cows, raising the calves, and getting them out the door. He was now running a cow factory. And a damn good factory it was!

A new kind of meat was the result: corn-fed beef, widely promoted as far superior to the lean beef that was the norm till then. (Kind of like the way smoking was once sold as good for you; this was now universally marketed as a much better kind of meat.) Corn-fed beef was marbled from the higher saturated-fat content, it was tender under the knife, and it was uniform in taste now that homogenous corn rations instead of grass from different ecosystems was standard feed. Even the cuts and portion sizes were standardized, now that butchering was done in bigger, centralized plants. All this consistency increased convenience for the American housewife working in the kitchen; it made dinner prep easier and more streamlined. Which was ideal, because everything that saved labor and was mechanized, and free from nature's unpredictable variation was now very much in fashion. (I still recall the first time I saw the words *grain-fed beef* etched with a red grease pencil on the windows of Mr. Scarborough's grocery store in Blakely. It was quite the hot item, my daddy explained, and the fact that it had made it to the shelves of our local store was cause for celebration.)

Commodity corn-fed beef spawned the new American fast-food industry, which surged alongside the processed-food industry, thanks to commodity sugar—and to corn, and corn's evil offspring, high-fructose corn syrup. My daddy's generation rode the crest of the wave of surplus farming, which paid farmers, through government subsidies, to produce more than the country actually needed and ensure food shortages never occurred. This strategy kept free enterprise from working as well as it should have. It also changed the health of Americans in ways we are paying dearly for today.

By the time I was born in 1954, my father was in the swing of industrialized cattle ranching, first in line for every tool it offered him. I don't think my daddy ever really *liked* the industrial methods, deep down. But he didn't let himself feel that—and to be sure, a cowboy didn't share his feelings, even if he knew what they were. Because another part of him relished being at the crest of the wave, no longer a jack-of-all-trades doing lots of things on the farm like his own dad, but a specialist—a cattleman of the first order, feeding America the affordable corn-fed beef that was its birthright. I can only imagine it felt a bit like being a heart surgeon—an expert in an enterprise that others couldn't fathom. Compared to the old guys before, who were handy at raising all kinds of things, a farmer in the fifties and sixties would've been fiercely proud of a narrower mastery of his trade, of having expertise that ran an inch wide and a mile deep. The pendulum was swinging away from the pastoral model based on animal husbandry, land stewardship, on-farm processing, and direct-to-consumer selling—and it was swinging *fast*. Which powerfully influenced opinion: soon everyone agreed that this kind of farming, and the food that came of it, was just fine.

And so did I. I'd hear all the stories about our pastoral past, of course, and I revered my granddaddy just like I revered my dad. But my father was running the farm now, and he was a force to be reckoned with. What he said, went; what he directed you to do, you did. Because he was damn good at it, because he could outwork almost anyone else around, and as Jenni puts it, because he was charismatic and demanding and could be surprisingly generous and also literally didn't give a damn what anyone thought, few people would have dared to question the methods he used or the thinking behind them. I certainly wouldn't have.

I loved growing up on this land. My dad and my momma, bless her heart, let me run feral over every inch of this property, and over its edges into the woods and waterways around us, hunting, trapping, and fishing, and almost never coming indoors. Like my father, I was an only child; also like him, I was feisty enough that I was always close to an ass whupping if I was anywhere indoors, so nature became my sanctuary. I came to know the hardwood bottoms and the rolling uplands like some kids know their Lego sets or toy car collections—I knew where everything was and how it all fit together, the different species of waterfowl and how they cohabited with the snapping turtles, and what an osprey was hunting for when he plunged into the alligator pond my daddy had made, and where the moccasin snakes would get you if you weren't careful. Our neighbors had a saying about us. "There are three kinds of people. There's good people that go to church. There's trashy people that don't go to church. And there's the Harrises." They didn't mean it disrespectfully—we were hardworking, tax-paying citizens. But in the heart of the Bible Belt, for the men in a family to shirk that white building in Bluffton was pretty damn unusual. (The only two instances I saw my daddy inside our village church were my wedding and his funeral.) I used to hear them say that as I kid, and I thought it meant we were not religious people; I was a grown man before I realized what the real deal was. Though anybody that is worth a damn has a church, in my opinion, it's not necessarily in the form of a chapel, or synagogue, or mosque. Oftentimes, it's very different from that—it's a passion that they are fiercely devoted to, that is freely given for the benefit of others. The Harrises are as spiritual as anyone else—maybe more so—but we have always felt closer to God in the pastures with our cattle than in that white building with its worshipers. For us, our pastures are our church; our waterways are our church. And I was baptized into it early, moving cattle every Sunday morning.

When I wasn't exploring this biome, barefoot and shirtless, I was closely watching my daddy on the farm. Even as a little-bitty boy, I wanted to be just like him. He had me on a tractor by age six; not posing for a picture but disc harrowing, which means breaking up rough land—not a precision job. More than one onlooker cringed at the sight of me on a metal seat with nothing but air between my pint-size body and the tractor's mighty wheels, but I puffed my chest out at the responsibility. And when my buddies declared, as eight- or nine-year-old boys tend to do, that they were going to be an astronaut, or a baseball player, or a firefighter, I knew that I was going to run our farm. All I ever wanted to do was run this farm. It never for a minute occurred to me to want to do anything else.

When I was eleven or twelve, I was put to work for real. In the rural South of that time, it was almost a rite of passage to put aside the cut-off blue jeans you ran around in all summer, pull on some long pants and boots, and step up to what your daddy needed you to do on the farm. I didn't begrudge it a minute; my life as a wild thing was great, but I wanted to have an influence, and an opinion, and to matter more around the place, and the only way you earn that on a farm is through hard work. As my father started to put me in charge of projects here and there—still at an incredibly early age to be supervising adults and making decisions, not to mention being held accountable for those decisions—I began to understand that the fields were where I worked, the woods were where I played, and there was a hard line between the two. One was organized, productive, and efficient, one was wild and unruly; it was agriculture on one side, nature on the other. They were as separate as church and state.

And the pull of industrial farming was *strong*. It appealed to the alpha dog in me; it was bigger, faster, and more intense than what my forefathers had done. It ran on more horsepower, had tricks and cheats, and got results. My father, tough as he was, was well respected in the community and had done well financially. I wanted to follow in his footsteps. (Besides, there were no other kinds of farming to emulate that I could see.) As teenagers eager for beer money, my buddy Rube Johns and I would load crop dusters with chemical pesticides, their fine powder raining down on our shirtless torsos before the planes flew off over neighboring row-crop farms. I helped my mom around the property, too, spraying the vegetable garden with newfangled pesticides that blitzed insects, happily eating tomatoes straight off the vine as I went. The commercials told us we had better living through chemistry—our fridges were stocked with new products like Tang and TV dinners, the doctor had all kinds of new cures for what ailed you, and none of us thought even a bit of what we were doing wasn't completely okay.

When I got through high school, my parents pushed me to go to college in the hopes that I'd land a "real" job off the farm. My daddy, successful farmer that he was, believed that white-collar professionals who drove Cadillacs, not pickups, *really* had it made. The farm as he ran it was still dependent on physical labor—he wasn't the type to spend frivolously on machines when muscle power could pick things up instead. To him, the life of the doctor or lawyer or corporate paper pusher was appealing—their lives were easier, they had more disposable income, they got to spend cold nights inside by the TV, not outside pushing cows around. Ironically, he was probably building more wealth than they were, in land and tangible assets on the farm. But the 1970s was all about "Big" farming: Get Big or Get Out was the motto of President Nixon's secretary of agriculture, Earl Butz. Historic family farms, the thinking went, should become obsolete; mergers, consolidations, and mega-farm operations were where the opportunity really lay.

Because I had no choice, I enrolled in the University of Georgia's College of Agriculture to study the methods and tools of modern animal husbandry—the major that any wannabe cattleman took but, more important, would also open doors to a respectable corporate ag career. When I graduated in 1976, I still wanted to return and run the farm. My father, however, didn't make it easy for me to do that.

Virtually everybody in my class had the same goal: to score a ten-thousand-dollar-a-year job with a Fortune 500 company. A salesman's position or a research gig with John Deere or DeKalb Seed or a company of that caliber was the holy grail. We'd give high fives to the person who scored a nine-to-five at Monsanto, and piteous looks to the guy going back to work the family feed store or farm. I began working in the agriservices division of a big conglomerate called Gold Kist, helping to run the company's cotton gins, peanut-buying warehouses, fertilizer-blending facilities, and grain elevators scattered around Georgia, Alabama, and Florida. I was good at what I did and over time I rose to become the youngest regional manager they ever had. But I hated every day of it. I was too young and dumb to know you were supposed to play golf three times a week with the higher-ups to advance your career. And I was such a chip off the Harris family block that I couldn't fit into the corporate mold. My style of management was extremely active. I made decisions swiftly and acted on them without doubt. *Ready, aim, fire! Aim, fire! Aim, fire!* Their style meant holding meetings about the decisions, hiring consultants, then holding more meetings about the consultants' advice. It was *Ready, aim, aim, aim, aim.* I quickly learned that being a trigger puller could get you real successful or real fired. I kept pulling the trigger nonetheless, and because my decisions were good ones, I ended up becoming the highest performer there—and the least popular. The landscape was changing around me as sophisticated networks of seed, chemical, processing, and grocery chain corporations grew quickly in the eighties, like grapevines that gradually got intertwined, dependent on the next one to hold them up. They began to consolidate into transnational corporations that set the terms and prices for food production. As a result, the export market grew, the independent family farm shrunk, and as a manager at Gold Kist, I was as deep in the belly of the beast as any sonofabitch you ever saw.

For a good ten years, I worked inside corporate agriculture by day, then worked our farm at night and on weekends, helping to run it as well. My father was getting older and he couldn't manage it all himself. But he wouldn't relinquish any control, so I played second fiddle to him, paying the bills at the kitchen table and cowboying wherever I was needed. My bride, Von, had the questionable pleasure of spending Saturdays and Sundays indoors with her mother-in-law. In my day job, I helped to sell all the tools science had given us to make beef production cheap and efficient; at my farm, we bought and used those tools, and in neither place did any of us question what their downsides might be. The feed was artificially cheap, thanks to crop subsidies, and the inputs were readily available, and both helped us extract the most from our land and animals, without thought of ever putting much back.

By the time my daddy was in his midsixties, he began exhibiting the first symptoms of dementia. When it became clear that he couldn't run the farm unaided, I left my managerial job and worked full time at the farm. We clashed constantly because when bull head meets bull head, things get competitive and combative pretty quickly, and neither side backs down. In retrospect, he was probably more right than I, and I probably challenged him too much, but he was not the type to mentor anyone, least of all his son. Only later did I realize how deep his misgivings were about his only child leaving a stable corporate career for a farm where, despite its relative success, he didn't see opportunity for the future. He had one thousand acres of land, all paid off, and a big herd of cows. But he would complain, "There's not enough for me and you to make a living here." Nonetheless, due to his health, he had to have me there. So Von and I raised our kids—Jenni riding the pastures with me every day after school, Jodi and our third daughter Jessica busily engaged in extracurriculars—and my dad's dementia gradually worsening. By 1990, my father's decline became too steep to ignore any longer, and the leadership of the farm became mine: I stepped in to raise the monoculture of cattle on this land just like he had.

I was a very industrial cattleman. It was a system predisposed to excesses—and I loved that part of it. The alpha-male, testosterone-charged person that I was relished the chance to play hardball now that I had control of things on the farm, and the game came naturally to me. When it became apparent that chicken manure, mixed with enough corn, cheapened the feed for cattle, I fed it to them, even though chicken shit is not what any cow would naturally want to eat. When a drug said on the label to inject the animal with 2 ccs, I gave 'em four. If a pesticide said to put out a pint, I put out a quart. It was like dosing your kid with two teaspoons of medicine instead of one. For me, a label rate was just the starting point and you moved *up* from there. I had a foot on the pedal and a hand on the brake—high-carbohydrate, grain-based diets promoted super-fast growth, then pricey pharmaceutical drugs took down the painful bloat and liver infection that resulted. The results were hard to deny. My calves weighed, per head, at least twenty pounds more at weaning than those of other operators, which, multiplied by 700-some calves, increased my take significantly. In my community, I was well respected for my success, a farmer with a leadership role, just like my father, grandfather, and great-grandfather had been. I was a hard-pushing commodity cowboy and I'd mastered the skills better than just about anyone else around me. Until one day I looked at what I was doing and said, *This sucks. This sucks real bad.*

Chapter Three

A Horrible Price to Pay

One day in the fall of 1995, I stood at our corrals and watched a hundred head of five-hundred-pound calves getting loaded onto a double-deck eighteen-wheeler that would wrench them out of their coastal savannah ecosystem and transport them to a massive feedlot thirteen hundred miles away in a very different ecosystem, the high plains of Nebraska. They would stay there for a year before being moved again to one of the high-volume industrial slaughterhouses that are common in the West and Midwest. I knew from two decades of experience what would happen when they left my farm: a thirty-hour ride with each steer jammed up against the next, deprived of food, water, or rest; the steers on the top deck peeing and shitting on the ones on the bottom. Transporting calves this way off the farm to big feedlots in Iowa or Nebraska was absolutely standard in our industry. We'd done it at our farm several times a year since the 1960s. But standing there looking at it on this particular day, something changed in me. I wish I could say that God spoke to me or that I saw a burning bush; but it wasn't that dramatic. It was just that something that had always felt reasonable and rational to me suddenly felt very wrong.

I had worked hard to raise these animals the best way I knew how, protecting the weak ones from prowling coyotes and circling buzzards after their birth, checking in on them in the pasture every day to make sure they and their mamas were okay, ensuring they got their fill of mama's milk and grass. And now this. Their natural existence ruthlessly curtailed; their value reduced to nothing more than a commodity with a price tag on it. It suddenly felt like raising your daughter to be a princess and then sending her to the whorehouse.

Probably, if I had played by the rules a little more, I wouldn't have gotten so disgusted. But I had pushed the limits with all the tools of industrial farming, tools that I had used with impunity. Not just the pharmaceutical drugs and unnatural feed I gave to my livestock, but the chemical fertilizers I used to squeeze more grass out of my pastures and the pesticides that I used to destroy anything that got in the way. When the disdain for what I was doing hit me, it was with a hard slap.

I don't apologize for how I farmed up until that point. Everything in my life so far had conspired to make me that kind of farmer—one with a heavy hand on the inputs and a healthy sense of bravado as well. I'd absorbed the John Wayne mystique of the cowboy like any kid of the fifties had—except it was personal, because they were making *movies* about cattle people like us! The culture of my family literally bred swagger into my genes, making the practice of arm-wrestling with nature more than okay. That was reinforced by how my father rolled—tough and macho, not inclined to back down. And then there was college, where industrial farming was the whole curriculum. The way I farmed was not only to be expected, I'd say it was destined.

You have got to remember, I come from the generation that lived the societal transformation from worshiping nature to worshiping science. Our parents were entirely seduced by their new postwar reality in which science and technology held all the solutions for staying well-fed, comfortable, and safe. I couldn't have articulated this as a kid, but I certainly felt it. There I'd be, slurping water out of the cattle troughs when I got thirsty outdoors—blowing on the surface to part the thick green scum before dipping my head in—while indoors, my momma was in horror at a speck of mold on bread. Her reality was vastly different from mine: to the parents of the 1950s, nature was full of invisible threats like microbes; and all microbes were germs; and germs were the enemy because germs made you sick. The universal quest—in nutrition, in housekeeping, in medicine, as well as in farming—was for a sterile environment.

And that attitude rippled across everything. To be a young American in the late fifties and sixties meant—unless you were really countercultural, and nobody I knew was—that manufactured was better than homemade, and sterile was better than living; that education was better than common sense, the laboratory was better than the kitchen, and the city was better than country. Flashy was better than authentic, and imported was better than domestic. The future was cool, the past was not, and the wise ways of our ancestors were entirely too antiquated. Productivity came from *technology* now— and it was some powerful shit!

I don't think America suddenly lost its *awe* of nature. Or its respect for the farmers and their amber waves of grain. But we bought into the new agreement that nature, working at its own speed, in its own cycles, was too *inefficient* to properly provide our food. The world's population was growing, sure, and there was a noble goal of feeding more people and avoiding hunger. But I think the belief came from a more subconscious place than logic. The human mind easily believes that since we are the only species that has mastered technology, we can use it to one-up nature. All puffed up about it, we start to forget that nature is in charge and begin to reinforce for each other how great it is that technology is in charge. From there it's a quick jump to the next concept: "Because we *can* do it, we *should* do it." Technology offers things nature doesn't: It is discoverable by us, and patentable by us, and marketable by us. Its benefits are immediately apparent, while its drawbacks don't show up till much later. It can make some people obscene amounts of money; it can make some people close to godlike. So we decided that technology was a worthier altar to bow down before than nature was, when it came to growing our food. I have been accused of being too big for my britches more than a few times in my life; but I can't help but think that this took too-big-for-britches to uncharted levels.

Should a nitpicker try to point out that today at White Oak Pastures, we employ technology in the form of drones that help us track our herds and flocks, and GPS to track our vehicles, and software to sell and ship directly to customers, let me be clear: I do not believe that technology is intrinsically bad. It's hard to argue that it hasn't helped farmers to have easier lives. First we got the domesticated horse or mule team and the plow; then that plow got upgraded to where it could plow two rows instead of one. Then the tractor sped up field work from three miles per hour to fifteen. And on and on from there. The problem, in my estimation, is not that technology is intrinsically evil. It's just that in agriculture, we misapplied the hell out of it. We never considered the unintended consequences that plowing might have on the land, or how those consequences might compound with each technological leap.

Instead, we put all our attention on a single goal: making the whole process of producing food more efficient. And the way we did that was through the use of reductionist science, which broke down the holistic and complex systems of the natural world into smaller and smaller isolated parts that could then be studied and mastered, and improved upon by technology. This reductive approach was applied to everything—to the way we treat health and sickness for one thing— and it completely changed agriculture. It was in full swing by the time I got to college. In my classes, professors with PhDs taught my classmates and me, the future agriculturalists of America, how to dial in the exact amounts of pharmaceuticals and hormones to get our livestock to grow fat more quickly and how to saturate the soil with killer chemicals so you could have a blank canvas, so to speak, for growing monocultures.

The academics at the lecture podiums were the gatekeepers to this new, efficient world, and they held the keys to unlock the farming puzzle. In my soil science class, Dr. Kim Howard Tan, our professor, would confidently declare, "You cannot build organic matter in coastal plain soil!" He meant that the carbon material from naturally decaying microbes, plant matter, and animals that mixes with inert silt, clay, and sand to create fertile soil was near impossible to increase here, where the very sandy soil allows soluble minerals and nitrogen to leach out easily. We all wrote that in our notebooks. The only way to extract productivity from our weak Georgia soils, Dr. Tan was telling us, was to use the tools of modern technology. And he was right. If you farmed the way they taught us, with mechanical tillage to break up the earth so that plant roots could penetrate, and with soil fumigants to sterilize the soil before you planted seeds, you couldn't go back. You would have fundamentally altered the way soil naturally works to such an extent that you'd need to pour on chemical fertilizers next, or you would have no crop. But that was okay; these man-made crutches were better than anything nature could have come up with on her own.

Raising livestock successfully, meanwhile, meant following the linear steps that had been proven to work by university researchers, whose studies, I later learned, were often directed and paid for by the companies that made and profited from the results. First, separate one species from the others and raise only one species on your farm— make it a plant or animal monoculture. If you were a cattleman, separate the calves from their mamas at six months, separate them from their natural foods of mother's milk and grass, and separate them from the land. Transport the animals to a feedlot (which might be a thousand acres but populated by about a hundred thousand cattle) and get them on a high-calorie diet of grains that nutritionists have precisely engineered. Blend antibiotics into that grain, at a low level, to hasten their growth and avoid or temper the sickness that might come from the stress of such a life. Give them hormone implants to disrupt their natural endocrine function, and thereby increase their weight gain. And on and on. We students were taught the how-to procedures of linear, assembly-line production that ended when the slaughter-weight steers got picked up by the double-decker truck from the feedlot—and our part in it ended months before that, when the animals had left our farm in exchange for a check. The art of farming, which has always been highly situational and intuitive, requiring a broad understanding of a complex living system, was reduced to a scientific instruction manual. Do each step right, the promise went, and use the indicated products at the prescribed times, and you, the producer, will reliably achieve your goal. And just like that, a new era of industrialized farming was born. It was about efficiency, at any cost.

This new, science-based approach to farming took one of the most necessary cyclical systems—the never-ending circle of birth, growth, death, and decay—and made it a linear, factory-line process to achieve plentiful food for the consumer and ample profits for providers. The appeal of this was undeniable. After all, a straight line is the quickest and most direct route from point A to point B. And once you've got an assembly line up and running, you can do a lot of things to increase productivity. You can develop hundreds of products to improve performance at each step; you can train specialists to go out and teach farmers how and why to use those products (what we generally term "inputs") and turn them into captive customers who cannot do without them. You can take the farmer's role and simplify it to where he no longer oversees the whole cycle but just a couple of parts of it: growing his livestock from birth to six months instead of managing the entire cycle from birth to slaughter to processing, distribution, and selling, and composting leftovers as my predecessors did. And you can get the farmer to send his food products—be it beef or wheat or tomatoes or corn or oranges—outward into a large national (or multinational) and centralized commodity system that buys raw foodstuffs in bulk, at set prices, then extracts value from them by processing and distributing the food through centralized facilities and supply channels that take food miles away from its source. The farmer loses out, because with all these other entities extracting value, he gets less for his products. But he makes the trade because this "hyperefficient" system promises him high volume to make up for the lower price per unit, and a (seemingly) reliable market for his goods, and a much more convenient, simpler job on the farm. In a (very simplified) nutshell, this is how the commoditized and centralized system was spawned by the industrialization of growing and raising food. It dumbed farming down.

Think for a moment of how profound a shift this was: The three ugly sisters of industrialization, commoditization, and centralization turned nature's complex, and still somewhat mysterious, supply *cycle* into a linear and efficient supply *chain*. A chain stretches away from its source to an end point far away. A cycle feeds back into its source, over and over. Which one, do you think, would sustain the farmer, his land, his animals, and his local rural economy, helping them all to thrive in perpetuity, and which one would leave all those things depleted and close to collapse? The right answer is obvious. But we must remember the need for corporate profit. The supply chain is much easier to scale up cheaply, creating a lot more money for all those bigger entities involved. Since in this model farmers follow standardized procedures, they can pretty simply be added in to the start of the chain as demand grows. (Kind of like adding more assembly lines into a busy car-parts factory, where every line is doing the same thing the same way.) This efficient machine model helps to cut costs (those costs don't disappear, but they do get shunted into less obvious places), and pretty quickly huge economies of scale are achieved. Linear efficiency is how the average American ended up being able to buy chicken on sale at a dollar a pound, anywhere in the country, at any time of year—even though I can tell you from decades of experience that the farmer's true cost of properly raising a chicken for market is over four dollars a pound.

I have heard it said that through the application of reductionist science, chemists have been able to isolate all the ingredients in seawater and they believe they know exactly what it comprises. But when they put the ingredients back together, a fish can't live in it. It's not the way the water and fish evolved. I think that's what happened through taking agriculture apart into all its separate silos and trying to put it back together again using technology. The food we ended up with isn't really food and the farming isn't really farming. There is a big ripple effect from that.

My degree when I enrolled at the University of Georgia in 1972 was called animal husbandry, but when I graduated four years later, it had been renamed animal science. The word *husbandry*, which is the old-world description of how a stockman cares for the animal's needs and the animal provides for the stockman in exchange, was too unscientific by 1976. Husbandry asks you to see the whole: to understand the herd and the land and the cycles of nature. Husbandry is something of an art, and it requires skills, experience, and knowledge. I can only assume that some higher-ups in the halls of academia had gotten wise to the fact that art was not good business, and since business paid the academy, the future agriculturalists of America had better switch sides. I'd entered college as the last of the old guard, and graduated as the first of the new.

I'll confess that I was never a great student of this siloed approach to agriculture. I wasn't interested in pursuing more and more knowledge about less and less. My brain likes knowing a little bit about everything—and knowing the hell out of those bits. I could swing a C in every class I took, and the buck stopped there. It was only decades later, when I'd adopted a more holistic way of farming, and when I was fortunate to be befriended by the great Allan Savory, that I could finally articulate the mismatch I'd felt as a student. Alan is a herdsman and scientist from southern Africa, and he is the founding father of holistic land management, the farming philosophy I follow. He describes how living systems are inherently *complex*—many parts interrelating in dynamic and unpredictable ways, with one part able to adapt and support the rest if any other part fails. The human body is one such complex system; an ecosystem is another. This complexity is what makes these systems resilient under pressure. In making agriculture factory-like, and forcing it into a linear system that could be scaled up and up—but that can also fall apart when any one component of the system fails—we were acting as if it wasn't. We humans used technology to make it complicated, like a computer network where countless separate parts had to all work perfectly for the thing to function, instead of letting it be complex. Our puny attempts to better nature turned out to be a big mistake.

But this was the late 1970s and early '80s, a period when the corporate trifecta of Big Ag, Big Food, and Big Grocery were rapidly growing into a superefficient food machine that was changing the ways we farmed, ate, and shopped. If a person wasn't sure by then whether technology was a stronger force than nature, they soon would be: the makers of the machine had large platforms and loud voices. Americans in their homes and out on the farms quickly learned that processed foods, convenient shopping, and feeding the world with technology was what it was all about. As a farmer, if you could elbow a few other producers out of the way to be an important cog in it, you did so. So that when I started operating the farm here in Bluffton myself, I lived and breathed what I'd absorbed. Efficiency was the holy grail—to accomplish more, by adopting new methods and investing in new tools, in order to gain quicker and bigger returns. As a stockman feeding your cows into the beef commodity system, you get paid by the pound; he or she who gets the maximum poundage out of each animal wins. That becomes the prize your eye is always on, and you throw at it everything you got. Just like my daddy seeing that grass explode into growth back in 1946, I was transfixed by the effectiveness of the industrial tools I used and I was hooked by the promise of the path they took me on. I still remember the day that "cheap" ear tags impregnated with insecticide came out—I think I knocked two or three guys out of the way to get my share, and probably their share, too. The flies got blitzed entirely. I felt like a winner.

As I took more and more control of operations at the farm, the returns on my investment were good. I couldn't complain; I had a nice house and a good pickup and took my kids on vacation every year. What I failed to understand, however, was that the technologies of reductionist science had an ugly underbelly. For each industrial tool I used, there was always a consequence—one that without fail was bad, always unintended, and always unnoticed until tomorrow or next week or next year or even next decade.

I failed to see that the unnatural grain I fed the animals, trucked in from industrialized monocultural farms, required substantial amounts of petrochemicals to cultivate and transport, using up nonrenewable resources—and also created painful acidosis in the animals, unnecessarily causing suffering.

I didn't yet see that those ear tags didn't work so well the next year—forcing me to buy more of them—and then less well the next, and then the flies started eating my ass up, and the cattle's asses after that. They'd annihilated all but the strongest flies, who'd bred and become super-resistant to the chemical, which no longer worked. Nor did I realize that the antibiotics we regularly put into the feed at low levels to help with the acidosis bloat as well as respiratory problems were helping antibiotic-resistant bugs to find their way into the environment.

Nor did I see that the ammonium nitrate fertilizer I applied to my pastures quickly oxidized the organic matter that gave the soil its biological force, and the pesticides stripped it of its microbial life. This reduced the soil's ability to hold water (changing it from absorbent sponge to hard tabletop), which in turn changed the temperature of the air, contributing to a broken water cycle that played out in extreme weather events. I did not see that nitrogen residues from the fertilizer escaped during large rain events into my streams, and then into rivers, and even, ultimately, to the Gulf of Mexico, contributing to the algae blooms in the waterways and the Gulf that kill aquatic life.

I wasn't acknowledging that shunting cattle away from where they were raised and into centralized meatpacking facilities over a thousand miles away was depriving my local economy of historic agricultural jobs, and that towns like Bluffton and Blakely were losing *their* life force as a result.

And though it shames me a little to admit it, I don't think I was even noticing how many species of animals that were my companions as a child—from crawdads at the gator pond I fished at, to toadie frogs in the ditches we played in—were now missing, no longer able to survive in a biome that was saturated with life-killing chemicals. When I first saw them coming back, some years into managing my land for the better, I was not only astonished to see them but also astonished that I hadn't noticed their absence.

I was slow also to notice the lowered resistance against diseases and pests in my livestock from relying on all the insecticides and antibiotics and vaccines; the weaker genetics in the herd from bringing in seed stock from outside; and the reduction in the diversity of grasses and forbs and forage, and the pollinators that liked them, and the predator insects that helped keep pests in check. Nobody else was seeing or talking about these consequences—not the teachers at my educational institution, or the authority figures above me, or my peers in Southwest Georgia—so why would I?

Instead, I spent my days as a conventional cattleman looking for the next problem to fix and the next enemy to kill, because this is exactly what I had been trained to do. As an industrial farmer, you were to go out each morning looking for problems and use your arsenal of remedies to rid yourself of the symptom. My mornings went like this: Big cup of coffee, check. See the sunrise, check. Drive out to whatever large pasture my six hundred head of mama cattle were stationed in that month, and then start running the list: What's the weed situation out here today—is it more weedy than I want to tolerate? If affirmative, I'd get out the herbicide, a good quart of Graze On P+D. Next, crouch down low, hands and knees getting dirty on the soil. Is there an infestation of fall army worms? If yes, spray some Pyrethroid to take them out. Search the blades of grass for leaf spot mold. Better get the fungicide. Test the soil for nutrients, then add nitrogen, phosphorus, and potassium. Now look over the cattle for bottle jaw, which is a sign of parasites; some of them might need a dewormer. And if there are over two hundred flies per head, the book says to spray insecticide on them, so I'd do that, too.

I was good at doing this—taking enemies out was a skill set I felt proud to have and I was always looking for a chance to use it. On a large cattle farm in a very humid environment, where the teeming biome encroaches on you from all sides, there is always some problem to aim at every single day of the year. When you have created a monocultural, industrial farming system, there is always something wrong that needs correcting. There are always what *appear* to you to be problems to fix. Kill the worm, kill the bug, kill the fungus, kill the parasites, kill the coyote, and so on and so on. But everything I was spending so much time and money on was actually just a symptom of deeper problems I was inadvertently creating by my farming practices. And you seldom solve problems by attacking the surface while ignoring root causes.

An ancient Greek said something to the effect that for every pestilence that nature sends, she also sends the cure. In a biome that is undisturbed, predators are constantly preying on other creatures lower in the food chain, doing the killing and taking-out for you. When you choose to farm industrially, however, you make choices that throw all that out the window. You spray pesticides to kill army worms in your fields because they eat the grass to death, and the unintended consequence of that is to kill the spiders out there, too, but the spiders had been keeping the army worms in check, and now you don't have their help. You have excluded the cure. Or you give your cattle a dewormer drug to kill internal parasites, and it kills the dung beetles in your pasture. But the dung beetles were keeping the horn flies in check, so now you have to spray them. And there is no end to it. You need more and more of the industrial tools—the insecticides and other -cides—to keep things in your favor.

I couldn't see the downsides of this system because what we were doing was so clearly *the right thing to do*. What kind of fool would deny that a big pasture growing nothing but Tifton 85 Bermuda grass was a smart idea? This cultivar was bred by the University of Georgia's Experiment Station in Tifton, Georgia, and was selected over years of research to grow the fastest and tallest of all the grasses that prosper in this ecosystem. You could count on it to get you to your goal of heavier cattle at sale time. Its claim to fame was that it could assimilate unnaturally high applications of chemical nitrogen fertilizer. Never mind that this led to the cattle ignoring everything else they could have eaten, which encouraged weeds, which required the use of herbicides. Who would question spraying gallons of Roundup along fence lines to keep them clear of the weeds that might rust your fencing? Never mind that the glyphosate in that Roundup killed helpful microorganisms, pulled minerals out of the soil, and drifted dangerously into my family's homes and water supply. That was called taking good care of things on the farm. And when my neighbors' monoculture crop fields boasted row after row of corn or cotton or peanuts stretching on for acres, every single plant in each field looking like every other plant, not a leaf out of place or a weed in sight, it was so very satisfying to the eye. As appealing to look at as the straight rows of brand-new automobiles I'd see outside the Ford plant near Atlanta—parking lot after parking lot of blue Tauruses, then silver ones, then white ones parked in perfect order, as far as you could see, every one just alike. To look upon such uniformity of *anything* appealed to my sense of order. It wasn't until later that I remembered what I knew instinctively as a boy: in nature, neat and tidy and uniformity and sameness don't happen. Uniformity is unnatural, brought about only by unnatural acts.

All this sounds disconnected when I look from the perspective I have now, because I *was* disconnected—in the first place, from the cycles of nature that spin off abundance, and from myself as well. That way of farming, which was working *against* nature, felt very normal to me, because it was normal for everyone else. The rapid rise of the corporate food machine, with its superefficient arms of production and distribution, had conditioned us to feel as we did. But it had made food obscenely cheap and wastefully abundant and boringly consistent. And because the cost of food was so much less than it had been just a generation prior and was getting cheaper by the year,

I think we were all dazzled, unable to glimpse the devastating toll paid by the land, the animals, and the rural communities—I know that I was. The power and prestige of being one of the families leading the parade still appealed to me.

I'll never forget a moment back in the late seventies when Jimmy Carter was president. One of his sons married a lovely local girl named Annette, who happened to be the daughter of Mr. Buddy Davis, who was a very successful industrial farmer in these parts, just like my dad. Annette brought her newborn baby to town to meet Buddy, and we crossed paths outside his office. She mused, "Just think! His granddaddy is the most powerful man in the world!" I replied, "Yep, and his *other* granddaddy is president of the United States!" The captains of industrial farming had that kind of eminence in our America back then.

I want to be crystal clear: none of the unintended consequences of postwar farming came because farmers did not care what they did to their land, and their animals, and their communities. Every farmer I've ever met believes that he or she is a good steward of the land and is compassionate to animals. All the farmers I've ever met work tirelessly and relentlessly to uphold their part of the deal, and to keep food products coming into the system. I also believe that the scientists who created industrial agriculture had many good intentions. But you start on the industrial trajectory with the mindset that germs are bad and that monoculture is good, and then you let the guy in the corporate corner office making billions of dollars by supporting that system call all the shots, and pretty soon you forget what you knew to be true before. Pretty soon the cyclical processes of farming are a "vertically integrated" food production chain with the guys in the corner offices owning most of it. Pretty soon, there are experts at the top of the whole structure who say they know much more about it than you could ever know on your own. They make the how-to manuals you need to follow to be cool and in the game, and make it pretty clear you're a loser if you don't, and there's no turning back. This complicated system developed in just two generations and today four multinational companies control 88 percent of the beef processing in this country. A handful of corporations control many categories of foods and drinks.

The apogee of this modern agricultural system as I experienced it back then was the annual cattle convention hosted by the National Cattlemen's Beef Association. It was held in venues across America. If you were in the cattle trade at any level, you wanted to be at this trade show. It meant you were relevant, hip to the times. You were a player. And it let a farmer from the fringe areas rub shoulders with the industry's high rollers. Cattle farming occupies a kind of stratosphere in farming, much more so than chicken farming or hog farming or rutabaga farming. It's a world where the ballers strut around in five-thousand-dollar custom boots, making deals for million-dollar stud bulls, where Fortune 500 CEOs run cattle on the side for the tax breaks, and money moves from hand to hand as fluidly as water. The rank-and-file cow people like me would make their way to Las Vegas, or Fort Worth, or New Orleans at their own expense, get a shitty hotel room near the convention center, and step into what was basically a carnival of consumerism. Hall after hall of sales booths offered the latest, greatest tools for enhancing your cow-calf operation, brought to you by Cargill or Tyson or John Deere or Monsanto or any pharmaceutical company. A good-looking model with shiny hair and white teeth would give you a pen and a peppermint just for stopping by. Even a levelheaded guy could find himself pretty quickly developing an appetite for products and services he didn't even know he needed and couldn't afford. Surrounded by bright lights and big smiles, a farmer could acquire everything required to succeed—from seeds or semen to deals with feedlots or cattle brokers—each thing priced just low enough to hook him, and just high enough to ruin him over time. But the message was clear: only an unenlightened yokel or an obsolete grandpa would try to farm without the whole inventory.

I admit I got a rush out of walking through it, as tacky as much of it was. Being inside this glittering technological showcase made me feel super advanced, like I would go home and crush the competition. Now, of course, I see it for the mirage it was. The throwaway swag and complimentary beers after five couldn't completely cover the sorry fact that the poor farmer was there to be duped. These people were "farming the farmer" for their profit and his loss. Their machine had long tentacles and deep pockets and it looped him into dependencies that offered short-term gains but came with steep undisclosed costs. Sure, all the products and services on offer promised to lower his risk or make his work easier or increase his yield. All of it was alleged to make his farm more profitable. But when you factored in the damage they did in the long term by disrupting his farm's own capacity to provide what it needed—something I'll share more about shortly—the numbers added up differently. The quick gains in pounds and profit were ultimately at the expense of his land and his animals, and they sucked the money out of his own rural community. The companies that extracted value from his products were not headquartered in places like Bluffton, Georgia. In addition, the more dependent the farmer became on these outside products and services, the more the multinational companies could charge for them: bound to entities that gained more and more control of his process, and kept fairly comfortable but cut off from options to leave, you might call this the definition of an abusive relationship. In just two generations, only a few decades after the fish fry my daddy attended outside the Bluffton Peanut Company, the little farmer's hand-in-hand journey with Big Ag had become a race to the bottom in food quality, health effects, animal welfare, and environmental impacts. Everyone lost out but the corporations. Those with the most power and making the most money were the multinational conglomerates. They were the least hurt by and the least likely to see the unintended and unnoticed negative consequences. There are none so blind as those who will not see.

On that October morning when I suddenly perceived the unintended consequences of squeezing my cattle onto a double-decker for their ride of misery, I was jolted hard enough to turn off that downhill path. I wasn't hurting financially; my farm was one of the largest cow-calf operations in an area where most cattle came from small farms with less than a hundred-strong herds raised alongside crops, nuts, and fruit. I had no debt. I paid plenty of taxes every year. I was respected locally. I was selected as Farmer of the Year for the state of Georgia one year, and Businessman of the Year by the Small Business Administration another year. I was sitting pretty, from anyone else's perspective. But *my* perspective changed—kind of like when a small corner of your house becomes the junk zone, and you lived with it fine unheeded, tossing your old socks and broken toys there until it gets so out of hand you can't not see it anymore, and you realize it won't ever go away unless you make a very conscious decision that *This sucks. I am cleaning this shit up!* That's about how it was for me, nothing lofty or philosophical or grand. Just a C-student's aha that he didn't like what he'd been doing, and now he wasn't going to do it anymore.

You see, I'd always been shown and told and taught, and had

experienced for myself, that animals that were well-fed and well wa-tered, kept comfortable, protected from predators and in no way abused, were enjoying absolutely fine animal welfare. And I'd always thought of my cattle as *looking* good, too, barrel-bellied and stocky, well on their way to being fat young teenagers. Now I saw more. My cattle were about to spend the next two-thirds of their lives on a feed-lot, eating ridiculously cheap subsidized corn and soy that would transform them from magnificent cellulose-digesting creatures graz-ing on pastures into crappy, grain-digesting animals gorging from a trough. They would be encouraged to grow obscenely obese, akin to a twenty-year-old human weighing four hundred pounds. By the time they would be slaughtered, they would likely be dying of the diseases of obesity and sedentary lifestyle that kill countless humans today. They would be confined to a high-density feedlot, where pharmaceu-ticals would be relied on to keep them alive (and keep the feedlot profitable), their legs sunk almost to their bellies into manure and muck when it was wet—their lungs filling with inhaled fecal dust when it was dry. They would be about as far as they could be from the land that they evolved to live in symbiosis with. Sure, as an animal scientist, maybe I had succeeded. But as a practitioner of animal husbandry—as the descendant of Harrises who had staked their rep-utations on the proper care of livestock—I was failing miserably.

I had heard about a new category of consumers, still small, who wanted to buy meat from producers who raised their animals accord-ing to high standards of welfare. This was the mid-nineties; there was no conversation among any consumers I'd heard of about the environ-mental impacts of industrial farming. Back then, there wasn't even an awareness of what grass-fed beef was. Mainly, these early adopters I'd heard about just wanted the livestock to have a better existence, and they were willing to pay a little extra for that. So I decided to stop sending my cows off the farm to feedlots and to stop feeding them unnatural feed on my own farm. I decided to not confine them in lots of any kind and, instead, to let them live on pasture their whole lives and eat grass as nature intended. In 1995, this way of ranching was very much on the fringe. The decision to change to grass feeding was a process of extreme fits and starts, infinitely challenging for a commercial operation the size of mine. Change came more slowly than you might think. But out there on my land, I liked how it felt to raise cattle on grass. It felt better to me.

Once I stopped that practice, I made more changes—a whole cascade of them. I gave up using the subtherapeutic antibiotics that had helped the cattle gain weight, and the hormones that did similar; and I continued to feel good, even when my bank account did not. I gave up more tools and made less money but liked it more. The impact this had on my cash flow was painful. The only reason I was able to do this was that I had no debt. I was farming more but profiting less. Yet some part of me saw that in my methods and practices, the downhill path was leveling out. I was starting to be free of what I didn't like.

Around that time, I had another epiphany. One spring morning, just after the pecan trees started budding, I was out in the hickory grove pasture on the northern end of the Home Place that my great-granddaddy established. Back there, areas of hardwood forest border the pastures, creating sanctuaries that offer shade on the hottest of days. I had always felt good in those woods where I had hunted squirrels and rabbits as a boy. That morning, as on every morning in those woods, the air was fresh with humidity and the pungent smell of decaying leaves invisibly transforming into new soil underfoot. I scooped a handful of the earth, rubbing it between my fingers, relishing how cool and moist it felt against my skin. Glancing over at the field where a crop of corn had been growing to feed to my cattle, I noticed how naked and barren the ground was in comparison. Nothing out of the ordinary, from a cattleman's perspective. But something about the contrast between the two types of soil struck me anew. Under the forest canopy, where cattle had grazed lazily for decades while seeking shade, but where no crop or grass had ever been cultivated by man, and most certainly no industrial tools had ever been employed, the soil's color was deep chocolate brown. Its texture was lush and full-bodied, its aroma mushroomy. The soil was alive with life. In the field where I was raising food to nourish the cows that would then nourish people, however, great areas of it looked like the gravel parking lot of a honky-tonk—hot, dry, and dusty. The soil out there was closer to a dead mineral medium than to a life-giving organism. Beyond my pasture lines, the fields of my neighbors were also in view. They were row-crop producers who farmed their soil as intensively as I did mine. There the earth was terra-cotta red, the subsoil fully exposed to the unforgiving Georgia sun after years of cultivation. I glanced back to the undisturbed earth under the oak trees, and the obvious hit me like a truck. *Shit, this is how soil is supposed to look!* I had never ever had that thought, and I don't think my peers had it either.

Knowing what I know today, I can better describe what I was seeing: the land that my neighbors and I were farming was starting to desertify. That may sound ludicrous in a part of the world where fifty-two inches of rain falls reliably throughout the year. But desertification can occur in any kind of landscape from lack of moisture held in a healthy soil structure. It can also occur from chemical damage. The inputs I used with such fearlessness had, just as Dr. Tan predicted, made me reliant on *more* inputs. I had unwittingly farmed this naturally lush environment into a degenerating, wet desert of sorts. My monoculture-crop neighbors, who used armfuls of inputs like I did, had farmed their land to death.

It takes powerful technology to create a desert in what is nearly the most humid part of the continental US. But intensive agricultural practices, used for years, can do it. And when you're steeped in the industrial paradigm, pouring on pesticides and ammonium fertilizer, you just go about life thinking that is what your land is supposed to look like. You think if it doesn't look that way, it has been unforgivably uncared for.

Today I see clearly how the practices followed by highly efficient, linear farmers such as I was were part of a system-wide sleight of hand—we were ignorant players in a game that was all about shunting the true costs of producing food away from the price tag the consumer saw. The food that came out of the linear system was artificially cheap—in reality, the price was subsidized by the environment, our wildlife and aquatic life, and our bad health. We just couldn't see those hidden costs yet—nor could we grasp how future generations would inherit the effects of our extractive, intensive farming methods. When you add up all the ways the bill is coming due, it takes the shine off the glittering promises of postwar industrialized food. The deal we made with our planet, its creatures, and our rural workforces, all so we could enjoy a slightly cheaper hamburger, might just be the worst deal that was ever made.

But changing back to a better way wasn't, and still isn't, easy to do. The industrial system has gone so far that we've just about reached the point where we can't function without its tools. You can't operate at a profit without them—not for some years, at least—and getting over them is like going through a wicked kind of drug withdrawal. After I quit using chemicals on my land, I would get to the time in the season when I once poured on the fertilizer without a second thought, and now I would have to hold back, relinquishing the easy explosion of green I'd gotten used to. I swear I acted like a heroin addict cut off from a fix. There were days I'd kill a man for a little ammonium nitrate.

What kept me straight was the gut certainty that I couldn't go back. I finally had seen the ugly underbelly of the reductionist approach. To make industrial fertilizers, phosphate and potassium are extracted from mines with no thought of what will happen when they run out. Aquifers, wetlands, and wells are drained to grow crops with no thought of their capacity to replenish. To squeeze productivity from pastures and fields, chemicals that hurt the land and caused rivers of water to run off are used, taking precious inches of topsoil with it. To make food production more profitable and efficient, the role of the farmer is reduced to being something akin to a widget performing a mechanized function, thereby losing the all-encompassing wisdom that had been passed down. Even with my C-student's comprehension of the natural sciences, I could predict that when you use up something you're dependent upon, it's gonna be a life-changing experience on the other end. I got to the end of the string and discovered that on the relentless quest for efficiency, I had given up resiliency, something much, much more important. The inconvenient truth is that efficiency and resilience are almost mutually exclusive. The more you strive for efficiency, the less resilience you'll have. It's incredible that we got it that damn wrong for that damn long.

This makes me sound very smart, saying it today. But I was no savant. Twenty-five years ago, a forty-year-old Will Harris did not spontaneously proclaim, "I do believe the climate is changing; I think I will mitigate it by changing the way I farm." That just didn't happen. Few people at all were talking about climate change back then, and a farmer in Southwest Georgia was not prescient enough to recognize it, let alone figure out how to mitigate it. Nor did I opine, as if holding a crystal ball revealing extreme weather events and power-grid failures and cyberattacks and pandemics to come, "I must build a more resilient farming system!" Though resilience is what we gained, as a function of the water getting better, the land getting better, the town getting better, and the animals getting better. I made the changes that I made simply to get away from practices I found displeasing and wrong. I didn't wear a sackcloth and put ashes on my head. It wasn't a philanthropic endeavor. But I realized that I had fought nature all my life and I wasn't ever going to win. That's why, midway into my life, I walked away from the altar of technology. I turned my back on reductionist science. I ceased to listen to the specialists sponsored by the corporations, the consultants with the corporate name tags, and even to other farmers and ranchers who followed all the corporate rules. And I started to listen again to nature, which knows everything and never lies. And the farm started working properly again. Because here is what I know now, unshakably and unequivocally: If you will just sit still and shut up and pay attention, nature will tell you everything you need to know. She will provide you with everything you need to make your farm work. Nature knows everything, forgets nothing, and bats last.

Part Two

Repairing What I Broke

Chapter Four

Restoring the
Cycles of Nature

I'll let you in on a secret. It's a secret not because it's so hard to figure out but because not many people know it. The few people who do know it, more than likely, you have never met. I've got most of their numbers in my cell phone, and I can confidently say: There aren't a lot of us. And we're busy. We're not out going door-to-door, passing out tracts, trying to convert anyone. But it's important to know, because it helps you take a much smarter, closer look at the way food is grown.

The secret is this: If farmers want to raise food in a way that is *better* for all concerned, and if they don't want to hand over a legacy of desertification, depleted soils, and polluted water to the next generation, they have to stop focusing on the end products and turn around to focus on nature as the source of life and growth. They have to ask if nature is functioning as it should on their farms. Are they working with or against nature? And then they must do everything in their power to collaborate with nature.

It seems obvious once you think about it. *Focus on the fundamentals. The start of the food chain.* After all, if you want a house that lasts, you start with the foundation. If you want to make a garment that fits, you start with the pattern. If you want to nourish people, and support life and support health, you start by ensuring that the cycles of nature that make seeds sprout and make water fall from the sky and make minerals available to plant roots are working as they should. You see, nature is designed to spin off an abundance. The whole phenomenon is geared for that to occur—if it's working right, that is. But over the last eight decades of industrial farming, we have horribly changed the game, so that now those ancient cycles won't spin off the abundance without the addition of a lot of man-made technology, in the form of agricultural inputs. It takes a helluva power to impede something as powerful and perpetual as nature. Somehow, we humans figured it out.

I'm not a genius who has giant eurekas. But I do have small eurekas every day. And when I saw that the soil untouched by agriculture was thriving, and the soil being used to grow food was not, it upset the applecart considerably. Having a flash of insight was one thing; figuring out what to do was harder. In taking those first steps on a different path, I wasn't making a bold, conscious leap toward "regenerative agriculture." That phrase and that kind of thinking didn't exist for me yet. (It didn't really exist for anyone at that point.) It was more like I quit digging the hole I had been digging. I set down the shovel, and just stopped.

What happened was that things started falling apart a little bit. For the first time in decades, the farm started to deteriorate. Without chemicals to annihilate the insects and the weeds, and without the fertilizers, the pastures began to look sick. When I ceased giving pharmaceutical cocktails to my animals, the unnatural diet I was still feeding started causing serious gastrointestinal and liver problems in the herd. When I did start to feed them nothing but grass, I over-grazed the land, and the cattle didn't have enough to eat. Humpty Dumpty hadn't quite fallen off the wall, but he was tottering.

Yet the problems served a purpose. They got my attention, fully and completely. I zoned in on what was *really* going on with my cattle and my pastures as I never had before. When I looked more closely, with a little less of the bravado and bluster that had driven me until then, I saw that all the things I'd been doing to pull more productivity and more success from my farm were destroying the basic operating principles of nature. In trying to force more food out of my land, I was undermining what was invisibly working *for* me. I was engaged in the business of providing food that sustained people, but I was overlook-ing the very gift of life by which nature sustained my farm.

Once I started seeing the changes in how soil looked and felt as a result of industrial practices, or in how water was being held in some pristine parts of this ecosystem but was running off easily in others that had been intensively farmed, I couldn't not see them. This was even more pronounced when I looked at the well-groomed monocul-tures of cotton, peanuts, or corn my neighbors grew, and the cruelly exposed earth left behind after they harvested their annual crops.

I can't tell you why it came so sharply into focus for me. Maybe, once I got off my industrial farming high and quit letting the back-ground noise of experts and inputs distract me, it was easier for me to remember the humility I'd had in the presence of nature when I was growing up. I'd prowled her forests for fun and foraged her bounty for food and gotten lost and scared in her wilderness, because I didn't have to come home after dark like other boys did. I'd had enough experience of her extremes—her six-inch rain events, her tornadoes barreling through cornfields, her snakes and spiders causing the only emergency room visits I ever saw my daddy make, because my people don't go to the doctor unless they can't stop the bleeding—to know that even with all our big-hatted efforts to outwit her and improve on her, humans are unworthy opponents. We could talk a big game and use the latest technology to try to override her rhythms or better her output, but really, from nature's perspective, we will always be a fart in a hurricane.

Plus, I'm a natural-born skeptic, a person who is not fond of outside authorities telling me what to believe, and certainly not telling me what to do on my own land. Once I realized that the tools of industrial farming weren't the silver bullets they'd been touted to be, the credibility of the PhD experts promoting the products and the technological gods pitching their latest innovations for my farm fell like a rock. It was not hard for me to scrutinize every line of what the corporate entities put out—and I did so, poring over their research papers and reading the fine print on their product claims, sitting at my farmhouse kitchen table late at night. Under the glow of a skeptic's lamp, the deal being offered to farmers began to appear a raw one: the farmer provides the monopolistic corporation with half of his promised benefit up front, by paying out handsomely for their array of inputs and technologies... which, it turns out, only delivers him *half* of the promised benefits because the bullet ain't so silver after all... and also dumps out *all* the negative unintended consequences, which are then distributed between the farmer and society at large, with almost none of the cost borne by the entity that offered the deal. It wasn't a giant leap for me to wonder, if those guys hadn't told us farmers about the damages their products would be doing to the soil and the water and the atmosphere, and to the health of the people using them (and the people eating the food that was being raised from them), then *what else weren't these smooth talkers telling us?* I had zero angst about discarding most of what they were offering. Cultivating food using the modern industrial system is like pissing in your pants to stay warm. It's okay in the very short term but a terrible strategy for the long term.

Once the forces of nature had won back my full respect, hanging on to technology's promises as a backup became non-optional. Jenni likes to say, *You can't ride two horses with one ass.* Once I made up my mind I wasn't going to keep supporting a system that was hurting my land and animals, and that had siloed what used to be a holistic, prolific system into separate and slowly degrading parts, and that had reduced the perpetual, self-generating, cyclical system of farming into a series of assembly lines spewing out products for short-term gain, I stuck to it. I accepted this choice, embraced it, and decided to ride the whole ride, through the storms, without switching sides.

A lot of farmers wanting to make this kind of transition struggle to maintain their conviction—and it's understandable, because giving up the treat-the-symptom approach, with its immediate gratification and its convenience and its relative low risk, is a lot harder than one might think. When you do, however, it's a much better deal. Because sure, there are significant costs and stresses involved in changing teams. But what you give up, you win back in spades: nature doesn't charge half up front and doesn't leave you with unintended consequences. You just have to come to terms with cooperating with what she's already got figured out for you, instead of fighting it. That mindset shift is the hardest thing to make.

That I was able gradually, slowly to deindustrialize my operation is not in itself earth-shattering. Though it took a lot of trial and error, even a person with limited intelligence could figure it out if they, too, quit listening to the background noise and just focused on what's in front of them. What *does* make me feel accomplished is that I figured out that the cycles of nature were broken to begin with, and saw they needed fixing, and decided something had to be done about it. Just like once you realize you are cold, you put on your vest, or when you realize you're hungry, you get something to eat. When you realize that you've gone and damaged or impeded the water cycle or the microbial cycle on your land, you take steps to fix it. Perhaps I'm underplaying it a little. By fixing it, I don't mean you press a button or make a call to some guy who'll sell you a suite of instant solutions for a price. Nor do you produce the answer overnight from some kind of analytical intelligence of your own. It's a lot slower and more internal and more ponderous than that. What happens is that you spend countless hours in observation of your land and your herds, wondering what's wrong and how to repair what's been damaged and how to restore the abundance that you know your farm is designed to give. You agonize over these things, and agonize some more; you lose some sleep, and probably drink a little more wine; and you go back and look at your land and herds again. At some point, you figure out what actions you are taking that are doing your land and animals harm, so you quit doing them. You suffer the withdrawal pains of giving them up for a while, then you start using the tools available to you to try to make the conditions around you a little better. And when what you do the first time doesn't work, you make a new plan and try that one instead. One step at a time, by planning, implementing, failing, and replanning and reimplementing over again, you start to figure out how to fix your farm. Plan; implement; assess; replan; implement; assess. It goes like that, and over time as you figure out what works, you build what I call "experiential wisdom." I admit I had an edge in doing this for a few reasons: I was an ecological and livestock abuser who had inflicted more damage than most because my abuse was so heavy-handed, so my motivation was higher. I had a quicker ability to see what nature needed because of my feral childhood. I had the financial wherewithal to make the changes once I perceived they were needed. And I was immune to peer pressure because I naturally didn't give a damn what anybody thought, kind of like my dad. But mainly I succeeded because there is no damn quit in us. Not ever.

Before we go any further, we probably should back up a little. For me, the cycles of nature are just about the whole story when it comes to farming and food. But I've learned the hard way that not everyone has read the book on it. So I'll give you my cowboy science interpretation of what they are—short and sweet and notably lacking in detail. (One vice I don't have is academic arrogance.) A vision of these cycles in action dropped into my mind when I was alone in the eastern corner of White Oak Pastures driving around the gator pond on the way to check on some goats. Our gator pond is a very special spot. My daddy created it in the 1950s by damming up a perpetual stream called Devil's Branch. An old fishing camp shack sat on its edge for many years, offering refuge for my daddy and his buddies and employees to fish for bass and chew tobacco once the cattle were seen to. To the testament of Von's saintly qualities, this shack was our first home, too, for the half decade before we had kids. I wouldn't even be so kind as to call it shabby chic. Let's just say it was real, real rustic. (Now it's been completely renovated into a cushy two-bedroom abode for farm-stay guests, complete with soft linens and gator-watching straight from the dock.)

The pond is framed on one side by a big swamp with great walls of foliage that appear to steam with humidity on hot days, as the plants release heat and cool off the earth underneath. Above the water, swallows streak the sky, chasing insects too small to see, and just under it, turtles zigzag left and right, searching for water bugs. Even if you only have two of your five senses firing, you'd instantly feel the sheer aliveness of this scene, in which everything in the biome is working as it should. As I drove, I pondered, What tremendous forces created this riot of life in the first place? A picture of this planet in its earliest iteration formed in my mind: A lifeless rock, spinning around the sun. Just a ball of black, brown, and gray shrouded in a poisonous atmosphere—incredibly hot on one side with all water vaporized and gone, and incredibly cold on the other side, all water frozen solid. And then somehow—and I'm not gonna debate how it started, but let's just agree that we do know it started—the Cambrian explosion occurred, several billions of years into this planet's existence. And then I saw a sequence of interrelating cycles beginning, which transformed the lifeless, inert rock into something else.

Plants evolved that could harvest the energy radiated by the sun. Through photosynthesis, the energy of light was taken into plants' tissues and turned into sugars, and proteins, and fats, instead of simply heating the lifeless rock and bouncing off it. Chlorophyll found so many different ways to show up in growing things, it was as if every color in a box of sixty-four Crayola crayons got scribbled onto blank paper. And all around were miniature solar voltaic panels—leaves—capturing energy and sending it down into the earth to be used for growth. The *energy cycle* began.

Photosynthesizing plants also absorbed carbon dioxide and the other greenhouse gases. By sequestering carbon, and nitrogen, and other elements present as gases in the atmosphere, the plants turned them into solid and liquid compounds to support other species' survival—such as plant biomass and liquid carbon and nitrogen captured in the soil. By turning that element of the periodic table into the basis of all life-forms, the rock became habitable for non-plant species, and the *carbon cycle* was in motion.

The liquid carbon exuded by the plants delivered nourishment to microbes like bacteria, fungi, and protozoa living around plant roots in the soil. The well-fed microbes worked to break down dying and dead plants into organic matter, the medium that makes soil viable for growing things. By decaying the plant matter, the microbes made the photosynthesized compounds bio-available as food for insects and other life-forms. Other microbes at the roots helped develop a kind of immune system for plants, helping them flourish. The sheer number of minuscule life-forms coexisting are almost beyond comprehension. Similar to what we now know happens inside our own bellies, the microbes became key agents that kept the whole system alive. The *microbial cycle* took off.

Minerals from rocks in the soil got synthesized by microbes, much in the way moss breaks down boulders, so they became biologically available to the plants. The microbes exchanged these synthesized mineral elements to the plants for the sucrose that they had made through photosynthesis, in an early example of nature's symbiosis. (Sorta like how cattle and cattle egrets coexist in my pastures—the roaming cattle flush insects up to the birds, and the birds reduce the volume of insects and stop them from becoming blood-sucking pests.) The *mineral cycle* was born.

As photosynthesis helped reduce the greenhouse gases in the atmosphere, and as plant tissues absorbed the radiant energy of sunlight from the rock's surface, the planet's temperature cooled. This allowed water to evapo-transpirate, moving through the plants from the earth to the atmosphere then falling back down as rain. The carbon-rich soils, meanwhile, had the structure to hold on to water, making water always available in the ground to drive more plant growth and move into the atmosphere. The *water cycle* was in play.

Flourishing plants and abundant water allowed herbivores to evolve. They roamed the earth bunched up in herds, pursued by predators further up the food chain. Herbivores ate the foliage from plants and turned it into manure. Their feces was assimilated by microbes, and then provided nutrition to plant roots so that the plant could further cycle minerals. When herbivores bite off the plant's foliage, it causes a portion of the roots to slough off before the plant can recover. This traps carbon, and other nutrients, in the soil. The plant literally operates like a carbon pump, breathing in greenhouse gases from the atmosphere and turning these gases into plant material (some of which is buried in the form of roots). When the plant dies, or is set back by being grazed, a portion of this carbon is sequestered in the soil. That is how much of the fossil fuel was trapped under the surface of the earth in the era of the dinosaur. The herds made the land lush and productive, as they themselves were nourished, and when they died, the decay of their bodies added to the organic matter in the soil—birth, growth, death, decay, repeat. The *grazing cycle* was at play.

Now I recommend you go back and read through again what I just wrote. I just explained the most beautiful, and complex, and important, and powerful goddamn thing that has ever occurred. It is what God is all about. And we humans, with our obsession on doing things better, faster, and bigger, have found ways to fuck it up. We are truly the most destructive species that has ever resided on this magnificent planet.

There are clearly a lot more cycles going on than those I just described. But six of them are enough to sketch a picture of an unbroken natural cyclical system, feeding around and around into itself for millions of years, so powerful that the abundance that it spun off turned a lifeless black, brown, and gray rock into a blue, green, and white planet teeming with life. So productive that for one time span at least, seventy-five-ton dinosaurs roamed some areas of the earth, achieving their astounding size through eating nothing but plants. (They were called Argentinosauruses—look 'em up.) They tell me that these creatures were almost four times as large as an elephant but had a head about the size of a horse's. And they only ate plants. Can you imagine how rich with diverse microbial life the soils must have been, and how filled with minerals, and how saturated with carbon and nitrogen they must have been, to have given rise to plant life that was nutrient-rich enough to support a seventy-five-ton vegetarian? And how capable the earth must have been of absorbing every single drop of precipitation that fell on it, to drive those super-size cycles of birth, growth, death, and decay? (Few people realize that humidity from a properly functioning water cycle is key to the processes of decay, which helps to build up the soil's organic matter. Moisture is essential to every aspect of nature's cycles, in fact—why do you think there is so much water on our earth? Nature provides.) And can you imagine what kind of cornucopia of plant species must have existed then— every different leaf shape and color photosynthesizing different bandwidths of light, so that not a single unit of solar energy was wasted, and resulting in mind-boggling amounts of carbon being captured and stored as deep reserves of oil, gas, and coal, way underground? I truly wish that I could go back in time, just for a minute, and see how beautiful it all would have been. Just the idea of that quickens my pulse.

All this cycling of carbon and water and energy and minerals would have enabled unlimited numbers of different plant, animal, and microbial species to live in symbiotic relationships with each other, sprouting and birthing and growing and decaying and feeding into all the cycles. It's incredible to imagine just how maximized the bounty and abundance would have been as a consequence. When natural cycles are allowed to function totally unimpeded and fully intact, they can really get rocking—they go full-tilt boogie—with all the cycles interrelating with each other, and a biome that's rampantly alive is what you get. I thought this vision of dinosaur-trodden fecundity was pretty profound at the time I had it. In all the many undergraduate soils courses I'd taken at the University of Georgia in the seventies, I'd never heard a thing that would've led me to think of soil as a living organism. We'd believed with the passion of zealots that if the world was only rid of all the germs and fungi and nematodes in existence, it'd be a much better place to be. Even now, as I look upon the forests and waterways and pastures where I farm, I am still in awe of the way the cycles functioned on and on, operating so beautifully, for millions of years, with no help from anything or anyone outside them. That's what makes even a gator pond with a swamp next to it alluring to my eyes. The cycles are humming so hard you can almost hear them. With all our man-made technologies, we Homo sapiens have never done anything remotely close to this feat. It should make even a mildly curious person question why we currently all feel so smart and good about raising hygroscopic vegetables under artificial lights and synthesizing fake meat by smooshing up soybeans.

Which makes it all the more devastating that we started to mess with this perfect system. Let's be honest: the Indigenous people of the Americas knew how to live with these cycles, in concert with them. They enjoyed abundance as a result. But once the Europeans came in—my ancestors—it all got fucked up. They started clearing the forests for arable land (taking down trees that help draw carbon down into the ground, sometimes by burning them); tilling the soil (breaking up the complex soil structure to destroy what they didn't want to grow and to ensure seed-to-soil contact), planting crops without replenishing nutrients in the soil (just moving on to the next piece of land after harvest). Slash, burn, repeat. If I'd been the chieftain of those North American Indigenous people, and knowing what I know now, I'd have killed all those Europeans as they came off those ships starving from months at sea—there were some that did try to do that, and I don't blame them. I'd have burned their ships and put their heads up on poles on the beach, as a sign to those who might come behind them: We got this—y'all go home.

The industrial tools that came later made it all so much worse. More pristine swaths of forests, grasslands, and other diverse ecosystems cleared to open up space for fields; more soil deadened as chemicals oxidized the rich organic matter, killing its magic; and more loss of minerals as microbes died off. Photosynthesis took a hit, because by practicing intensive monocropping of single plants, you lose the diversity of leaf colors and shapes that should be there to capture the maximum amount of sunlight, and you have good foliage available to perform it for only a third of a year, not year-round like nature does.

Exposing the earth to the elements after harvesting made soils even more lifeless and fragile, less able to hold water, and made the earth's surface even hotter. Constant tillage hurt soil structure and killed microbial life. Not to mention, growing only one crop at a time starved the soil microbes of the diverse foods and decaying plant materials they need to survive (kind of like our own bodies), forcing us to use more inputs as crutches, to prop up what we'd made wobbly and weak. Tapping fossil fuels for all the production and transportation of modern food pulled vast amounts of carbon out of deep reserves far beneath the surface, where it had been stored as oil, gas, and coal, then spewed it back up into the upper atmosphere to trap heat like a blanket covering an already hot greenhouse. Our confinement feedlots (more monocultures of livestock) screwed the natural microbes in nearby fields by dramatically changing the nutrient balance through over- or under-application of manure; and unpleasant artificial catchment systems called manure lagoons, built to handle all the shit coming from cattle and hog operations sent more carbon into the sky via methane, as well as seeping antibiotics from the animals' bodies into the nearby environment. Along the way, all this activity drove thousands of species of plants, animals, insects, and microbes, which had naturally evolved to serve some function on this planet, into extinction.

The misapplication of technologies to make monoculture crop production more efficient quietly caused the cycles of nature to sputter. It was like taking a top of the line, eight-cylinder engine and forcing it to run on one. Entire books are written on the details of the ecological disturbance that has occurred as a result of intensive modern food production. But it's safe to say that through our technologies of crop and livestock cultivation, as well as logging and mining and construction and urban development and any number of other invasive practices, we turned what was a productive paradise into fields that are as degraded as those honky-tonk parking lots—or worse. I've watched a lot of critters over my life, and I can safely say that no creature breaks the cycles of nature that exist to spin off abundance except humans.

It's astonishing how wildly disproportionate our human impact has been, relative to the very short amount of time we have spent on this planet. It's so obvious to me what a horribly destructive direction we are headed in; I scratch my head about why it's not as obvious to everyone else. I guess it's because our entire economy and society incentivizes all of us, including me, *not* to take the thirty-thousand-foot view. We expect to have infinite energy from fossil fuels, and AC on demand, and full tanks of gas in our cars, and cheap food, and a million different jobs that in one way or another depend on extracting from nature's reserves, but we lack comprehension of what it took to put them there or how fragile the cycles that made them can be. So most of us avoid thinking about it—until, that is, that hurricane or flood surge or pandemic or the chemical-related cancer diagnosis hits close to home. Coming to grips with what we are doing is a paradigm shift from hell. We just about can't do it.

Farmers are equally incentivized not to take the broader, bigger look. I've had countless agricultural experts and scientific specialists on my farm over the years, sometimes as hired consultants I'm hoping will help me solve a stubborn problem. I've come to see that every one of them—well-intentioned as they always are—have a worldview fully shaped by their silo, their personal hard-earned area of knowledge. Presented with the same systemic problem, the soil biologist will diagnose that the bacteria-to-fungi ratio is off; the plant geneticist says the genetics are awry; the livestock specialist says I should purchase the seed stock they've got on offer; and five different people give five different solutions based on their discipline. None of them are thinking of the farm as a complex organism in which every part is interconnected and influencing the next. They're watching the whole ball game through a sliver of missing plank in the fence. I get why that is—our land grant agricultural colleges have been teaching this approach for decades. But I think when you get that focused on your silo of knowledge, you learn more and more about less and less until you know all there is to know about almost nothing.

Because when you're dealing with a natural biome and the cycles operating in it, you aren't dealing in separate pieces. You're dealing in a complex whole with its own nuances that may be different from a biome not too far away. As a farmer, you're also working toward a context you have chosen—that means the goal you are working toward with your land. On this farm, my context is a functioning coastal savannah biome that produces ten species of meat I can monetize, as well as a bunch of other food offerings we use in our system and sell on the side. That's not the only context possible; someone else might raise fruits and nuts in orchards on this same land, in an agroforestry setup with hogs and ruminants around the trees. Perhaps some economic impetus will drive my kids to do that here one day. But I am the son of a cattleman, and I'm forever, first and foremost, a cattleman. So my context is shaped by who I am. It would be nice if some outside expert could hand you a step-by-step guide for building or operating your regenerative system, but it just wouldn't work. That kind of thing only works for complicated systems, like spaceships. No one can write a how-to manual for a complex system.

When I decided to fix what was broken on my farm, I most certainly didn't have a book or a template to follow. I just started making the shift intuitively. After I made the bold (and many thought foolish) decision to raise grass-fed cattle where previously I had supplemented with grains, and to keep cows on pasture for their entire lives, I was tested. Before, I'd never had to worry too much about running out of grass in my pasture. If it was running low, I'd go get some feed. The cows were never gonna get hungry or quit growing in that model. If I had to pay some money for feed, so be it—I'd get it back from selling more beef. But in giving up corn, I had to ensure I had better grass, more grass, and sweeter, more nutritious grass, or I wouldn't have animals big and healthy enough to sell. I couldn't go out and buy more acreage to make this happen. I had to manage better the acreage I had. And that led me to revisit what I am sure my great-granddaddy James Edward Harris and my granddaddy Will Carter Harris would've told me, if I'd ever been able to ask them. *You gotta move your cows every day.*

The industrial grazing model we modern cattlemen followed had us leaving the herd out on vast swaths of pasture for a month at a time. It was convenient that way. Didn't take a lot of effort. Fix some fences, check on the water—not too much labor required. But you know what cattle do if left to their own devices for that long? They spread out wide and slowly graze their way around, eating the best plants down so low that they can't spring back into new growth. They literally eat them to death. This lets the most undesirable plants take over, reducing the diversity of plant species and creating such weed problems that I had to spray the pastures with costly chemicals. The cattle also compacted the earth by spending weeks circling around one area. Slow degradation over time was the result. I was raised to believe that our soil in the coastal plains of the Gulf of Mexico was the best land in the world. I guess a lot of American farm kids hear that growing up, no matter where they live. The truth is that the soil here is fragile and not very robust, because it is sandy and low in minerals, not very good at holding on to nutrients. (It is an ancient seabed, for Christ's sake!) Our soil just doesn't have the resilience of midwestern soil, so any insult hits it harder. Once the natural grazing cycle of herds moving across the land, slowly chased by predators, had been broken—mankind deciding they had a better idea, again—all the other cycles had been brought down with it. Microbial diversity, mineral absorption, water storage, plant growth and health—each one was quietly taking a hit.

What I have come to understand is that you cannot separate any of the cycles of nature from the others. One of my heroes, the famed naturalist John Muir, said—to paraphrase—that when you pull a thread in nature, you find that everything is connected. When you deplete and damage one cycle, you deplete and damage them all. But the converse is also true. Fix one, and you start to fix them all. So I started by fixing the grazing cycle. Which meant going back in time.

Millions of years ago, large herds of bison had moved across the coastal plain savannahs of southern Georgia. They were pushed from behind by the slow chase of predators—gray wolves in the uplands and big cats in the riparian areas—looking to take out the easiest targets, the old, or crippled, or weak animals, or animals with genetic malformations. The herds, which were prey animals, stayed in tight formation because it was their only real protection. The predators, in picking off the weak animals, were playing their evolutionary role in keeping the herd strong and resilient.

The impact of a huge, constantly moving herd on the land was intense, but brief. The weight and motion of all those animals disturbed the earth and the plants—but in a good way. A certain percentage of the plants got eaten down and others got trampled into the earth by thousands of cloven hooves, where they covered the surface like a slowly decaying blanket. Seeds got worked into the soil to bring about new young plants. All kinds of animal fluids got deposited: saliva that broke down plant cellulose, and nitrogen-rich urine and manure that was superfood for the soil microbes (including a strain of bacteria that could metabolize the methane from all the belching and farting that occurred). And then the herd moved on and often it would not pass that way again for a year or more. This gave the plants a long time to recover. The roots got longer and stronger, holding soil in place, trapping lots of moisture, and storing carbon and nutrients under the earth. This drove lush growth aboveground, so there was always enough foliage left to protect the soil from relentless sun or driving rain. The cycles of nature kept spinning, and the results were spectacular: the grasslands with their diverse, deeply rooted plants, established themselves as miracles of life, capable of producing and sustaining untold numbers of species, eventually including humans. There are other, more famous grasslands than our savannahs in Southwest Georgia—the Great Plains and other tallgrass prairies of the US, or the Serengeti in Africa. But the fundamentals were the same here as anywhere else. What is so profound to me is that the pastures evolved in symbiosis with the herd. No intervention from man. Land and animals (and insects and birds) living and flourishing in symbiosis. Operating through all kinds of planetary changes, morphing and adapting but always continuing. The way it's supposed to be.

So when my pastures started looking a little tragic, I began thinking differently. If evolution got it right, I pondered, maybe we ought not just say *I got a better idea.* I guess that was another small eureka.

Constant grazing on one piece of land was unnatural, to say the least. And nature had already put land plus creatures together and proved that one plus one equaled three—so much more abundance than we could even imagine. To take it further, maybe the land *needed* the intense, hard impact of the bunched-up, slowly moving herd to be healthy and productive. I figured I should try giving the land what it longed for. I should heal the split between the land and animals that we industrialists had created.

I'm not an academic; I'm an implementer, and pretty far to the left-brain side of the spectrum as well. When I do things, I don't need to know everything there is about *why*, I just need them to work. And I'm not afraid to say I know enough to try something long before the next guy might have the guts. My barely passing-grade knowledge of evolutionary biology was enough. Mimicking what I loosely understood had happened for eons in the past, I bunched my cattle up tighter and started to move them more frequently. To be fair, it was an act of imperfect biomimicry. I couldn't bring in the exact conditions of yore—no bison, no wolves—but I could emulate those conditions the best I could. By dividing up the farm's expansive hundred-acre-plus pastures into dozens of much smaller paddocks using temporary wire fencing (which I later replaced with permanent post-and-wire fencing), the herd would tighten in formation out of necessity, as if bunched up in protection. They cleaned the land pretty good, selectively eating the nutritious plants that they instinctively knew they needed the most, but they didn't get to bite the grasses off but once. I played the pseudo predator at their heels, driving them from one paddock to the next after they had disturbed the plants just enough to encourage healthy regrowth but not enough to obliterate their potential. It was my way of emulating the wolves' or big cats' slow, steady chase. I came to call this technique "prescriptive grazing"—others now call it rotational grazing or sometimes "mob grazing." (About fifteen years after I started doing it, I got to know the work of Allan Savory, who, in his native Zimbabwe, had been perfecting this technique to repair land for even longer than I had. I said, "Damn, that is what I've been doing!" The biomimicry that I had found to work in Georgia was exactly what Alan had already figured out in Africa. Ecosystems will vary dramatically, but the fundamentals never change. Nature is constant and consistent.)

I quickly discovered that I had the right kind of animal to restart the grazing cycle. Cattle are large and they are heavy; they eat a lot of forage; they saturate the land with constant streams of nitrogen-rich urine; and they drop a lot of shit. I spend a lot of time looking at it. Cow patties are the first clues you get to the state of your animal's health. They're also extremely valuable. When people walk through the pastures with me and go "Yuck!" at the piles of manure, gingerly stepping around them as if they were lethal piles of hot lava, I tell them, "That is pure currency right there—the only kind the soil microbes can cash!" The minute the manure comes out of the cattle, the microbes can spend it and put it to work. One of my other heroes, the early-twentieth-century agronomist, inventor, and agricultural scientist George W. Carver, famously said that in nature there is no waste. Manure is a prime example. Because when ruminants consume and digest perennial grasses and legumes—which they do for about half of their waking hours when they're out on the pasture—they are doing two things simultaneously. They are converting the cellulose that humans can't eat—packed with proteins and carbohydrates—into pounds of flesh that we can eat. They are also fermenting the fibrous strands of plant material, which soil microbes cannot immediately assimilate, into nature's best soil enhancement: cow shit. Think of each cow as a portable, forty-gallon fermentation chamber, blessed with a four-section stomach, or rumen, very different from our own. The naturally occurring microbes that populate that chamber—the cow's microbiome—feast on the fiber as it passes through the digestive system. They increase in number, and then they come out the back end, riding on volumes of predigested fiber. This mix of microbes and predigested fiber, dumped wherever the cows move—the steadily released by-product of their continuous grazing—gets worked on by dung beetles and other insects, which help to carry the manure through the top layers of soil and into its deeper layers. The community of soil microbes go to town on this organic matter, feasting, reproducing, and thriving on it, and in turn doing *their* job, making minerals available to the roots, which drives more growth, which drives more photosynthesis of foliage, which contributes more feed for the cattle, which releases more manure into the earth, which feeds more microbes... and creates a never-ending cycle of improving the land. This makes me think we should quit using the word *shit* in a derogatory manner like we do. It's a liquid asset falling for free out of the cow's back end that is constantly deposited and easily exchanged (just like currency in a financial market) from one part of the cycle of life to the next, creating more and more wealth over time—healthy animals nourished on a diverse array of grasses and forbs, and strong, enduring grasslands to sustain them. By doing just what herbivores have evolved to do, my herds are building my farm's biological capital, so I can leverage that capital to produce good food, year in and year out. It is a beautiful system, far, far greater than anything man has ever built. It's hard to fathom how, in confinement livestock farming, we turned animal manure (as well as compostable carcass parts) into a burdensome waste product, a pollutant costly to manage, instead of using it as a tool to generate more and better food.

Once I got the prescriptive grazing going, I had to make a decision to make things better for the land. Before then, I had a lot of small herds of cattle, sorted by category—old mama cows were in one herd; they needed a little pampering. Young females were in another. Middle-aged were in another. Each group needing my eye on them in a slightly different way. But I needed more numbers in my herd to truly succeed in making a hard, short impact followed by a long recovery time. I started combining the many small herds into three large ones—a summer calving herd of mama cows (and their babies) as well as the heifers that hadn't become mamas yet; a winter calving herd; and a smaller herd of bulls. It made things a little less good for the animals, maybe—not as much specialized care as they were used to—but a whole lot better for the land. That's the holistic part of what I do now. I consider things from all sides—land, animals, community— and make decisions to benefit one aspect today, and another tomorrow, not just focusing obsessively on one outcome like whether or not the animals are quickly gaining weight. I do this all day long, seven days a week. It's why you'll never be able to condense holistic land management into a freshman-year textbook or measure your understanding of it on a standardized test.

The only way truly to know the power of the herd is to stand right up close to it, letting all your senses take it in. Moving cattle might sound like a slow, fly-swatting amble between one paddock and the next, the cow version of a lazy stroll to the corner store. It is anything but. A cattle move is a stampede of up to fourteen hundred beasts at a time. A phenomenal force of a million pounds of animal flesh impacting the land for the better. A mesmerizing river of sleek-coated beasts, rippling like a ribbon of silk under the bright Georgia sky. It's not a stampede born of fear—there are no gun-slinging cowboys shouting *yeehaw* at their rumps. It is an unchecked instinctual behavior: high-energy animals competing to get the most palatable and nutrient-dense forage. The gate gets opened and the cowboy in charge— oftentimes Scott Cleveland, our cattle manager—quickly steps back. The animals, salivating like Pavlov's dog at the sound of the food bell, charge toward an all-they-can-eat buffet of cow ice cream—the sweet and succulent grasses, clovers, and forbs that they've learned will await them in the next pasture, bursting in peak greenery, because no cows have been there for a month and a half. It's a battle of the fittest. Evolution in real time and technicolor. And the strongest animal wins. Each one of them will get food, but the best will get the best.

We do this every single day at White Oak Pastures, and I've watched thousands of visitors take in this scene. A kind of giddy thrill comes over even the uptight ones who were repulsed by all the shit. It's not hyperbole to say there is something incredibly powerful, almost holy, about the herd moving across the savannah, and you don't need to know a thing about raising livestock to feel it. I believe it comes from feeling that you are inside the cycles yourself—you feel as charged as you do standing on a beach untouched by human development, or soaking under a waterfall, or looking out across a windy valley from a mountaintop, alive to the weather on your skin. Everything's working as it should. *The land is doing what it longs to do.*

The better I got at prescriptive grazing and managing the land holistically, the more my view of my animals changed. I could no longer see my cattle as commodities, individual widgets on the assembly line that I raised efficiently to convert to maximum cash. Nor could I see grazing as a science, the way they taught me in school. I began seeing the cattle the way my ancestors most likely did before me, as my companions and as a tool that helps me improve my land, my corner of planet Earth, and to shape it and coax it into what it yearns to be—in this case, a fantastically productive savannah grassland with a generous serving of handsome shade trees. My generation never learned how to use animal impact to shape the land. My father's generation was exposed to it, but they fell so in love with internal combustion engines, the tools of reductionist science, that they forgot. Remembering how to do it feels right in a core place inside me. The cattle are still a product that I'm going to sell, but more importantly, they are the instrument that helps me keep making this place what it could and should become. They're the paint, and the land is the canvas. The picture will never be so finished that I can sign my name at the bottom, but I sure do enjoy getting better at the art.

Over time, I added more and more colors to the paint box. Other species of animals got added to the land. When you change one thing in a complex system, it changes everything else. That's how these systems work. Take out the chemical pesticides you used to control the weeds and clear the fence lines, and now you must find another solution that fits the ecosystem. Take out the industrial fertilizers, and you need to recover that enhancement naturally. That's one of the challenges of changing to a regenerative land management model; it makes you perpetually rethink your whole program. I knew I couldn't stay locked into just being a cattleman. Even a regenerative one. After all, nature abhors a monoculture—that's day one, lesson one stuff. If you can't reject that coming out of the chute, you're screwed! And my vow was to emulate nature. So I had to abhor monocultures, too. Which meant introducing more species.

You see, in nature, a landscape is never solely populated by one type of animal eating one type of food. That just doesn't occur. Diversity is everywhere—in the forage and in the animals that consume it. Cows graze grass and certain forbs; other types of forbs get grazed by sheep. Brushy browse gets nibbled by goats, while hogs are drawn to roots buried in the soil and the insects that live around them. Each species brings a certain kind of disturbance to the land that it needs, in reasonable amounts, in order to be healthy—a kind of shaking up of the status quo that adds to the total resilience of the land and the animals. Different species also have different susceptibilities to parasites and pathogens; when species coexist in a polyculture—multiple species of animals, plants, insects, and microbes thriving in synergistic relationships with each other—this variability helps to keep the bad guys in check. When you force a livestock monoculture, you not only over-disturb the land by leaving your herd in one place for far too long—like I did habitually for twenty years without realizing it—you also create a breeding ground for certain species-specific strains of parasites and pathogens to run rampant, causing disease. You've gone against what nature intended. So one by one, I started adding the sheep and the goats and the hogs and the poultry onto the land to add their impact, making a complex system even more complex.

Getting it right was not an overnight kind of deal and was a perfect example of why no manual could tell you exactly how to do this kind of farming, and why teaching it hasn't caught traction in land grant universities, where curricula are required to tell young agrarians *exactly what to do.* With a polyculture, it is just as easy to over-disturb your land as with a monoculture, I found out. Like when I tried to leave hogs in a stand of unwanted pine trees just long enough—so I thought—to take down only *some* of the trees. The pine stand was so dense that the grass underneath wasn't getting enough sun to grow. I wanted the animals to thin out the stand. But it turned out that hogs can't think in partial terms. They destroyed the whole lot of them. Or like when I let scores of big laying hens stay out too long in a pasture that had no downward slope and wasn't getting enough rain. Way too much nitrogen-rich defecation landing in one flat spot, where no rain could wash it away, obliterated the microbes in the soil. It nearly killed the fertility before I figured it out. And don't get me started on the strategy for rotating the different species on the land. I got that wrong at first, too. Thinking that my practice of moving my cattle herds daily was pretty neat, I tried to impose that approach on the other species, making them keep up with the cattle. But foolishly, I wasn't considering *those* species' instinctive behaviors. Cattle are pasture-grazing creatures capable of traveling great distances. Sheep are meadow-grazing creatures that graze and travel differentially. Goats are scrub browsers who graze and travel differentially. Hogs are forest creatures. Poultry are most at home in the edge between forest and pasture. Though poultry flocks happily trailing herds of cattle makes a pretty picture in theory, I've found that doesn't work in practice. When we tried driving the poultry flocks to follow the cattle herds, it took an incredible amount of labor, it was stressful on the animals, and it pissed everyone off. I nearly ran off all my good livestock people before I relented. After all, have you ever heard of a big chicken drive across the West? There's a reason for that. Hogs and poultry just don't want to move so far or so fast; the laws of physics and biology don't allow it. And the benefits of moving them with the cattle were minimal. I quickly determined that the juice ain't worth the squeeze.

By accruing experiential wisdom about raising multiple species on this farm—plan, implement, fail, replan—we eventually hit the right balance of things. Now the cows graze the grass, the sheep and goats eat the weeds and shrubs, the hogs open up impenetrable jungle, doing a world of good, and the five species of poultry (chicken, turkeys, geese, ducks, and guineas) peck at the grubs and insects, all of them enriching the soil with their effluvia and all of them active participants in restoring the cycles of nature and improving the land.

Today, what I call a well-managed pasture is not what I used to. In my previous life, the only sight that'd win my approval was an unbroken sea of Tifton 85 Bermuda grass—a specially hybridized cultivar that I paid for and planted to convert my fertilizer into high-calorie cow food with supreme efficiency (just like certain breeds of cattle are bred to gain three or four pounds a day). I wanted to see great swaths of that Tifton 85, consistent in height and color and not a blade out of place. Now my idea of what is beautiful and well managed has radically changed. The *more* things I see on my land, the *more* pleasing it is to my eye: hundreds of plant species per square yard is what's appealing to me, because diverse plants occupy diverse root zones and fix and accumulate different nutrients, making the whole system so much more productive. A good pasture in Bluffton boasts Bahia grass, several different Bermuda grasses, Johnson grass, Dallas grass, white Dutch clover, arrowleaf clover, purple verbena, fennel, Italian rye and ragweed, pigweed (spiny amaranth), millet, sun hemp, and crabgrass. It's the opposite of monoculture; it's the world's biggest salad bowl and it looks like you could put some Ranch dressing on it and eat it yourself. Fringing the edges, we've got a multitude of other plant species in the form of vines and trees and shrubs. Busy populations of microfauna like butterflies and bees and mosquitoes hover over the grasses, intent on their important jobs—lightning bugs do the same thing at night. Worms and ants and termites and other much smaller soil organisms work the earth under-foot. Rodents and reptiles scurry and slither, occasionally catching your eye. Birds of all kinds chase the insects, helping to reduce the need for insecticide, as do all the dung beetles in the shit, working through it so it hosts fewer fly larvae. In the ponds, crawfish have come back, and snapping turtles and huge toadie frogs, too. (When I was a little boy, there would be greasy spots all over the road from the amount of frogs we had getting run over by cars. That phenomenon disappeared completely until we stopped using chemicals, and the frogs found their way back.) Alligators might even cross your path, on their way to a creek somewhere—nature's scavengers, helping keep the cycle of life going. In fact, you can't not see the cycle of life—birth, growth, death, decay—everywhere you look.

Sure, some of my fields may look a little raggedy to my neighbors, who still get weak-kneed about uniform, clean lines and pruned corners. But they don't look that way to me. Biodiversity is an indication that the cycles of nature are switched on, and a sign that productivity is high. It proves that we had the guts to stick it out: after making it through the initial pains of withdrawal from the performance-enhancing drugs, the farm had a brief period where it went to crap, like championship athletes weaning themselves off steroids. But slowly, everything built back up. And like the athletes, maybe we won't ever win medals in one narrow category like we used to, but the total picture of health is so much better than it was. Natural fertility has come back. We've got a landscape that is teeming with life.

When I was a cog in a complicated system, running a factory cow farm—any monoculture is a factory, in my opinion—my day-to-day job was pretty simple. The key to being a good farmer was to be able to spot a symptom, know what to kill it with, and relax in the confidence that you'd profit more than you would have if you hadn't killed it. Now we've circled back to what Jenni started calling radically traditional farming. To me, that's not an oxymoron. It's a complete statement: Farming is the occupation, the thing that we do here. Traditional is the descriptor, describing our style of doing it, one that harks back to this farm's roots and the knowledge that all farmers used to have of natural systems. And radical is the attitude we bring to what we do, showing how damn hard we go after it. Unlike many of our peers in American farming, today we are radically oriented to making everything *live*. So it's a more complex job, and I spend a lot more time in observation than I used to, making connections in my mind—probing the universe around me like John Muir did, looking for the way threads tie together. Instead of scanning for what's wrong out there on my farm and in my fields, I'm looking for what's *right*. I'm looking for the biological activity that I can support and will maximize production, instead of killing biological competition to try and reach the same goal. It takes more time and you can't do it on autopilot. Kind of like baking sourdough bread from scratch instead of making cake from a box. But that's a good thing. There is no resilience in that cake mix box, only efficiency—and empty calories.

Radically traditional farming has deepened my connection to this place in a way I profoundly enjoy. Ever since I set aside the canoe and frog gig spear and put on real shoes to help out on the farm, the message had been clear: the field was where you worked, and the forests and waterways were where you played. I lived that way for the first half of my adult life. But now there's been a reconciliation. Now, the whole biome is where I work and play. There is no separation at all in how I experience it.

My job title changed as a result. I used to have a business card that

had WILL HARRIS III, PRESIDENT OF WHITE OAK PASTURES grandly emblazoned on it. Now I use a boiled-clean cow rib that I tuck in my shirt
pocket. You can take a picture of it if you need the info. It has the
words WILL HARRIS III, LAND STEWARD AND HERDSMAN etched in it. My responsibility is to keep the biological systems spinning, and sometimes
I'm like the guy at the circus spinning plates on sticks, shifting left
and right and back and forward so that none of them fall. Farming
this way is a constant dance of situational responsiveness and going
with the gut. But it's a much more satisfying career as it turns out.

I cannot understand the way software works in a computer. I cannot play an instrument or carry a tune. I was even unable to mem-
orize the multiplication tables or the damn Gettysburg Address. But I
have developed a good practical grasp of the cycles and forces of nature and how they do their work. It is my gift. I've figured out that if
you manage your land and herds so that they function as they should,
you will always cash in on God's promise of abundance. The pledge *you*
make to God as a regenerative farmer is that you keep *all* the cycles
going, not just one or two.

When I go to bed at night, I close my eyes and picture the cycles
still spinning, right outside my window. It's the only vision that allows
me to find sleep. I feel reassured that I'm taking care of what's outside
the way my granddaddy and great-granddaddy likely did. They always
taught that the best thing a herdsman can put on his animals is his
eyes, and the best thing a land steward can put on his land is his feet.

Chapter Five

Returning to the Humane—Anti-Factory Animal Welfare

The first few years of raising cattle the new way were rough. I tried to take my whole herd to a fully grass-fed model, which meant I had up to eight hundred head of cattle per year to sell that were now not your average made-in-USA corn-fed beef. I no longer wanted to sell them to feedlots at seven months old; I wanted to raise them till they were fully mature, feeding them only on grass. It quickly became clear this was a more expensive and much harder way to raise cattle. I couldn't even do it at first—many them still went to the feedlot in the beginning. Holding on to the rest meant that the three-quarters of a million dollars in cash flow I really needed was not available to me, and I incurred another quarter of a million dollars in expenses to feed and care for these cattle for an additional year. It took all the strength in my hands to carry that ball.

It also left me with what was, back then, very much a niche product. Of the sprinkling of "grass-fed" producers out there, most still finished their cattle by feeding them commodity corn out on the pasture for the last four to five months of their lives to help fatten them up. I didn't want to do that. When I quit feeding corn, I quit. That made me an outlier.

My first market was made up of local buyers interested in purchasing freezer locker sides of beef—half carcasses straight from the local abattoir to fill their home freezers for the year. But those customers weren't especially curious about grass-fed beef or willing to pay much of a premium for it. I could price this meat only a little bit higher than average. The rest of my mature, slaughter-ready animals were still funneling into the regular commodity market because I didn't know where else to put them. The truth started to sting when I began to lose significant amounts of money for the very first time in my life: I couldn't farm in a manner that was good to the earth and the animals and the community without making changes to every part of the process. In getting off the industrial system, I was internalizing a whole bunch of costs that had previously been externalized for me, keeping things artificially cheap. I was incurring additional costs to put extra quality into my product that I could not extract by selling it to the commodity market. If I didn't come up with a new and better way to monetize what I was doing, I'd bleed out financially. There were a lot of sleepless nights.

I still remember the moment I first detected that there might be a better way, back in the early 2000s. The new issue of *Drovers Journal* was on my desk, a magazine that a lot of industrial cattlemen subscribe to in order to stay up-to-date. As I was flipping through it, a line in an article jumped off the page. It announced the formation of a newly formed nonprofit called "humane farm animal care." It was about the fledgling organization that became well known as the Certified

Humane project, headed by Adele Douglass Jolley. Strange as it may sound today, I had never seen the words *humane* and *livestock* used in the same sentence. Until then, anything I'd seen about humane treatment of animals referred to pets and rescue animals and animal shelters. Stumbling across these two opposite-seeming words side by side was so startling that I reread them three times. Though I was rethinking my animal welfare protocols at my farm, I thought I was the only one doing it. Discovering that other people cared about this was exciting. First, because it seemed that if I just raised my animals compassionately, I'd be spared the job of educating my future customers. I could get this new "Certified Humane" outfit to certify what I was doing, and surely have steady business. (It turned out to be a little harder than that.) Second, because it suggested that a new kind of customer was emerging, a customer who wanted meat raised in better conditions, without the cruelty of confinement. They were willing to pay a little extra for it. I just had to find them.

I decided that if I was going to raise this kind of meat, I had to get it to consumers more directly. To do that, I needed a grocery chain to take me on as a supplier of 100 percent grass-fed beef. A *big* grocery chain with a lot of stores, and hundreds of thousands of customers. Likely you have never tried to pull off such a feat yourself, but I can tell you that securing a supply contract with a household-name grocery chain is harder than taking a calculus class in Russian. For an average farmer, it is almost unheard of—no matter how well-known your farm might be in Bluffton, Georgia. The big grocery chains have a very fixed supply chain and fixed needs. Their professional meat buyers need to be able to pick up the phone, call their guy at Tyson or Cargill and place a purchase order of gargantuan proportions—six 48,000-pound loads of 8-ounce filet mignons, for example, delivered to six warehouses, every single week, for the next quarter. White Oak Pastures is bigger than most farms, but we will never see six 48,000-pound loads of 8-ounce filets leave our gates.

But I guess it's true that fortune favors the bold, and as the first person at the grass-fed beef dance, I had won a good spot to start from. Or perhaps it's just that there are enough Dead Harris ghosts around me, hungry to see this farm survive, that I've gotten a little extra. Somehow, my craziest ideas have had a way of actually working out. My dad used to say, "Will, I do believe you could shit in a swinging bucket." I have done the business equivalent of that a number of times.

One day a woman who was a relative of one of our cowboys came to visit the ranch. Their family was from Lakeland, Florida, which also happened to be the corporate headquarters of Publix Super Markets, one of the biggest grocery distributors in the Southeast. This lady was the head secretary in the management offices. When I told her what I envisioned for our beef, she got excited. She made a call to one of her bosses, John Telford, then the senior meat purchaser for the chain. He agreed to a meeting and just like that, I had a shot at what I wanted. When the day came, I walked into their headquarters in Lakeland, my plan for supplying them with grass-fed beef roughly sketched out on a napkin, and said, "I'm Will Harris the third and I am gonna help you sell the first pound of American grass-fed beef your customers have ever seen." John had all kinds of resistance. "Grass-fed meat tastes different! It cooks different!" he insisted. "It isn't uniform in taste and marbled with fat!" His shoppers, he said, would find it nothing but confusing. But I insisted there were customers who appreciated meat that came from outside the industrial system and who would pay a premium for it, too. He sighed and said, "You have no idea how far you are from getting this product in our stores."

I asked John to tell me what I lacked. He didn't want to get into itemizing my shortcomings, but I persisted. He gave in and told me. First, I'd need to complete an endless amount of paperwork, and figure out processing and packaging and Universal Product Codes, and build a website. I would have to ensure that I got USDA-certified processing and bought product liability insurance—and an unbelievably long and detailed list of other things that were completely foreign to a cattleman working out of his kitchen.

I wrote down everything John said on a yellow legal pad, filling two full pages of it. Then I asked if I could come see him again after I got all that shit done. He laughed and said, "Yeah, you can, but I don't expect to see you again, Will." I didn't say anything. I'm pretty sure John figured I would quit and that would be the last he would see of me. But I knew I'd be back.

Checking off all those to-do's took me a solid twelve months, and I don't know how much expense. Along the way, I landed on our name, a much better name for this new grass-fed brand than I'd planned on using. Up until that time, you see, this family farm had been known as Tenac Oak, something my great-grandfather came up with in homage to the old white oaks of our ecosystem—tenac being the colloquial term for the tree. I figured I'd make "Tenac Oak Pastures" the official name of our grass-fed beef. Until, that is, I went to get our first-ever website made—from the Baptist preacher's wife, the only person I could find who knew such things back then. Flipping open her laptop at her breakfast table, she asked me, "What are we going to call this website?" I told her. "How do you spell that?" she asked. "Well, some of the old folk spell it *Tenak*. But the Harrises have always written *Tenac*." She squinted a second and closed the laptop. "You really want to spend the rest of your life spelling *Tenac* for people? Just call it

White Oak!" I agreed. It was the best spur-of-the-moment decision I ever made.

A full year after our meeting, once my due diligence was done, I called John Telford and asked if he remembered me. He said, "Yeah, the crazy cattle guy from Georgia," and told me to show up in six weeks. On the designated day, I showed up at his office with two bankers boxes full of paperwork that probably weighed sixty pounds. Everything he'd asked for was complete and done first-class. The poor guy swallowed hard and said, "*One* store. And your product will be sold in the coffin case." I didn't know what that was, but I soon found out. It is the weird open freezer where strange meat products—turkeys in March, or squab—go to expire. There was another condition, however: I had to do in-person demos to lure consumers in for the sell. I would have to spend eight hours in a suburban supermarket, handing out meatballs to busy moms and sugared-up kids and retirees with lots of questions.

Spending my Saturdays and Sundays off the farm dispensing meat-balls on toothpicks under bright strip lights was about as appealing to me as getting beaten with a sack of catfish. I also had the cost of paying an Atlanta chef, Athena Penson, to do the cooking for me. But the experience taught me more than I bargained for. I would tempt shoppers over with a sizzling skillet—because who can resist a free morsel of hot meat as they stock up on toilet paper and frozen peas—and say, "Ma'am (or "Sir"), I'd like you to try some of my grass-fed beef." More than a few took a step back in alarm. "Your *what*? "Your *breast*-fed beef?" The knowledge gap was real. So I would tell how my cattle were raised out on the pastures, eating grass their whole lives, and the lady (or the gentleman) would interject with a bemused "Don't *all* cattle eat grass all their lives?" I could practically see Old MacDonald himself dancing in their minds. Then I'd break the spell that modern food marketing had cast, explaining that no, they did not, and that in fact I could almost guarantee that every pound of beef they had eaten until that day had a much less beatific origin: crowded, filthy feedlots, bloat-causing feed, and slaughterhouses where fast-moving conveyer belts hauled four hundred head per hour of traumatized animals to their deaths, and workers labored perilously close to danger in order to keep up. It was a shock to me that this was a shock to them. I hadn't realized just how powerful the pastoral myth of farming still was, and how little the average shopper knew about the production of industrial meat. To be honest, most of the folks stopping by for a free snack probably didn't believe me. They thought I was spinning a story to sell them some product. But thank God a few of them did. They'd turn ever so slightly pale at what I was describing, but they wouldn't walk away. They'd lean in to hear more.

Sometimes I'd throw in another meatball, because these suburban shoppers—good people, curious, and concerned about doing right, for the most part—wanted to know what we did differently on our farm. I'd like to say it was my rangy good looks or cowboy-hatted panache that had them spellbound, but in reality it was the tasty food that did it, and the sheer surprise that a food producer was telling the truth. These folks had never been told that what they *thought* they were buying when they picked up "USDA-inspected" supermarket beef—an all-American, small-town product steeped in feel-good special sauce—was no such thing. No wonder they were confused. The beef industry doesn't exactly label its product as "confinement-raised, pesticide-laden, soy-bean-finished beef." It had never occurred to them that there were hidden costs to the cheap meat they enjoyed, and that the cruelest of these costs were heaped onto the animals themselves. But authenticity is the real deal. Folks recognize it when they see it. So they listened.

That first demo was a success, and Publix gave me twelve more demos at stores in the region serviced from their Atlanta warehouse. After those were done, they gave me another twelve, a little further afield. Our grass-fed beef got bumped up from frozen meat in the coffin case to fresh meat located at eye level in the meat department. Publix put White Oak Pastures beef in their Atlanta warehouse, which meant it got stocked in about two hundred stores. I kept at the demos weekend after weekend. Store by store and shopper by shopper, my regionally produced, independently farmed, fully grass-fed beef caught traction.

These customer meet-and-greets, resistant as I was to do them, laid an important foundation. They were the first glimmerings of what became a much bigger Know Your Farmer movement, involving a lot more farmers than just me, that helped producers and customers to connect in person again, through farmers markets and farm tours, and later on podcasts and social media. Our longest-standing White Oak customers still recall seeing life-size posters of me, emblazoned with MEET WILL HARRIS OF BLUFFTON, GA, behind the meat counters at my second wholesale customer, Whole Foods, with a description of our welfare standards. They'd made me the unlikely poster child of the humane meat movement, which pained me a little, but since my friends and neighbors don't drive three hours to shop at Whole Foods in Atlanta, I was spared the worst of the embarrassment. You could say that all the demos and long drives to far-off stores, my truck packed with meat coolers, my whole body itching to be back on the farm where I belonged, were an atonement for the unintended consequences my generation had helped to cause. Or you could say that they were a years-long initiatory experience that would ultimately give me the unshakable understanding that, in the fight to establish a new market for a better kind of meat, the only weapons I had against the industrial system and its greenwashing were transparency and authenticity. (*Greenwashing* is the term that I use to describe a deceptive marketing practice that is increasingly utilized by Big Food. They routinely use creative words to trick their consumers into believing that the industrially produced food they are selling is grown in the same manner that mine is. It ain't. My transparency and authenticity are my sword and my shield, and they are powerful.)

You see, the big players in the conventional meat industry don't really care about the market share that relatively small, grass-fed farmers or ranchers take away from them. They spill more than we sell. Even with our success today, we still don't threaten even a corner of their multibillion-dollar take. But our story of how we do it—that's different. When people hear about our farm and our animals and how we go about raising them, they invariably start to wonder, If this is what *you* guys are doing out there for all to see, on your pastures and in your slaughterhouse that are open to the public, what are *they* doing behind their walls and gates and their security guards who will call for backup if you try to get inside to look? That comparison gets the consumer to thinking. And Big Food doesn't like it when folks think. In fact, it scares the hell out of them.

I can easily tell a curious consumer how animal welfare degraded to deplorable conditions over the last seventy-five years. I see that pretty clearly. It started with a fundamental shift in how we thought about the animals we rely on for food. Prior to the advent of the factory farm system, farmers naturally thought of their food animals as essential parts of the cyclical system on their farms; they played an important role in benefiting the grass, the land, and the entire landscape. They were also the monetizable abundance that resulted from the proper working of the cycles. But when the linear system replaced the ancient, cyclical one, the animals became products, plain and simple. That change had huge implications. When you see a living creature as a product, when you *produce* meat instead of *raise* meat, and when your holy grail is efficiency, you can rationalize a lot of sins.

You can rationalize taking the animals off the land that they co-evolved with and confining them in indoor spaces where you can control the climate and keep the lights on, so that chickens keep laying eggs even when their bodies don't want to.

You can rationalize crowding them together in cramped pens or lots where there is none of the symbiosis between species that occurs in nature. From the standpoint of efficiency, this crowding is no problem. It ensures high volumes of product, which is critical to amortize the expensive techno-facility. The same treatment applied to humans is called *incarceration*, and it is utilized only when one has been found guilty of a criminal activity.

You can justify feeding herbivores unnatural, hard-to-digest grains that have been formulated to pack on pounds without any consideration of their health. Or worse, feeding them newsprint waste and poultry shit and even bone meal from other animals, or remnants of distillers' grain that make health-damaging Omega-6 fatty acids proliferate in the meat. Then you need to add a steady stream of low-level antibiotics to the feed for nobody's good but your own. This is a cheap attempt to make sure that infectious diseases don't spread in the cramped conditions. This means pathogens get resistant to the antibiotics that humans sometimes need.

And you can talk yourself into employing fewer humans to care for the confined animals, because every increase in the cost of labor decreases your bottom line. Instead, you add technology; your smart facility can handle the climate control, feeding, watering, and just about everything else. The remaining employees, low-paid because they don't need animal husbandry skills, can get rid of the dead animals. You can crowd in more animals to make up for a high death rate. When the overworked, underpaid employees become a little unglued and, from sheer stress, treat the animals cruelly, you can look away. Unrelenting stress makes humans desensitized; the result is nobody calls out the horrible acts as wrong.

You can even justify engineering your chickens to have massive breasts, your cattle to be unnaturally obese, your hogs to be so muscular they can't walk. I can only guess that this gruesome manipulation feels like being a muscle-bound bodybuilder who was force-fed steroids and can barely touch his toes.

I'm not here to villainize the folks who make these justifications—I get how they arrived there. Each small decision made in the name of efficiency, and making food as abundant and cheap and consistent as possible, has an unintended consequence on how welfare is carried out. And these practices are validated as benign to the farmer by PhD researchers paid by Big Ag. For the producer who is working his or her ass off to keep their farm going, the incentives to meet anything but the minimum standards gets slowly stripped away, because the commodity system won't reward anything higher than that. So a farmer may just go along with it. It's easy not to notice the standards inching lower, because it happens at a glacial pace, a little bit lower each year. Joseph Stalin said something to the effect that if you take a person's freedoms away from them slowly enough, they won't even notice that they are gone. We did that to the welfare of our livestock. This is how one day you arrive at a point where deplorable conditions like cattle standing knee-deep in shit in the feedlot, or mama hogs imprisoned 24/7 in gestation crates, unable to turn around or lie down lest they crush their piglets, or chickens that never see the light of day but end up crushing each other to death, is unremarkable. Just fine. *Nothing to see here, people!* And now you've got the opposite of healthy, happy animals—instead, they're stressed, obese, and well on their way to many of the diseases that strike humans and cause our deaths. It's bewildering that so few people find eating this meat to be problematic.

I can only surmise that this is what made me oblivious to the welfare on my farm for so long. I kept many of my own cattle in outdoor confinement here on my ranch and sent plenty others away to feedlots that I sometimes visited (in some cases I retained ownership of my cattle until they were slaughtered—a type of contract that's a terrible deal for the farmer, as it happens). But I was not appalled or aghast at any of what I regularly saw and didn't feel complicit in any kind of inhumane activities. The monocultural mindset of convenience and efficiency just seemed to make sense: produce your product, call the feedlot, set a date for the semi to come, take the check, repeat, repeat, repeat. That process worked well for me, and that system rewarded our farm well. I was confident that good animal welfare during that process meant keeping them fed, watered, sheltered, and just not intentionally inflicting pain. The whole way of life that my ancestors knew, in which humans and livestock herds lived in a reciprocal relationship, their fates deeply knitted together—you take care of me, I take care of you—was reduced to a one-liner. When that gets passed on generationally—my daddy did it the new, industrial way, my teachers taught me to do it this way, and all my contemporaries were doing it this way—then no wonder it becomes the new norm.

It was only as I got more distance from that system that I saw how separating one part from another made all this possible. Smart people working in the corner offices of Big Food and Big Meat corporations crunch the numbers, figuring out how to maximize the efficiency, setting the rules of the game. The actual animals they trade in are out of sight, out of mind, for the most part, many miles away from where the number crunchers work. Meanwhile, the folks working out in the feedlot or the confinement hog house are standing there with boots in the muck, looking at the miserable creatures before them, and also racking *their* brains about how to make things more efficient, because if they can, then maybe they'll make it to that corner office one day, too. Where's the room in that equation for compassionate animal welfare—where's the incentive? There's no incentive for making the animal's quality of life better, unless it has the economic impact of making a product cheaper—which I've never seen occur.

As a consumer, you rub right up against this when you shop for food in your local store. A budget-cost pork loin or bargain-priced skirt steak, wrapped and ready to toss in your shopping cart for dinner, can make even the most miserable meat appear pretty good. I have compassion for that—when you don't know where that meat came from, why wouldn't the price tag be the main thing you consider? But I can't help but think, if you could taste the suffering in that underpriced meat, you might not want to eat it at all.

I didn't want the food I raised to taste like that. So I led White Oak Pastures in the direction of what some might call an "anti-factory farm"—one that returns multiple species of animals to their rightful position at the center of the farm and gives them the quality of life that position deserves. The way we've done it is probably different from the way someone else might do it. Our welfare practices reflect our unique attributes: a polycultural ranch in the semitropical coastal plain of Georgia where we have been blessed to acquire land year by year. This gives us options others might not have. Because we have more land available, for example, we have been able to make the choice to never castrate our bulls, as we have the acreage to keep a large herd of intact bulls (over a thousand head) where other farms might not. (We used to castrate anything that was born on the farm that wasn't named Harris, but that was one of the first industrial practices we ditched. We also allow calves to nurse their mothers until they are up to nine months old, instead of six, among many other examples.)

I would never want to decree a set of universal laws of good welfare. Context is everything, and each producer's checklist will look distinct. But I can share the broader considerations that I think need to be there, and that I know *can* be there, after doing it on our holistic, resilient farm. These are the high-level goals that farmers or producers should have in mind when they make a transition away from industrial production to something better, and you as a consumer can use them to navigate better meat buying, too. These considerations can help you enquire into whether a producer is truly invested in animal welfare. (It's tempting to rely on a third party to verify good welfare. I felt that way too, when the first certification programs came out, not just for humane treatment but all of them—certifications for ecological, environmental, labor fairness practices, and the like. At first, I went after certifications for my farm like a Boy Scout going after badges—I wanted to collect them all. But despite the good work done by some of these outfits, a larger certification industry was soon born, and these days a farm can get a certification for getting the low-hanging fruit—and too often, the certification raises the bar half an inch instead of a foot.)

If you truly care how the food you consume is raised, the only way you can really find out for sure is to get familiar with these compassionate welfare concepts and learn what questions to ask your farmer. I would hope even a person who chooses to not eat meat at all but who is interested in the ways livestock are raised for other reasons—like the impact on the environment and the potential for better land management—might agree that these kinds of questions are good to ask. They're born out of what has worked for us, and they help you think about things differently. By following them, we've proved that it is possible to perform high-level animal welfare at scale, for years.

But first, an important caveat: livestock welfare is not going to look the same as pet welfare. Don't go out there expecting to see the latter. That's not what farms do. I've learned that I have to set this expectation early in the conversation, unless the person I'm talking to has grown up on a farm. If we're gonna get anywhere better at all, we all need to start on the same page. And that page is one that has a *complex view* of human-animal relations. We are dealing with complex systems here, after all—an organism of a farm in which livestock (and perhaps multiple species of livestock) exist in a varied ecosystem, alongside a bunch of humans who seek to make enough money to sustain the organism. So it's helpful to take a second and just notice if you expect a farm to be treating all animals the way you might treat your companion animals—your dog, or cat, or pet parakeet you love. I'm a very simple guy in many regards, but I've learned from many a meatball demo, interacting with well-meaning shoppers, that when it comes to animal welfare, most nonagricultural folks have a much simpler worldview than I do. These people would earnestly ask how I could care so deeply for animals that I've jeopardized my bottom line many a time, yet also slaughter those same animals and process them and eat them. I would tell them, not being flippant, simply being honest, it doesn't bother me a bit.

You see, their view of the entire animal kingdom is filtered through the lens of companion animal relationships. The good human in that relationship acquires an animal, lavishes it with attention and affection for its entire life span, stays with it until it dies, and then buries it and gets another one. I understand that because I have companion animals that get special treatment, too—my dog Judge gets the passenger seat of my jeep and the sunny spot next to my desk. What's different for a farmer is that relating with animals becomes so much more complex and multidimensional than that. Out here on my farm, I have a relationship with my companion animals like Judge, and I have a relationship with my working animals—the horses my cowboys ride and the dogs that guard the poultry or the dogs that help to herd the cattle. I have a relationship with my livestock and a relationship with the wildlife that exists alongside them. I have a relationship with the bees that buzz around, pollinating the plants, and I have one with the microbes in the soil. I love all these creatures and put an incredible amount of energy and effort to ensure their well-being—it's the core of everything I do. But each relationship is slightly different, much as my relationship to my daughters is different from the one I have with my spouse, which is different from that with my neighbors, and from that with my working colleagues.

What you have got to understand is that the reason a farmer can raise animals and take their lives for people to eat is that we love our herds, and flocks, and droves instead of loving the individual animals. Individual animals come and go in this system. But the herd, like the land, is perpetual. It evolves, generationally, and the way it continues to live and to replicate itself is a beautiful thing. The best way I can describe it is this: The person whose only experience of animals is owning a pet tends to love that animal like they would a lake—a still body of water that doesn't flow, move, or change. My love for my herds is like my love for a great river that is always flowing. It replenishes itself over and again. I love my herds and flocks for their continuity and for their impressive genetics that date back generations. I love to see their offspring born, and grow, so that they can support this farm and ensure it survives, and then I love to see their remains go back to the land to fertilize it, to feed the herd and flock and keep the cycle going. I look forward to calving season, kidding season, and farrowing season, so we can have another crop of animals; but I equally look forward to the harvesting season so they can make way for the next ones. To me, this is a profound kind of love—it's an awe for something universal and ancient, something that happens whether mankind is in the picture or not.

Until you can see from this perspective, you risk having a perverse concept of what a farmer's animal care should be. If you look for it to be more like a petting zoo, or a retirement home for aged cows, you risk missing out on seeing a compassionate farm when it's right before your eyes, because you can't see that those baby goats and their mamas would much rather be sheltering under hedgerows in the rainstorm than snuggled up on your couch like your Pomeranian or poodle. You might even get caught up in judgment against raising meat at all (and I've met a lot of those people; they're called militant vegans). So while the simple and complex views have much in common—both want to avoid pain or suffering for their creatures—please don't overlay your expectations of pet care onto a farm. You have to appreciate that a good stockman or stockwoman expresses their love for their food animals not through fluffy pet beds and treats but by stewarding them through every stage of their life cycle and by turning their back on what science has determined to be cheap and efficient and instead turning toward emulating nature. (Besides, running a retirement farm for aging cattle and hogs and turkeys would never financially survive, nor would it feed anyone unless a philanthropist with bottomless pockets took on the cause.)

Compassionate care the way I practice it means returning to the roots of animal husbandry. I act as a caretaker, creating conditions for my animals that are as close to what nature would provide if I were not there at all. When I started my new program at White Oak Pastures, I kept asking myself, "How would nature husband these animals if I weren't in it for profit?" It's a question that keeps you honest. It's not that I'm a hundred percent true to it. Plenty of times I make a choice to do something that isn't exactly how the animals would do things, but it's gonna go that way because the land needs something specific, or my employees need something a certain way. Even so, the emulation gets pretty darn close. From this understanding, the first goal of the anti-factory farm, and the first question for the consumer to ask is this: Are the animals free to express instinctive behaviors? If you've ever seen a confinement animal up close, you can tell they are clearly unhappy. They are living in a constant state of low-level stress, and that stress is because the animal is being restricted from expressing its instinctive behavior. To my mind, robbing them of this is cruelty in action, just not as overt or obvious as kicking or hitting or yelling at them. It's pretty simple: cows were born to roam and graze; chickens were born to scratch and peck; hogs were born to wallow and root. Deny them that right, and you have poor animal welfare. Sure, if you keep a cow on a feedlot or a hog in a farrowing crate or a chicken in a chicken house, you might be keeping them safe, perhaps even reasonably comfortable, but it's like raising your child in a closet and saying, "This is great! You get a nice seventy-two degrees year-round, lights on 24/7, and you'll never break a leg playing football or get run over by a bus because you're locked in. And by the way, go ahead and have all the Doritos you want." Would that be considered good child rearing? To have a healthy, happy child, you need them out on the football or soccer field getting knocked around, exposed to microbes to build up natural immunity, and building the resilience that comes from responding to a dynamic, ever-changing environment.

Think about it: through confining animals and restricting their natural movement and exploration and socialization, we've inflicted on them the level of punishment that in human society we would inflict only on those who had committed terrible crimes. But somehow it's a perfectly accepted way of raising livestock. To me, seeing animals in confinement is like watching the general population of a prison when they're in their cells; there's nothing pretty or attractive or compelling about it. No person should enjoy looking at it. By contrast, when you practice animal husbandry you seek to reduce stress by allowing instinctual behaviors, such as maternal instincts. A mama cow or hog will experience great stress when their young are taken away from them, just like a human mother would. In nature, all mother animals wean off their young, at some point, to make way for the next birth. We leave the calves in the pasture with their mamas, drinking their milk and eating grass, and enjoying their mama's presence until she's ready to have another baby. That makes them up to about ten or eleven months old at weaning instead of six. At that point they need to be taken away from their mama so the new baby she's soon to birth can survive; it's humane to do that.

The hogs are smarter than cattle. Mama hogs in nature watch each others' piglets so that the other mamas can forage. They build nests on hillsides so gravity carries urine and feces away. Letting them far-row outdoors in wooden farrowing shelters may not be as *efficient* as industrial hog farming—we get about eight babies per litter versus twelve to fourteen in confinement—but it allows the maternal instinct to flourish, and that makes for a strong and resilient drove.

Sometimes, the animals' instinctive behavior is not pretty, and we have war stories to prove it. Putting the goats in with the hogs during kidding time was a mistake; a birthing mama goat with her head stuck in a fence and a hungry hog are not, it turns out, good bedfel-lows. As Jenni likes to say, farms are not Walt Disney World and farmers doing this kind of farming are perpetually figuring it out as we go. Even this kind of thing, however, deserves some respect and awe. It's animals expressing their natural instincts.

The long and the short of it is that products don't express in-stinctive behaviors, but animals do. And in my book, if you are not orienting your whole operation to allow them to express those behav-iors, you are failing miserably. I've had some wry skeptics ask, "Sure, Will, you say you prioritize animals' welfare, but who's to say any of us know what a 'happy cow' even is?" I tell them, I can most certainly describe what a happy cow looks like, because I have a lot of them. A happy animal is shiny-coated and gleeful! It has energy and curi-osity and gusto. Much like a kid in a playground, a happy cow kicks up her heels with joy as she discovers fresh grass; her contentment is as clear as day. To have that happy, satisfied livestock, you put them in an environment that allows them to express instinctive behavior: their natural habitat. This is the second vital aspect of animal welfare to consider.

Separating animals from the landscapes they evolved to live on—grasslands for herbivores, forests for hogs—was our original sin.

Moving them indoors into industrial-scale houses, or fully away from their natural environment in concrete feedlots, was the ultimate arrogance. It's likely clear by now how irked I get by the philosophy that we humans can improve on nature. When we broke the connection between land and livestock with such impunity, it was more than irksome. It was downright criminal. Everything went to hell from there. Just look at it this way: from the holistic perspective, animals and land live in symbiosis. They co-evolved for many purposes. It wasn't just about the animals surviving off the land, *taking* from it; they *gave* to the land as well. Ruminants regenerated grasslands by impacting them with their hooves and mouths; poultry scratched the surface of the soil to help spread microbes around; hogs rooted and wallowed around tree bases to aerate the soil with their snouts. Just as we celebrate the way the plants perform photosynthesis to turn energy, water, and minerals into amino acids and fatty acids and carbohydrates, we should herald the herbivores for performing the next necessary step, turning those plants into meat for us to eat, and into feces for microbes, and ultimately becoming more food for microbes when they die. These animals do not perform these functions for the benefit of others. They perform them to benefit themselves, but there is symbiosis, and the activities benefit the environment and other animals. We should treat the animals like royalty for the simple reason that they keep the cycles spinning. Doesn't that prove that there is something very, very *right* about them living their lives on the land? If the animal component of this greater evolution suddenly went away, it would be a very different world. We are certainly not smart enough to figure out how to do it without them—no matter what the tech gurus proclaim. So we should work *with* them, not against them.

We should also do everything we can to respect this timeless bond because, when animals live in their natural environment, they express their full genetic potential. I see this everywhere I look on my farm. The cattle are fit and athletic, always moving, never sedentary. The hogs, goats, sheep, and poultry live fully exposed to all the elements that Mother Nature can throw at them and have greater fortitude and resilience because of it. The animals are in sync with nature's rhythms of light and dark and seasons, which supports successful reproduction. They are eating the food they evolved to eat—with a little help from us where needed. For example, a herd of buffalo might cover hundreds of miles in one direction. But White Oak Pastures is only four miles long; our cattle cannot roam as widely as the buffalo could, grazing grass that is high in copper one day, then grass that is high in phosphorus or sulfur the next. So I came up with a simulation by filling a cafeteria-style trailer with trays of many different minerals and leaving it out for them to pick from. Their bodies tell them their need, depending on what they're deficient in, or if they're pregnant or nursing a baby. That's just one example of our imperfect emulation of nature.

If I granted my cattle a presidential pardon and decided not to slaughter any of them, I am confident they would live to twenty-something years old, medication free. The confined creature, eating its high-carbohydrate diet, wouldn't make it much past its scheduled slaughter date. A disease like obesity or a heart attack or a stroke—or some other kind of scourge of sedentary living—would take them out. The same goes for our hogs, or poultry, or goats.

I'll never forget seeing a series of vintage photographs of cattle on the wall of a hotel in Fort Worth, Texas. Fort Worth is the epicenter of the industrial stockyards and home to a major cattle show each year. The hotel had photographs of every grand champion from 1936 until 2008, the year I visited. The physiological changes from decade to decade were striking. The bulls from the late 1930s were stocky and barrel-chested—what we call spring-sided—with a short, thick crest or hump on the neck, the epitome of masculine secondary sex traits. They could hold their own in a pasture and survive and thrive in nature with all its variable conditions. The bulls seventy years later, by contrast, were taller and slab-sided. They were entirely less virile-looking but more able to slot side by side in a crowded feedlot. Their longer legs meant they wouldn't sink into the inches of muck and manure as they stood there, barely moving. Their high-carbohydrate diet had piled on gobby fat atop their slab-sided bodies.

I stood looking at the photos, struck by the difference between old and new, for a good five minutes. It was a little like when the scales fell from my eyes about the beauty of straight rows of monoculture crops. I had always relished the look of a fat feedlot cow. It had always looked absolutely prime to me. I had brought in outside seed stock for years to ensure that I bred the biggest, juiciest cow DNA in my herd. (Seed stock introduced through artificial insemination is another technological input that is commonly used by cattle farmers.) But squinting at those photographs, I saw how the more that industrial farming methods had selected for unnatural traits, the more our idea of a healthy, handsome animal had changed. Cattlemen had gotten used to doing all kinds of perverse things because of that, like sono-gramming bulls to check the size of their rib eyes, and making the bull with the biggest rib eye—the freak-of-nature bull—the most desirable and expensive stock to breed from. None of us thought about the unintended consequences of selecting for freaks of nature, though now I understand that these outliers are never the good "all around" animals. The steer that has been bred by man to have a supersize rib eye or to pack on weight extra fast, or the dairy cow that has been bred to produce great volumes of milk, likely has weak legs or low libido or an inability to tolerate different kinds of grasses, and poor health as a result. These are all things that natural selection would have taken care of if we'd just let it be. When you select for *one* trait in a species, you do so at the expense of all the *other* traits in that species. The same as if you enforce one species in an ecosystem, you do so at the expense of all the other species.

Looking at those pictures in Fort Worth that day was another small eureka moment. I couldn't fawn over a fat animal ever again. I almost pitied it. Bred to become a victim of the same diseases of overconsumption that strike humans these days, he had to get slaughtered young. He wouldn't make it long.

I have worked hard to breed my herds backward in time ever since. I want my animals looking like those 1930s steers, and generation by generation, I get closer. Part of what made me quit castrating my bull calves was that it gradually became clear that I was raising better bulls in my own herd than I was buying. The herd had been a "closed herd" back in my great-granddaddy's day, which means no outside animals were *ever* brought in to breed and reproduce. He only bred from the bulls and heifers of his own breeding that met his own standards. But somewhere in my granddaddy's or daddy's era, they started buying purebred bulls from expensive bull dealers to improve the herd— to improve the yield. In the quest for bigger, heavier animals, all kinds of breeds got mixed in over the decades. Between my father and me, we've had one of just about every breed of bull to have walked American soil, kind of like a flavor of the month club: Brahman, Hereford, Akaushi, short horn, Charolais, and Simmental as well as plenty of Black and Red Angus. This gradually mongrelized our breeding to a more generic American beef cow, one that had unnatural ability to digest and assimilate the grain and soy feed they'd later get at the feedlot. But the female side of the Harris herd had always stayed closed. We have only ever had mamas born from our own herds. When I ceased castrating the bulls, I closed the male side, selected my own breeding bulls from the ranks of my own herd, and never ordered seed stock again.

Having the wealth of diverse DNA in the testicles of my herd proved a blessing. I selected for the attributes that I liked the most, picking the most virile and healthy bulls, the ones that performed the best overall in my ecosystem. Doing this has, over time, helped to repair the disconnect between land and livestock even further: we've got a breed of our own at White Oak Pastures that is highly adapted to this land, animals that can get full nourishment from the grass we grow here and that stay healthy on these pastures from birth to death. I still have to watch myself, however, or my old cowboy conditioning can easily take over. Twice a year, when I select the lucky devils for our herd sires, I stand at the corrals with my son-in-law John, who is the farm's director of livestock, and watch over the guys separating out the bulls we want to keep. John is six foot four and lanky. I'm about six inches shorter but a generous amount heavier. I tell the guys who are working the chute that separates out the keepers into a small corral, "Remember, we want the Will bulls, not the John bulls!" Over time, that's gotten the kind of cattle I want: stockier and more resilient than their confinement kinfolks.

I remember going to an industrial hog farm, not long out of college. They made me undress, shower with antimicrobial soap, put on a sterile jumpsuit and hairnet, and stash away every piece of clothing in a locker before going in. I remember thinking, "Hogs are wallowing in *mud* and I've got to take a shower and wear sanitized clothes, just to take a look?" But the fragility of the industrial facility made it necessary. With the animals crowded together, isolated from the exposures that would naturally strengthen their immune system, one little speck of unexpected bacteria could take the whole operation down. Back then, of course, I didn't have the sophistication to understand that. I just thought that it was high-tech, and that was the way that it ought to be. Now I know the cost of that isolation.

When I fixed the disconnect between land and livestock and began emulating what nature would do—natural diet, natural environment, constant movement, little stress—so much began to go right with my animals. They got healthier than they had ever been before. This created a positive feedback loop—fewer health problems meant less need for drugs with unknown side effects, which ensured even greater health for the animals. I was able, for example, to taper off the annual doses of dewormer drugs I'd relied on for every cow. Because the cattle were no longer stuck on the same patch of land for days or weeks, they stopped accidentally eating neonate parasites that typically get transferred from one animal's guts onto the grass in their shit, and into the next animal's mouth. Moving the cattle frequently broke the parasitic breeding cycle on the grass. This corrected about 90 percent of the problem. The parasites weren't completely gone—they never are, and if an animal looks wormy and is struggling, I might still spot-worm her with medicine. It's a situational decision. But the parasite population is so reduced that the cattle's own gut flora and immune systems can mostly keep the upper hand. They don't get overtaken by the parasites, or as sick from them. (I don't know if I want to fully eradicate them anyway. I believe that these "unwanted" species probably have their purpose, even if I don't know exactly what that purpose is.) The *positive* unintended consequence of taking dewormer drugs out of my system is that the dung beetles have flourished. The great quantities of dewormer drugs that used to poison the cow manure they feast on have gone. Now, thriving colonies of dung beetles work the manure into the soil, which helps keep the face fly population in check. Meanwhile, cattle egrets and other birds flourish in the pastures. Their presence helps keep the population of blood-sucking flies down, which avoids the need for toxic insecticides. And who needs subtherapeutic drugs on tap when constant exposure to naturally occurring pathogens in nature enhances the resilient immune function required to withstand those pathogens? No drug can match that level of health.

These benefits hit home about eight years after starting my poultry program, in an episode that was gut-wrenchingly stressful but ultimately vindicating. I was away from Bluffton, speaking at Michigan State University. The Georgia state veterinarian called me and said there was a serious situation going on at my farm. He put the fear of God in me, because when the state vet calls me, it's usually to tell me about a disease running rampant, or threatening to. He said, "Your guys brought a chicken to the diagnostic lab"—something we do semi-regularly to test for disease and make sure all is well—"and it has tested presumed-positive for high-pathogenic avian influenza. We gotta do some more tests to confirm, but if they come back positive, you'll have to depopulate your farm of poultry." I fell utterly silent and went numb. *Depopulate* is a code word for "Kill everything with feathers."

At the time, I probably had fifty or sixty thousand birds at the farm. No insurance policy would cover such a loss. The next twenty-four hours were agony. But when the vet called back, he had good news. "The bird did test positive for avian influenza," he said, "but not the high-pathogenic strain. I don't think influenza had anything to do with its death, so no further action is required." I exhaled like a man saved from a pack of hungry wolves. Then the vet added, "There was one really unusual finding. That bird's bloodwork showed antigens that seem to be antibodies *against* the high-pathogenic strain of avian influenza, which is highly unusual. Was it inoculated against the disease?" "Nope," I responded. We were momentarily quiet, both of us confused. Then I said, "I know you're the vet, but I got a degree in animal science, so let me throw some spaghetti at the wall here. What if a wild duck living in my ecosystem had that highly pathogenic, deadly virus, and what if it flew over my pasture, crapped on my soil? And what if this chicken got exposed to the virus, but because she had been exposed to millions of microbes all her life and had a strong immune system, she got the illness, got over it, and developed the antibodies to protect her for the rest of her life? Could that have done it?" He thought for a while and said, "Mmmm, that *could* have done it." I responded, "Well, what's something *else* that could have done it?" He didn't have a something else. For me, it was a confirmation of everything I had done so far. I had put livestock back in the environment they were supposed to be in.

In the early years of changing my farm, I evaluated the success of my animal care program through *process*—the fact that I'd stopped using drugs and returned to grass and forage, and established rotational grazing. Now, I measure it through *results*. My results are that my animals are vital, fit, and remarkably unstressed. For the humans who work with the livestock, life feels good and, for the most part, is uplifting and enjoyable. Before, I *liked* working cattle. It was my core competency. I went at it like a football player intent on winning the game. Now, in a strange way, taking care of cattle has become a kind of service. Husbanding the herds is enriching; it is the source of the feeling that pervades my farm that all is right with the world. I take that as a testament to how being around confined animals will stress even the hardest of humans to some degree, whereas being around animals expressing their instincts is eminently pleasant—like the deeply contented feeling of sitting by a campfire or a flowing creek. So I think the animals that help this rightness to happen deserve an idyllic existence. They also deserve a death that is as stress- and pain-free as possible. Which brings me to the last of the three welfare considerations I think a person should look into, when it comes to buying their food: How and where do the animals die?

I believe that if I want to take full responsibility for the welfare of my animals, I must also be responsible for where and how they die. In the industrial system, farmers are forced to outsource or hide most of the birth, growth, death, decay cycle of life. Baby poultry get trucked in from hatcheries, and farrowing hogs are hidden away in cruel cages. Death happens far away from where the animals lived, at the hands of total strangers. Even decay is lost—major slaughterhouses certainly don't compost carcasses to feed soil microbes. They sell every single part left over from meat production to other industries: hides are sold to the leather industry (overseas where the toxic production methods wreak havoc) and glands are sold to Big Pharma. So are the fetuses of pregnant mama cows. The farmer's primary job is to ensure that one part of the cycle of life gets maximized: growth. Growth is the step of the cycle that counts.

But that doesn't make sense to me. I believe that husbandry involves caring for the whole life cycle of my animals. Growth, breeding, conception, gestation, birth, growth . . . and death and decay. This is where the non-farmer often gets squeamish. They tell me that they wish this last part didn't have to occur. But I explain to them that, first of all, there is no end, from a cyclical point of view. If they could step out of a linear mindset for a second, they might see how everything that has ever lived has died, or will die. I tell them, this is true for me, for you, for the microbes and the sequoias. Furthermore, every living being gets its nutrition from something that has previously lived but is now dead. This, too, is true for me and for you, and for the animals, the plants, and the microbes. Taking it further, in a healthy ecosystem, nothing that dies *stays* dead. It goes on to provide nutrition for another living thing. From death springs decay. From decay springs new birth, and then growth, and then death again. This is how nature works. I feel better about my own death when I think about it this way.

Playing a proper role in that process is nothing to hide from or feel shame about. When I select animals for slaughter, I am emulating that natural process. I am the pseudo predator and, just like the wolves took down the old ones or weak ones, I do it more methodically. I scrutinize the herd thoughtfully, and I select the animals to take out, literally saying, "I don't want that animal in the herd anymore." When we thin the herd and take out an older cow or the ones that fail to reproduce, it is not because we don't care about a particular animal. It is because we care more about the herd as a whole. The great mamas, the great breeders, and the virile bulls all get selected to stay because we need them for our herd to be strong. But we need some others of them to get turned into a form we can monetize. To put it another way, we need the cash. If we just blew the numbers up in perpetuity, never culling a single animal, we wouldn't have a herd or a farm at all.

None of this is done frivolously or arbitrarily. But it must be done. As the orchestrator on this farm, I make the call of when they're ready to go. It may differ from what the individual animal would articulate if it could. But if we go with *their* program, they're going to be out there till they get old, and arthritic, and blind in one eye, and vulnerable to predators. Panic and pain, the insult of predators in packs, will likely surround their death. The sticking point for so many folks is that they think nature, because she can be so beautiful, must also be inherently kind. She ain't. Nature is not kind or cruel. She just *is*, and she is beautiful as she is. And death is part of her. Coyotes run down calves and eat them alive (or eat them as they are being birthed) because they are hungry; hogs pile on each other not to keep each other warm but to keep *themselves* warm. Strong chickens peck at the weak ones, to establish dominance. (The phrase *pecking order* exists because runts in the flock literally get pecked to death; the word *bully* exists because bulls gang up on each other. These unbecoming terms do, in fact, come from animals expressing their instinctive behavior.) I am being neither kind nor cruel when I select an animal to die. I am supporting the beautiful system to continue.

The simplistic worldview of animals—filled with furry friendships and cherished animal companions—does make the issue of humane livestock slaughter hard to tackle. But we have to have the conversation. We have to think about it from a complex systems point of view. I believe that to raise food the right way, humane slaughter *must* be brought under the farmer's oversight—whether it happens on their own farm is not as important as whether the farmer has a direct connection to the process, and some influence over how it is done. This is extremely unusual even today. The exact figures are hard to verify, but my experience leads me to believe that less than 1 percent of the pasture-raised meat available comes from producers who oversee the whole life cycle the way we do here. (With *far* less than 1 percent of it in the case of some species like poultry and pork.) It hasn't been easy to reclaim this link in the chain. As I'll share shortly, we didn't set up our own slaughterhouses—one for red meat, the other for poultry—motivated purely by animal welfare concerns. The motivation was to keep our business going. But the positive side effect was that it allowed us to bring this important step under our complete control. (Many regenerative farmers and producers are, I'm happy to say, working closely with small, independently owned abattoirs. This can ensure high standards and oversight.) By having our own facility, we can ensure that the process of slaughtering the animals we raise is done with respect and care, and without unnecessary suffering. I think we do as good a job as anyone I've ever seen.

Unlike the industrial system's slaughterhouses, the biggest of which kill four hundred head of cattle per *hour*, ours handles thirty head of cattle per *day*, four days a week. On the fifth day, a much smaller number of hogs, or sheep and goats, move through. Our poultry plant can do about a thousand chickens a day, compared to a quarter of a million in an industrial facility. Where an industrial plant unloads truck after truck of cattle into crowded holding pens—imagine a sprawling penitentiary filled with noise, pollution, and chaos—our animals get driven just a quick mile from our fields to our processing plant area, five or ten at a time. They have a night in a spacious pen together, in full view of the meadows they know as home, with plenty of water and an atmosphere of quiet. When it's time, the pen is opened and each animal moves through panels built high enough to keep human activity obscured, so they don't get frightened and hurt themselves or other animals. It's only a few steps from the pen to the kill floor—unlike the big slaughterhouses, where scores of animals move through maze-like metal alleys, the cacophony and panic around them causing their fear to rise and adrenaline to spike. Our cattle move fluidly and calmly, like water through a pipe and our regulatory compliance manager, Paul Bouet, ensures that the only employees interacting with them are those who are professionally trained in humane handling. No hot prods are held to the animals' skin to move them through, no mechanized conveyers (no mechanized anything, in fact) grab them from beneath their legs to move them up a terrifying escalator, as they do in the huge facilities. Instead, the animal takes only a few steps inside before our very experienced stunner, Cedric Jones, a man who has spent years perfecting his skill, renders the animal unconscious with a captive bolt—a long rod with a blank 25 caliber cartridge in it. In one split second, the animal is rendered senseless. Only after this is confirmed by a man running his hand past the animal's eyes can the animal be hoisted from the ground. A knife is put to their heart, and the heart stops beating. The animal is dead.

To be sure, animals die here every day; I'm unapologetic about that. And we cannot sidestep the fact that death involves suffering. But I think the animals that we dispatch suffer less than almost any animal raised for food today. I've seen a lot of animals die in nature, too, and I think the animals we dispatch suffer less than the animals killed by predators. The fish grabbed by spike-taloned ospreys from my pond, the rabbit mauled by a coyote—those creatures suffer, too.

After the meat is harvested and packed for sale, any part of the animal we cannot sell for human consumption, or use to make a nonedible product that we can sell, goes to compost, feeding back into the cycle so that it all starts again. Though White Oak Pastures is known as a multispecies farm raising ten kinds of meat, plus bees on the side, we sometimes say that we raise *eleven* kinds of creatures on this farm. The number eleven is perhaps more accurate; it includes the microbes that make the abundance grow in the first place. They work hard, never stopping. And they need to eat, too.

Given all that we've discovered is possible, it is extraordinary that there is so much pushback against improving the welfare of farm animals. Big Food and Big Meat will tell you that it's way too expensive to improve confinement and intensive farming conditions; they say the consumer will never stand for the extra cost. Agribusiness trade groups who claim to be fighting for the industry's survival will push back against improving things for ludicrous reasons. They will even claim that the only alternative to confinement is letting livestock run wild in the country, where they'll fall prey to terrible endings in storms or get lost. (Yes, that was actually written in a trade group letter.) Underneath the rhetoric, they know there's no real need to change; most consumers aren't pushing hard enough for it, because they either don't know enough about it or don't care enough to complain. We'd be happy to host any of those agribusiness groups, or their writers and photographers, on our farm and show them the better way. So far, none have come. We have developed a close relationship with several animal rights groups, however.

The takeaway is that improving the welfare of farm animals falls on a different group of people: the consumer. You. Do you care enough about the animals that provide you with nourishment to go out of your way to look deeper? If you don't, then carry on buying the cheap, factory-farmed meat. But if it does matter to you, even just a little bit, then you've got to find and support a different kind of farm. One that, like ours, has rejected the minimum standards of the linear industrial system. And that over time—and inch by inch, foot by foot of improvement—has arrived instead at maximum quality: quality of life for the animals, and quality of the monetizable product they ship out the door. I'll give you the CliffsNotes version of how to know if that's happening: Go visit a farm you're interested in supporting. Watch the animals for a while. Get out there and look. If observing them is a pleasant experience, one that makes you feel good, then the farmer is probably following good animal welfare. You will know it when you see it. So try to find out. Get involved and get out there, with curiosity and questions. Vote with your dollar for producers who make it all the *best* it can be. This is a way different mindset than making it the worst it can be and still earning a passing grade.

Chapter Six

Rebuilding Rural—
Bringing Bluffton
Back to Life

Once I had my cattle living their full lives on pasture, and a grocery chain client in place to buy my White Oaks Pastures grass-fed beef, I had a major challenge on my hands. I had to figure out how to process my animals and produce the meat to sell. For a producer who's trying to succeed at regenerative farming, restarting the broken cycles of nature is just part one of the story. Even the slowest among us—and I count myself in that group—can accomplish that part. To take a plot of land, convert it from its former use, and develop it into a system that produces grass-fed beef is not easy, but it's doable if you've got the gumption and the patience. Getting your animal welfare to code—a better kind of code, one that you have written yourself—is fairly within reach as well. Raising several other species alongside your cattle, as I started doing a little later, ups the challenge a few more levels, to be sure, but that isn't rocket science either, once you've trudged your way up the initial learning curves. The hard part comes *after* you've got those pieces in place. You are forced to ask yourself, *Now what?* And you quickly discover that the answer is *a helluva lot*. Because even though it might feel to you, out there in your fields, knee-high in thick grass you grew without chemicals, smelling the unmistakable aroma of healthy herds living as nature intended, that you've triumphantly reached the top rung of a ladder you painstakingly built yourself—with repurposed planks and borrowed screws— in reality, you're still only standing on the first step.

You see, consumers don't buy cattle and sheep and chickens and hogs. Consumers buy beef and lamb and poultry and pork. And there are things that need to occur to get from the former to the latter. Processing the livestock—slaughtering, butchering, packing the meat— must happen if you want to support your farm. Nature only gets you so far—then *you* have to take over and turn the abundance coming out of your cyclical system into cold, hard cash. I quickly learned that when I opted out of the industrial system, I couldn't just opt out of one part. I was opting out of all of it. Back in the early 2000s with a potential customer base finally appearing for my new type of beef, I faced a serious dilemma: How would I get my fully grass-fed cattle slaughtered and processed and ready for selling without using Big Ag's slaughterhouses and meatpacking plants of the commodity beef system?

If you're not in this business, it can be hard to grasp why this would be such a challenge. The reason is centralization. Centralization is the third ugly sibling of postwar farming that brought us cheap, on-demand food, and it brought its own cascade of ill effects. The first sibling, industrialization, hit the land and the environment and the animals hard, through high-input, monoculture production and factory farms. The second one, commoditization, hit the health of everyone eating the food, because it forced farmers and producers to meet the minimum standards of quality instead of making food the best it can be. Centralization's ill effects, by comparison, have been less obvious. They have changed the fabric of American life for those in rural areas and "flyover" states, though this has been barely noticed by people in the cities or on the coasts. Centralization separated the categories of agricultural production from each other and relocated them to different geographic regions—vegetables grown at huge scale in the California Central Valley; cattle predominantly fed and matured in the West; corn and soy grown in the Midwest; cotton and peanuts grown exclusively in the South. In so doing, it blew up farming the way my granddaddy and great-granddaddy did it, as owner-operators of diverse and independent small food systems in their small corners of rural counties. It consolidated the processing of food trucked in from many different areas into big, corporate-owned facilities that were miles away, or states away, from the farms where the food was grown and raised. (Then it consolidated the distribution of the final product through huge, corporate-owned retailers and chain stores.) Before this happened, small communities of people across America had enjoyed meaningful livelihoods from either raising food or playing some kind of part in getting it from field to table as mill owners or slaughterhouse owners or bakers or butchers or brewers. These food-based livelihoods wove people together in a fabric of community, and the weave was tight because individual families relied on each other. They were interdependent and they valued that connectedness. But centralization sucked the life force out of all that. As it consumed the local farming and processing networks dotted across the country, it tore that fabric apart. Dollars no longer circulated around the community—they hauled ass to corporate facilities and trickled up to Wall Street instead. By pulling all the economic benefit up and out to faceless entities in faraway locations, centralization rendered small rural towns economically irrelevant and culturally obsolete.

In seeking my own production process, I found myself right up against this conundrum. I had deindustrialized my practices on the land and decommoditized my product by starting to sell it outside the system. By selling my grass-fed cattle to Publix's southeastern stores, I had ceased to be a commodity cattleman and became a regional beef producer. My product had changed, from weaned calves sold at auction to cut-and-packaged beef. This was starting to take off by 2004. Our Publix account grew to where we were supplying all four of Publix's warehouses, which distributed our beef to almost a thousand supermarkets in the South. Along the way, we sold Whole Foods the first pound of meat they ever marketed as "American Grassfed Beef," launching a second major outlet that would change everything for our farm. This interest in our new kind of beef meant that I had to continue building a whole new kind of food production system. What that challenge would eventually lead to was something profound, revolutionary even: a revitalized small town and a resuscitated local economy. But it took some serious growing pains to get there.

The human side of this story was not very impressive in these early regenerative farming days. For quite a few years after I switched to grass-fed beef, it was still just me and three farmhands working the herds. I hadn't yet fully developed my process of rotational grazing, so what did I need a bunch of cowboys for? And back then, I hadn't yet added hogs and sheep and poultry, so I didn't need a lot of extra help. My farmhands did what farmhands always did—fixed fences, moved cows, and one of them would load a farm truck with a few head at a time that had reached slaughter weight. The social fabric of Bluffton was stretched pretty thin, too. I checked in on my mom, who was aging alone after the death of my dad while Von stayed busy shuttling our daughters to school in the nearby town of Damascus, and to basketball and cheerleading and karate. A scant few of my childhood friends remained here, like my pal Tony Smith, who was raising peanuts, corn, and cotton. Had I been a churchgoer, my dance card might have been a little more filled. But since I wasn't, I'd gotten used to the opposite. The village of Bluffton had become aged and awful slow, the equivalent of an old man with a walker and a pretty limp pulse as well.

I'd like to boast that this fading of a once-bustling village bothered me, but it didn't. Your perspective narrows when you've been part of a slow decay and it becomes hard to see what's in front of you. The decline of Bluffton, like that of countless other farming communities around the country, had happened as slowly as the decline of animal welfare. Besides, as a kid, I'd always thought we *did* have a town. With my cousin Jim Knighton and my buddy Danny Williams and the other boys, I could get a football game going any Saturday afternoon with enough kids for offense *and* defense. There'd be a trickle of tourists stopping by during vacations, heading south to Florida, stocking up on Coke from Herman Bass's general store before hitting the snaketoriums and alligator farms ahead. When my cousins visited, we'd sit on the porch while the old folks reminisced, hustling for quarters to spend on candy and then disappearing into the jungles of the ravine to play cowboys or space explorers. We hadn't known Bluffton in its heyday, like the old-timers had, as a busy little trade center for the surrounding few miles. So to us, it was what it was—kind of poor, getting poorer, and nothing that we could do about it.

I knew that my father felt disturbed about it, though. He'd come of age in a proper southern farming village, and for him the town's heyday was still recent and vital, especially when it was colored with stories he'd got from his daddy about earlier times. The thrill of the trains bringing passengers from Dothan, Alabama, and Albany, Georgia, into nearby Blakely twice a day and taking local goods out; the reassurance of the steady traffic of wagons and buggies, and later trucks, moving between farms and feed mills and peanut co-ops and cotton gins, as goods and cash circled energetically through the immediate environs. I know that my daddy had been excited to make that postwar deal with the fertilizer salesman at the fish fry—though it feels a little like trading his soul to the devil to me—and he probably felt the charge of even greater possibility run through his town. But then he'd watched as more than a few of his peers fled this backwater town for a better opportunity elsewhere, the beginning of a rural brain drain that's lasted for generations. I remember him telling me that the A and B students went away to become professionals; the F students probably wound up in jail; and the C and D students stayed in the rural communities and farmed. Apparently, in his desire that I wear a coat and tie and get a weekly paycheck instead of following in his footsteps, he hadn't realized which one I was. Industrial farming had given a younger generation a get out of jail card if they wanted it; anyone smart, pretty, or talented enough to make it off the farm packed their bags and left.

This exodus of the best and brightest caused a hollowing out of a town that had once been a vital, well-rounded community. You can understand the changes here by looking at the broader patterns in farming. Successful farms shape-shifted in the modern era from one farmer, a couple dozen acres, and some mules to one farmer, 150 acres, and five high-tech machines. Making things worse, many of the youth who fled the farms chose not to return when their elders died. Farm properties that had remained intact for generations started getting split up into parcels when they were inherited, allowing other, bigger farmers to acquire parcels of land and fold them into their large monoculture farms. Smaller subsistence farms that had provided for families and contributed their excess product into the local economy began to fail. And when farmers and their families started to sputter, all the businesses that supported them—the local feed mills and the mechanics, the small slaughterhouses and hardware stores, the utilities and service providers and the schools and health clinics—struggled, too, and began to fade out with them. This trend played out in countless rural communities nationwide; it was by no means unique to Southwest Georgia. But the fact that Bluffton had nothing *but* agriculture going for it, no jobs to replace the ones that were lost, made the change especially harsh.

I don't think that my daddy or his neighbors and peers blamed this diminishment on the very system that he was participating in. I can only imagine he was caught between a rock and a hard place, benefiting financially from the industrialized system in which he was succeeding, while also grieving the demise of a way of life that no longer had a place. Each successive generation of Bluffton families found it harder to raise their children here. Many of them moved away. Little by little, as livelihoods eroded, the town eroded with it. It's how we ended up like we did, where the only thing I could buy in Bluffton up until about 2016 was a stamp—from a post office open for one hour a day. And where three churches became two churches that host more funerals than baptisms or weddings and may have only a handful of congregants on any given Sunday. And should my wife need a gallon of milk or a tube of toothpaste, she was looking at a twenty-four-mile round trip in the car.

I wasn't trying to solve this problem when I set out to reinvent my processing methods. Lifting up an impoverished rural village was not on my to-do list. I just needed cattle killed, skinned, and cut up, somewhere closer to me, at a facility that I could access any time I needed. I first turned to a small abattoir and freezer locker in Blakely, just a few miles to my southwest. The guy who ran it was aging out of the business, with no young blood to take over. So he did his best to help me but wasn't hungry enough to go the extra mile. I'd call and say, "I need twelve cattle processed this week," and he'd say, "I can do six." It was his plant, so he'd win. I made it work for a little while, but out of necessity—or better said, urgency—I reached out further, to a local slaughterhouse in the town of Tifton, ninety miles east of my farm. I was glad to buy whatever excess slaughter capacity this abattoir had. Their business, like so many other small slaughterhouses nationwide, was struggling, another victim of centralization. They were one of a tragically small number of independent local processors still operating in America, still serving their communities, much like the old freezer lockers that were abundant fifty years prior. A note to the uninitiated about freezer lockers: refrigeration was well-developed long before most rural communities even had electricity. But rural town dwellers and country people actually needed refrigeration more than city folks, because they raised so much of their food. The answer to this conundrum was freezer lockers. Entrepreneurs in towns that had electricity—usually the county seat—built large freezer rooms beside their abattoirs (which were also called kill-and-cut shops). They put metal lockers of various sizes in the freezer rooms and rented these lockers to folks who didn't have electricity, mostly the country folks. You could bring the vegetables that you had grown and processed at home and put them up in your locker, or bring your live animal—the abattoir owner would kill it, process it, and put it in your locker for you. Once a week or so, you could take out what you needed. The Harris family actually used to rent one of the five really big freezer lockers at Mr. Hughey Johnson's facility in Blakely, where Mr. Johnson had several hundred available in various sizes.

For a few years, I shuttled cattle to the Tifton facility as best I could. I was still deeply in the process of figuring out how to make grass-fed production work. They would dispatch the animal and cut carcasses into quarters for me. Some of the quarters were ground into prepackaged meat for Publix, and some of them got sent intact to Whole Foods, where their butchers would cut the meat and put it in their butcher cases. As my sales volume grew, however, the Tifton plant couldn't keep up. Which meant that my business got trapped in the bottleneck that just about every independent farmer I've ever talked to hits when they try to do their own processing. To really make good on my vision of sustaining a grass-fed operation and to achieve profitability, shuttling a few cows ninety miles each way in a farm trailer just wasn't going to work. With the local processors maxed out and unable to crank up their production any further, and with me putting so much value into a higher-end product, I started losing money hand over fist. Things got rocky—on my farm and in my mind. I'd done a lifetime's worth of heavy lifting, and dodged bullets that couldn't possibly be dodged, only to get within sight of the finish line and run out of gas. Figuring out how to fill the tank came with a lot of anguish: I had been raised to believe that encumbering the farm with debt was the worst of taboos, yet if I didn't find a way to expand, all the work I'd already done, and risks I'd already taken, would be in vain. For a short but agonizing time, I teetered on the edge of losing it all.

I heard about a group of ranchers in Carrollton, Georgia, who were proposing to come together and create a co-op abattoir for processing their cattle. It would be jointly owned and run by a bunch of them. For a brief moment, the sun broke through the clouds. I raced north to the group's first meeting, as hopeful as if I'd found the golden ticket in Willy Wonka's candy bar. I recited a couple of awkward prayers on my drive for good measure. But within fifteen minutes my heart sank. I could tell these guys were light-years away from getting anything done. They were sharp thinkers, but they were off in their calculations. They thought that processing could get done for a dime on the dollar of what I knew it would cost. Once it became clear that they thought they could add thousands of dollars to the value of each cow, and that they believed the co-op would run fine if they all took turns managing it, I bowed out. I drove back to Bluffton, faced with the hard truth. *Shit. I've got to build the sonofabitch myself.*

Most everyone I told about this plan had misgivings. I still remember one of the most respected cattlemen in the area, Ernie Ford, exclaiming kindly but sternly, "You can't do *that*!" It wasn't the raising grass-fed cows part that he was worried about; it was all the rest of it. The processing, the marketing, the distribution. He had the wisdom to know that taking on all of that myself was a huge, risky stretch. And he was right to be worried. But I just knew that I had to take care of the short stave in the barrel, which is transforming what you raise into something you can sell. *Short stave in the barrel* is one of my favorite analogies. If the wooden staves, or slats, that make up a tall barrel include one that is short, the barrel will never get filled to the top. The short stave will sabotage it, letting the contents drain out. Even though I had minimal financial experience—I hadn't borrowed a cent until age forty—I knew enough to know that a lack of processing capacity was my farm's short stave. If I didn't fix it, my barrel—the farm's capacity for success—would always sit tragically half-full.

With that fire under my ass, I hurtled headlong into building an on-farm processing plant. I had no fully mapped out plan for how I would execute it. There were precisely zero examples for me to follow back in 2007. I heard at the time that there were no on-farm, USDA-inspected red meat plants east of the Mississippi and only one to the west of it—Prather Ranch. I wasn't about to call them up and ask them to walk me through it, and I'm pretty sure they wouldn't have told me if I did. But I figured I knew enough to get started. I picked out a spot next to the original pastures where James Carter Harris had founded the farm and I started pouring concrete. Taking pains to conceal the full scope of the financial risk from my wife and my aging mom, I hired Colorado State University professor Temple Grandin, now internationally known as the authority on humane animal handling, to draw up plans for a plant that hewed to the highest standards of humane handling. (She wasn't nearly as famous back then.) It took a year and a half to build.

When it came time for the opening party, my family and my local friends gathered to celebrate and cut the ribbon. I had already brought on a twenty-four-year-old from Lake Placid, Florida, to manage the plant. Brian Sapp was fresh out of the meat science master's program at the University of Florida and he was itching to oversee an operation like this. Brian's worst nightmare was to end up in a job doing food safety testing in a cubicle at a midwestern corporation. I could tell in an instant that he was a chip off my block, so I hired him immediately, handed him the keys to the brand-new plant, and told him, "Don't break it." Brian was my first professional hire, and that one renegade choice would come to change everything about White Oak Pastures, growing it from one decision maker at its helm, me, to a team of us, and ensuring the growth of this farm as a regenerative business and as a deeply bonded community. After working with him every single day for half of his life, Brian is like a son to me. Blood makes you kin, but love makes you family.

But I didn't know any of that was to come on our plant's opening day. Underneath all the festivities, I was concerned. We had the regulatory and technical side of a processing plant covered—I knew Brian could handle that. But hands-on skills were still lacking. Even with his solid academic training, Brian had only ever cut meat in a college lab. It would take him about a day to carefully and deliberately process just one of our cows. How we were going to get enough beef moving through this new facility to pay it off and stay in business was mystifying. And terrifying. I was flying blind, traveling fast, and working without a net. In retrospect, it was a really foolish position to put myself in.

But the bucket must've swung in the right direction again. Because one Sunday morning shortly after the plant opened, I was walking around the plant, feeling doubts start to stab at my gut. An old man I'd known all my life, named Othar Adkinson, drove up and parked his truck. He was about seventy-two years old, tall and lean and in pretty good condition for a guy his age. Othar had taken over Mr. Johnson's freezer locker in Blakely and run it for years. He called out, "Hey, Will, how you?" I replied, "Okay." He called back, "Whatcha doing here?" Everyone in the area knew, but I told him anyway, "Built a kill plant." "Show it to me!" he said. So I walked him through the building, watching him take a keen interest in every piece of it. As we exited, he said, "You know what I'm doing here, don'tcha?" I replied,

"Nope. I don't. What?" He laughed. "Come to get a job!" He knew every step of the process—stun, skin, cut. He had done it thousands of times. And he had sought me out to do it again. It felt like some kind of miracle, aided, surely, by the Dead Harrises, who have always watched over my reckless ass. The answer had come straight out of the local community.

Othar, God bless him, was the first skilled worker on the plant floor. He worked there for a few years, and he trained a cohort of younger guys in all the methods he knew. With that unlikely kickoff, our plant started putting some of the jobs back into agriculture and food production that science and the scaled-up food system had taken out. This started with our plant crew. When you do your own meat processing, there are multiple skilled jobs involved. Not just the guys on the kill floor but the ones who haul the carcasses to chill for twenty-four hours, then break them apart and into sections. And the ones who cut the meat, and pack it, and ship it out the farm gate. And the ones who roll out the big barrels full of trimmed fat we can't sell, and transfer the leftover bones and hides and poultry beaks and feathers from the plant to the composting or added-value programs. So right away, we had about a dozen full-time jobs available where before there were none.

Inside the cutting room, there are eight guys around the table. The only cutting tools we use are knives, just like a hundred years ago, with a couple of exceptions: a splitting saw to split the carcass and a band saw to cut bone-in steaks. These guys have got to get as good with their tool as a hunter who just bagged a deer in the woods. We seldom have anyone come in who is already skilled as a meat cutter, however. That's the downside of being in a forgotten part of Southwest Georgia. There isn't a skilled labor pool to draw from. So we teach them. A cutter typically starts at the bottom end of the table, learning the trimming, then the deboning, and then working their way up to more complicated things like breaking down the carcass. You might think that splitting the six-hundred-pound carcass is Herculean work, but even a little guy with skill can do it, because they know exactly where to cut. In all these years, I haven't come close to the knowledge or craftsmanship that the cutters have.

The atmosphere in the cutting room is not, however, old-timey. Music pumps loudly, and the guys move to it, keeping their bodies limber and warmed up in the forty-degree room. Their knives appear to move in sync with the rhythm, flashing and glinting only a few inches from each others' bodies. I have come to appreciate the sight. A risky job becomes a little safer when everyone is coordinated. Plus, I like to see people happy, and music keeps them happy. I would never dream of telling them to turn it down. (Though Jenni once did. When she first came to work at White Oak Pastures, she and I worked together in the only office on the farm, a tiny room that shared a wall with the cutting room. The rap music would sometimes get so loud it would rattle your teeth. Frustrated by it drowning out an important business call one day, Jenni just about turned her chair over trying to get to the offending radio in the other room. I caught her, and had her look through the glass window that divided our office from their space. A dozen strong young men were rocking out to that way-too-loud music. They were also cutting meat at breakneck speed. And they were doing it without anybody pushing them to do it. I said, "You know who's benefiting from these men working like that, right?" "Yep, I do," she replied. We left the music blaring.)

I would hope that anyone who has been inside a large, centralized meatpacking plant and the one on my farm could see that they are as different as sugar and shit. We don't use workers up and spit them out here, like can happen at Big Meat's facilities. At our plant, workers do not stand in one place making the same cut over and over, their rapid pace set by the speed of the chain moving the meat. We ain't *got* no chain. Our people become skilled at the art, and the trade, and profession of slaughtering and meat cutting. In an industrial plant, this skill is intentionally dumbed down so that they will not have to train people and they can replace anyone at any time. There might be a few downsides to losing that anonymity: when everyone knows your name and where you live, they probably know something personal about you that might make you blush. But the payoff's worth it. Many of the guys who work on the kill floor have been with us a very long time. That longevity is testament, I hope, to the fact that they somehow know that I respect, appreciate, and love them. (I just hope that they don't read the "love" part, because cowboys don't say shit like that much.) These are very physically demanding jobs and the work may look gruesome to the inexperienced. But these are also noble jobs. These workers hold down the heart of this whole operation in some regards, and they are recognized for that. (We have always had male employees on the kill floor, scalding hogs and skinning carcasses, by the way, as well as in the cutting room. It's just the way it has worked out here, but I'm the first to say that might look different somewhere else.) I hope we are harking back to a system that has more human dignity baked in, more pride involved in the work. Just like my ancestors enjoyed.

Once the plant got running—and there were some significant hiccups I'll soon share—things began to really flow in the business at last. That began to clear some of the stagnation that had built up in this town. It's not entirely a metaphor to say that the blood started circulating in Bluffton again. Ours is a business of blood in some ways; at the plant, we literally let blood out of our animals to create food product we can sell, which infuses cash into our system. That cash flow pumps through our farm business as powerfully as blood in the body carrying the oxygen and nutrients that allow life to go on. So even though it was immensely challenging to add processing into our system, it reversed the decades-long trend of money flowing out of the farm along with the livestock, money that drained into the coffers of middlemen and corporations well positioned at each link of the food supply chain. In the industrial scenario, there is only a trickle of cash coming back to the farmer. It just about pays the bills but doesn't leave much to expand, hire, and grow. You don't need a biology degree to know that blood in a healthy body is meant to circulate well and vigorously, not trickle, dribble, and stop; and it's certainly not meant to pour out of it either. Capturing more of the dollar back got the circulation going again in Bluffton. It reinvigorated things.

Very simply, the reason for this is that I stopped paying for pesticides, chemical fertilizers, hormone implants, subtherapeutic antibiotics, and the like, and instead I started paying for local labor. The labor builds the community. Instead of my money going to Wall Street and Silicon Valley and wherever else the entities behind industrial ag may be today, the money stays right here in the poorest county in America. And because human labor is one of my biggest expenses in raising food properly—compared to labor being one of the *smallest* expenses in the industrial model—that money begins to add up. (Some people are surprised that raising food the right way is such a people-intensive business. I tell them, if that isn't the case, it may not be real food you're eating.)

As the red meat plant found its groove and business improved, we were able to add more and more of the lost jobs back into our farm. In 2010, we added a poultry plant next door to the red meat plant. That required about ten more employees. With our production volume increasing, we hired about eight more field staff to handle the fencing needs and our growing husbandry needs. To feed this expanding workforce, we hired three or four folks to cook lunch, working from a makeshift farm-to-table café under a pavilion next to the plants. Then, when we added hogs and small ruminants—sheep and goats— we needed a small staff for each species. As the farm got more complex, maintenance jobs became important, like grading roads and fixing trucks. People got hired for those. Once we established our composting program, which traffics nine tons of viscera and hooves and beaks and feathers per day, five days a week, out of the plant and into huge composting piles, we needed a couple of people who can drive extremely large dump trucks and are not afraid of blood. (Their jobs also include running the aerobic digester machine, which turns blood from the red meat and poultry plants into blood meal for fertilizer.) Unlike at the centralized meatpacking plants, where the waste stream can exert terrible collateral damage on the surrounding environment and community, our system of huge compost piles exists benevolently. They're almost unnoticed. These massive piles of decomposing animal matter, mixed with wood chips, get relocated every few years; they're currently located close to Jodi and John's house, and the only time they might smell is when someone slacked on the job of using enough wood chips. That's how low-impact nature's waste management system can be, when you let it do its work right.

As our farm departments multiplied, we needed managers with the experience to run them. But we couldn't find candidates who had it in our local tri-county area. So for the first few years, we imported skilled young managers from further afield. Crazy or inspired as these people were, they were attracted to the idea of deindustrializing agriculture and willing to move from Los Angeles and Seattle and Chicago and New York (and all kinds of places in between) to do it. They were not, in most cases, the offspring of farmers; they typically had not been raised in agrarian families; and they very often didn't come from the South. I'd go so far as to say they were typically urban types who had fallen in love with farming as a calling, and felt deeply moved by how much it matters.

Our first managers brought their off-farm educations and skill sets to Bluffton and, with almost no hand-holding from me, set up the systems that our farm would thereafter run on, and even dreamed up entire new departments. People like Tripp Etheridge, who arrived as a young market gardener from Florida and developed what became our flourishing organic garden, and pioneered methods of making biodiesel out of beef fat. And Frankie Darsey, who launched our soapmaking program using quantities of tallow we otherwise were not able to sell. And Lori Moshman, who innovated our black soldier fly program by feeding meat scraps to fly larvae that became grubs to feed the poultry; and Jaime Scoggins, who started our leather craftsmanship program from our hides. This program now produces dozens of gift items from earrings to pet accessories to fine purses and laptop bags. Most of these first-wave managers moved on to new opportunities after a few years, but the handover was easy: employees who came from nearby towns like Blakely, or Cuthbert, or farther into our tri-county area, took over their spots. These people, our second wave of managers, had deep roots in the local culture. They weren't looking to leave, as long as there was good work to do. This rooted a cohort of middle-class, well-employed folks into Bluffton, people who were starting families and owning homes in a place where none of them ever expected they'd want to forge a career and a life. It wasn't an overnight occurrence, but slowly the Bluffton brain drain began to turn around.

All this activity created a kind of updraft for other members of the local community. Local folks would come in to a job on the farm without skills or experience, but would learn it, master it, teach it to others coming up behind them, and then move up to managerial positions. Like Lisa Brown, who dispatched chickens on the poultry plant line for a few years before becoming the manager of the whole plant. Or Buck Wiley, who started out as a fresh-faced nineteen-year-old from Cuthbert on the cutting room floor. After learning everything about the red meat plant, he became a manager. Or Lashona Butler, who was a food truck cook at first and then took over the commissary that produces broth and pickles and tallow we can monetize. The more complex the farm became, the more possible it became for smart, capable people from our immediate area to establish meaningful careers in agriculture again.

There were more hiring sweeps in the years that followed. In the order fulfillment center we needed people to pick the products to order, and pack them for shipping. Customer service staff trained to handle the e-commerce business became necessary. Visitors to the farm increased, so we needed crews to maintain the grounds in an attractive way; and we hired a beekeeper because we had pollinators returning, and why not harvest that for honey we could sell? When I got the idea to fix up Mr. Bass's general store, which had been built in the mid-1800s but had been sitting unused and deteriorating on the corner of Church and Pine Streets for five decades, we needed local labor to do it. I pretended not to hear Von asking, "Why you gonna fix up that falling-down building when it'd be cheaper to build a new one?" My instinct told me that folks who came to our farm would rather walk into Bluffton history, complete with creaky floorboards and the odor of aged oak, than feel the sterility of poured concrete floors and LED lights. Once that was renovated, we opened a restaurant adjoining the store to serve our staff and the general public, so we needed a team on board to cook twenty-one meals a week. Opening our farm-stay cabins and houses required cleaning staff and capable people who could run guest activities like horse riding and farm tours. As we began hosting educational events and workshops, we needed a competent manager handling that part, too. And with so many different facets to the operation, we needed an administrative team to handle the unending tasks of keeping every part of it running smoothly: bills paid and bills sent; hirees hired (and occasionally fired); insurance paid for and claimed; and paperwork filed and regulations met.

Little by little, the life force in the area started to pick up. Bringing talented, passionate, educated people in and paying them a living wage meant they needed places to eat, and sleep, and play. We needed offices and spaces for our staff to meet and work. So I began acquiring every house in town that came on the market; usually ones in pretty bad shape. For thirty or forty grand, I would snap them up; the same amount again went into making them habitable. The old courthouse became my office. The Methodist church that had languished unused got fixed up, its pews moved to the side to create meeting areas, its side rooms becoming serviceable offices for administrative staff. We built an artisan workshop to make our leather goods on-site and produce candles and skincare products from our beef tallow. After renovating the general store, we built a new administrative building (we quickly outgrew the church, which became our training and events center) and rebuilt the horse barn. All this required workers from towns nearby to take on the jobs, and required us to pay them. Person by person, job by job, building by building, the gaping wound in our local economy began to heal. This historic family farm grew to be the largest private employer in any of the local counties around us. At my desk in the courthouse, I sign payroll checks for over $100,000 every Friday.

Unless you have personally lived in one of the poorest counties in one of the poorest states of the nation, it might be hard to grasp how much of a change this has wrought. Our employees make nearly twice the county average, and they get benefits and health insurance. (I believe you have to pay people fairly, because one thing I've learned is that a dog that is so hungry he's hunting food for himself is not going to hunt for you. I also believe in compensating people fairly for their skill sets, which is why some of my employees make more than me. I think when the founder or owner works shoulder to shoulder with the skill set provider, he or she appreciates those contributions a helluva lot more than when they're worlds away from those providers, trying to run the operation from a stock company boardroom. Another reason I hate big companies.)

That money doesn't all get spent locally, but most of it does. One of our employees might rent a house that has been sitting unused. Or they might buy an old home near the farm or in a nearby town and start to fix it up. They go to the hardware store. They buy food and eat out and buy beers and get their cars worked on. They use the local services and utility companies and pay taxes here. The money starts to circle around and local business become viable again. The rising tide floats everybody's boat.

I'll be honest. I never really wanted to employ close to two hundred people. Managing people is a heck of a lot harder than managing land or animals; egos get involved, and feelings get hurt. That person's got a better job than this one or this one's all up in that one's business. Out here with a hardy lifestyle, great food, and close quarters, young people couple up like yellow housecats, and then sometimes break up like them, too. Complaining can abound as temperatures rise and humidity, insects, and rain increase with it, on top of the hard work. (I tell whining interns to use Triactin. Try actin' like you have a spine.) But figuring out how to manage the human dimension has also created something I didn't realize we lacked, but now love to have: a town character of our own. We are, as my children like to declare, a weird but wonderful shiny little rhinestone on the Bible Belt. One that's surprisingly collegial, despite the differences in our extremely diverse workforce. (The lifers who root down with us sometimes joke that our farm T-shirt should read WE PUT THE CULT IN AGRICULTURE. A few Harris "Circle H" tattoos, based on the original cattle brand design my forefathers used, have even been reported).

There are a lot of assumptions about life this far south. I think we throw a wrench in most of them. The culture down here is not what you might think. We're an unconventional assortment of people, but we work together, and eat together, and drink dark liquor together and sometimes snip and bitch at each other, and somehow it all works out. It's not uncommon for me to look around the table where a few of us are eating lunch, and declare out loud, "I'm the only southern-born straight person at this table!" In Bluffton, we are all completely okay with however someone rolls—gay or straight, fat or skinny, white or black, Mormon or Muslim, made mistakes in their life or lived squeaky clean. We just expect them not to be lazy and we will not, under any circumstances, tolerate an asshole.

The significance of what was getting restored down here began to fully land when Jenni told me she was coming back to live and work here. None of my three daughters were raised cowgirl. They were not expected to do chores around the farm or chastised for watching TV on Saturday morning instead. I never tried to suggest farming as a career for them. Had White Oak Pastures remained a conventional farm, returning here would never have appealed at all. Once I got on a better track, I suppose I should have known that Jenni would eventually hear the calling. Jenni was always my shadow on the farm; of all the kids, she was the one who had the bug I had as a child. She had a natural inclination to be on the land, always at my side in her free time as a girl. We'd joke that, since I have some kind of genetic inability to smell acutely, she was my nose for anything awry—typically nasty things, like undiscovered dead animals—just like daddy had been the eyes for his father, the first Will Harris. When she got older, I told her in no uncertain terms that she couldn't work at White Oak Pastures until she'd done at least a year of working off the farm. My reasons weren't the same ones my daddy had back when he forbade me to return. Mainly, I didn't want her (or either of her two sisters) to come sailing into the family business straight out of college, riding on the back of privilege. That would have been devastating to the team building I'd been working so hard on. Subconsciously, I think I was also hesitant to hurt our relationship—too many memories of the bad old days when my father and I fought over every little trivial thing that came up, like two big old bulls.

After college, Jenni went to intern and then work for a large meat distributor called Buckhead Beef near Atlanta, learning the business of selling meat from the inside out. She also came out as a gay woman. Which made her, by her own admission, an extremely unlikely candidate for returning to a dot on the map in the middle of the Deep South Bible Belt. But I guess the same holds true for people as it does for microbes, plants, and animals: when you support complexity in an ecosystem, you get the gift of diversity. Jenni saw a place for herself in this growing community she thought she'd never see. And just like that, she was back, moving into her great-grandaddy's 1920 house with her wife, Amber, to establish what would become one of the most critical arms of our business, our marketing division. Amber, meanwhile, founded the artisanal goods department, expanding it to include not just leather goods and tallow products but extremely popular dehydrated pet chews as well. The two of them pioneered new things for the farm, and for the local culture as well. Their son Jack, born in 2016, was the first child adopted by the second parent of a same-sex marriage in the Early County courthouse, and also the first of the sixth generation of the Harris family to make White Oak Pastures his home. Their daughter Lottie Ann, named for her great-great-aunt on the Harris side and her grandmother on Amber's side, was born in 2022.

Jenni's younger sister, Jodi, followed suit in 2014. She had always had an affinity with horses and was a very competent barrel racer growing up, and she always sought to stay close to Von and me, but she spent her obligatory one-year post college working off the farm. She got back here as quick as she could, though, never doubting that Bluffton would be her forever place. Moving into the house that my great-grandfather built on the farm in 1878, Jodi set up home with her husband, John, who was not raised to be a farmer but who's become as cowboy as anyone I've ever met. He directs all livestock management on the farm. Jodi oversees all the consumer-facing experiences, like hospitality, lodging, events, and tourist activities—

businesses that literally did not exist before she saw the pressing need for them. These things not only bring more cash flow into the farm—adding more diversity and a broader range of things to sell, just like the old days—they deliver effective marketing for a farm with a non-existent advertising budget. When people spend time here in person, as a visitor or restaurant diner or workshop participant, they almost always pollinate our name and story and products wider when they leave. They go home and talk about us, and get the word out on social media, and that's the best kind of promotion you can get. Jodi and John's children, Hattie Bell, Harris Paulk Benoit, and Haisten James, along with Jack and Lottie, are the sixth generation of the family at White Oak Pastures. My third daughter, Jessica, chose to become a schoolteacher like her mama and follow a professional track in education some forty miles away from Bluffton while raising her two children, Maggie and Paxton Miller.

Jenni and Jodi and their spouses are now four of the farm's seven department directors; Brian Sapp is the fifth; and our indispensable, almost unflappable, and extraordinarily patient COO, Jean Turn, is the sixth. I'm the seventh. The five younger directors are a good three decades younger than Jean and me, but we all have equal voices at the table and each director makes their own department decisions. For the first four generations, White Oak Pastures operated with only one male authority figure on the whole farm. But I decentralized how we run this place—no one old geezer holding on to all the power. Now seven directors manage twenty-five managers, who manage about 150 other employees. What was a family-*run* farm is still a family-*owned* farm. But now there are a lot of folks helping to run it.

Having daughters who made the bold leap back home has given me more empathy for the ways my daddy tried to stop me coming back to run the farm. He really did believe there wasn't enough for both of us to live well on. He didn't want it to become a situation where I tried to make a go of it, then ended up taking a job at the automobile parts store, waiting for him to die and hand me the farm as some kind of asset—which was really a liability, keeping me there to see about it but without ever really spinning off any return. He didn't want a semi-productive White Oak Pastures to get passed down one day to my kids, who, like many of the third-generation farm kids, might eventually buckle under the burden of responsibility and say, *I'm gonna sell this farm and go buy that condo at the beach!* He didn't want the family heritage to evaporate.

So to have the next generation come back out of free will to a viable career—not coming because they *have* to or else the whole thing will implode in their parents' aging hands, and not pining to return but barred from that because there's nothing to come back for either—feels like I won the lotto. Of all the gauges measuring the right order of things here, having the young blood return to raise their kids on the farm is probably the most meaningful for me. It's not my charm that did it, that's for sure. But when I returned to my roots, it pulled them back to the family center, whereas otherwise they more than likely would have drifted off. I don't know from personal experience how life on an old established family farm was 150 years ago, but I'm pretty sure it was not all about how much money you could make or what return you could get on your assets. I think the motivation was to build a different kind of wealth, a multigenerational and resilient and comfortable existence that was appealing enough to keep the next generations close. It's a very different kind of code from what the mainstream offers, and once I reclaimed it, my kids decided they were willing to go out on a limb to claim it back, too.

It turns out that a lot of other people their age feel the same. In the last few years, we've seen a real turn of the worm—a steady flow of educated, passionate, smart, sophisticated people are choosing to come work here, or to intern with us. Most of them had careers in the corporate or academic world and became disenchanted. These are not folks who've failed at what they've done so far in life. Far from that. But I guess they feel that city living and suburban existences and all the things their parents' generations pursued, like promotions and two-car garages, no longer work as motivation. They want to live closer to nature and more connected to other people, and less isolated in their cars and condos and cubicles. They want to feel in harmony with their own mind, and body, and spirit. They want to eat real food and do real things, and feel the satisfaction that comes when you work with your hands as well as your brain. Some of the women and men who make it down here, as interns or employees, could make a lot more money somewhere else. But they won't do it, because they want something different from their parents' and grandparents' version of the American Dream.

I think this is happening because farms like ours, and the regenerative movement at large, are making rural and agricultural lifestyles feel relevant again. It's not that these folks want to work on just any farm. The monocultural farms near mine are really catching hell trying to recruit people to work these days. I can see why. When you go to work on one of *those* farms, your career path goes straight from one end of the field to the other and back again. You do much of the work sitting inside a tractor cab with the a/c blasting and the radio on. And it doesn't change much. The equipment may get bigger, from four rows wide, to eight, to sixteen or even thirty-two, but the job is the same, day in and day out. That's not remotely the kind of job description we have here, where the rain comes in hard overnight and makes the ground soggy and now the animals won't do well where we planned so we have to change the plan this morning. A regenerative farmer has to be able to roll with situational changes coming by the hour. It can give him grief, but it also gives him the satisfaction of think-on-your-feet responsibility, without the energy drain of worrying about status and appearances and keeping up with what's cool. That doesn't get you far on a farm like mine, especially in this corner of Georgia. It's more about how you show up. You have to get comfortable with yourself to live here. But I think the life offers better mental health because of it. I am not surprised at the large number of talented, aware people who choose to come and work at my farm. I just wonder why the rest of them haven't figured it out yet.

A friend of mine recently stopped me in the street. He asked, with a laugh, what I'd done to piss off a Bluffton biddy who I won't name. She's an elderly lady who's lived here for years and she was feeling pretty grumpy about our oyster-shucking farm dinners on the lawn outside the store (the oysters get driven in from the coast, and visitors come down from Atlanta). She was irked about the interns playing volleyball and music on a summer night. I guess this stuff was disturbing the cemetery-like silence she'd gotten used to in this town. I told my friend that, with all due respect to her, I refused to feel guilty for injecting educated, conscious, genuinely good folks and their families, who all have a passion for their community and fistfuls of good ideas, into a town that had fallen into a state of decay. I've seen what the alternative looks like, and it wasn't appealing in the least. An old white guy and his farmhands getting geriatric together, hoping that someone younger will take over before they croak, but not betting on it. I'd much rather have the energy of youth cycling through. It's made Bluffton a much more pleasant place to be. There's nothing "bougie" about it, as my daughters would say. No cute coffee shops, and the streets are still punctuated by empty lots overtaken by foliage. You'll still be the only person out on the street after dark, and there aren't streetlights to make you feel less alone. But I love what *isn't* here now. The town's lost the sad inertia of going nowhere that it used to have.

Don't get me wrong. Decline still riddles the communities around here. When I drive ten miles in any direction from our farm, I pass through plenty of towns that have seen hard times and still are largely seeing them. These rural towns are dying, and if the trend is not changed, they will soon be dead. It is as simple as that. I don't want that to happen, but I think it will be averted only if, as a society, we start asking hard questions. Such as, if you seek out nutritious food to build up your kids' health and your own, but if what you're buying leaves a trail of degradation on the people and towns that work so hard to produce it, or even wipes out the towns entirely, can you really call it "healthy"? That opens up a whole can of worms.

Furthermore, if you're seeking food that's fairer to the animals or kinder to the land—both of which I encourage—can you really leave out the fair, kind treatment to the towns and communities in which it's raised and produced? I think you can't just pick one attribute to focus on. You have got to support a system that betters the whole: animal, environment, and human. That has become my criteria for a truly regenerative food system. It has to allow for humans to thrive as much as it does the animals and the land they live on. You can't separate out one from the others. The Garden of Eden included two human beings living in it after all.

If neither of those reflections get you, how about this one. The more that consumers keep reinforcing a centralized food system, the less opportunities regular farming families have to own and manage land.

The takeover is already happening to an extraordinary degree—agricultural land is falling out of the hands of farmers and into the portfolios of other parties, like multinational corporations, investment funds, public entities, foreign businesses, or megalomaniac billionaires hell-bent on dominating the food supply. Few of these mega landowners have any idea how to manage their terrain the way landowning families do, and some of them have much, much worse ideas that will accelerate the damage already happening to the cycles of nature, the land, the animals, and the local communities.

There's been a preview of this damage that we should heed. Only a few centuries ago, wilderness was the predominant landscape all over the world. Growing up as a kid in the 1950s and '60s I was keenly aware of it—I yearned to voyage to see it, far away to Africa or the northern territories of Canada or the Amazon. I explored it all around me in Georgia as well. But over the last few decades, our actions have caused wilderness to become a memory. Wetlands have been paved over, forests chopped down to the nub, wild flowing rivers dammed and diverted. That was a sin against nature and culture and it was accomplished in a shockingly short period of time. Now the wilderness is almost entirely gone, save a few remote spots. I am afraid that in just a few more decades, we will do the same to the rural, because we do not value it enough. That societal travesty will be even worse. When we eliminated the wilderness, we lost part of our souls. I think the same might happen if the rural goes away.

While all this can feel like an abstract kind of concern, just think for a minute about how essential the rural towns and villages of America are—its little town squares, its main streets, and its farms and ranches. The rural is our country's heartbeat. It's our music.

Our country song. It's what our whole nation's progress has been built upon. Imagine being on a road trip in what seems to be the middle of American nowhere. You exit the highway for a moment to stretch your legs. You turn into a thriving village, where highly nutritious food is for sale, freshly harvested, straight from the field. People are bustling around happily, satisfied with their endeavors, feeling connected to each other and secure. It might feel pretty good to be in that village, don't you think? You might even decide you want to stay a while.

I'm not in the business of selling rural real estate, but I can't help but say that there might come a time when you and your family *want* to live in a place like Bluffton, Georgia. Maybe relocating to a rebuilt corner of rural America will be the only way you or your offspring can afford to own a home and to start building wealth the way your parents or grandparents did. Maybe you'll find yourself wanting a simpler, land-centric lifestyle. Maybe you'll just need a reliable way to get food on the table—food that you can trust, that is nourishing and not tampered with by science or Silicon Valley or megalomaniac billionaires. In any of those cases, you might be real glad the rural still exists. The story of Bluffton might start to feel extremely relevant to you.

I don't know much physics but I do know that you make anything stronger when you bind it to itself. If you're building a gate, you put the crossbars in; if you're making a tire, you wrap the bands around and around. When you complete these circles, binding what you've got back to itself, you get resilience. That's what we've done on our land, and with our herds. It's what we've done in our town. We have turned around a trend that anyone with a more cautious mindset than mine would say just couldn't be turned around. Unlike the changes

I made to the animals and the land—which were deliberate, and studied, and pretty well-thought-out—this one occurred as a side effect. It's one of the few unintended consequences of anything I've done that ended up being powerfully, transformatively positive. And I'm exceedingly grateful for that.

Part Three

||||||||||||||||||||||||||||||||||||||||||||

The Fight for
Resilient Food

Chapter Seven

No Risk, No Reward.
No Pain, No Gain.

I'm invited to a lot of regenerative farming conferences these days and get a lot of articles and interviews in my inbox every day. I don't go to many of the events (the cost of leaving the farm usually outweighs the benefits of appearing), but I do follow the gist of what's being shared. And while I'm pleasantly shocked at the speed in which interest in this movement is surging, I can't help but notice that many of the experts and consultants talking about regenerative agriculture leave out half the picture. When they give talks, appear at online summits, or write guest articles on websites, these well-intentioned folks have a way of making reinventing your farm sound less perilous than it is. (At least I hope they are well-intentioned, and not motivated by fame and speaking fees.) Excuse my skepticism, but I wonder if that sunny worldview ever comes from actually farming regeneratively themselves, at any kind of scale. I remember visiting the farm of one such figure, well admired for his smooth way with words and big ideas.

The place was beautiful, no doubt. But it was a little-bitty farm and somewhat underwhelming. My daddy woulda said it looked like the mule died and the plowman ran away. It's unfair of me to compare our operations; I've come to realize that one business model is selling knowledge, the other one, mine, is selling product. But I get angsty when gospel spreaders make it sound like you can make eighty thousand a year on twenty acres of land working eight months out of twelve by simply embracing the regenerative principles and having a bold enough vision. I'm not sure that is replicable in real life. Actually, I know damn well it isn't.

When we host workshops on our farm, this is the part that tends to turn happy faces to frowns. Farmers, wannabe farmers, and the agriculturally curious come from all over the country to learn how we think about resilient and holistic farming. Without fail, they're as excited as sophomores on prom night about the in-the-field stuff, scooping up moist soil with gusto and peppering us with questions about breeding heritage hogs. The production part of regenerative farming, which means the actual work done out in the pasture or field to raise the animal or plant, is fun and satisfying; you can relatively swiftly put points on the board. But when we get to talking about how to make the resilient farm work as a functional business, there's a lot of knuckle crunching and shifting in seats. I can't help it, because I'm not a coddler; I rain on their exuberance just a little. I tell them, "You can be Michelangelo knocking out masterpieces every day, but if you sell them to a guy on the corner with a picture store for a hundred bucks apiece, you have not perfected your system." Then I explain, "If you can't also figure out how to turn your good farm into a good business, a resilient business, it's not just *possible* that you'll go broke becoming a great regenerative producer, it's likely." The trail of good farms, run by good people, is littered with corpses.

You see, when a person decides they want out of the industrial system and want to run a farm on their own terms, with proper treatment of the land and the animals and the people involved, they have to change everything, not just the production methods. That takes what they're doing way the hell beyond the complexity of what they imagined. The first bubble that gets burst is the false notion of low-cost that modern, linear farming, with its massive economics of scale, created. Modern farming is a low-reward endeavor, but it's also low-risk, and the farmer can get a skewed sense of what producing food without all the crutches actually costs. When the blinders come off and you drop those crutches, the truth hits pretty quick. In making this noble choice of rejecting the poor deal that's been given to industrial farmers, where it's increasingly normal to barely break even (even in the good years), you also give up the tools that reductionist science gave you to take the costs out of production. The dubious reward for being a worthy outlier is that the costs get added *back* to the bills you've got to pay. You find yourself faced with a huge array of expenses that the industrial system had hitherto absorbed. (As an example, a big packing plant that kills several thousand cattle a day can do it for a few bucks a head because of the monetization of their waste stream and their economies of scale. The value they receive out of the "drop"—the hide, organs, and other remnants—typically covers the cost of operating the plant, which means the cost of processing can be considered "free." I only process 120 cattle a week, and even after factoring in the value we get from our hides and organs, it costs me about six hundred dollars a head.)

In the case of White Oak Pastures, we started with a significant advantage. I inherited one thousand acres of paid-off land thanks to ancestors who took risks and made sacrifices for me, in the expectation that I would take risks and make sacrifices for my descendants. But when I decided to double down on transitioning our system, I discovered very rapidly that when we tallied the costs of labor plus land plus the value-added services like processing, the food we had to sell to consumers was not obscenely cheap anymore. So then we had to find new customers and educate them about why it was worth it to pay extra. It's tempting to rail at the conventional food system that takes 85 cents out of the food dollar and leaves the farmer, at latest calculation, with only about 14.5 cents, give or take a few pennies depending on what they're producing. I resent the Big Food and Big Ag mega entities more than most, yet it's important to remember that they provide services for those 85 cents that the farmer otherwise has to provide themselves, and doing that hurts. At my farm, we might keep a hundred cents of the dollar from our direct-to-consumer sales. But to make that happen, we write a hundred grand in payroll every week. I'd be lying if I said I hadn't occasionally wondered if the folks farming conventionally are the sane ones, and I'm the stupid one for going rogue. When I decided to make my farm the whole machine again instead of just a cog in it, I transformed what had been a streamlined business—raising cattle for a little over 1,000 days each, when you add their 283 days of gestation plus about 730 days of growing to slaughter age of two years old—to a much more complex business. When it all came together, it was beautiful; but getting there was bloody at times.

The sheer grit required to switch your system and offer better food to consumers is hard to see at first glance. Visitors to our farm can easily see the $30 million of assets that we have amassed when they tour our acres, but they would never know about the $10 million of debt that exists alongside those assets if we didn't tell them. Nor would they know about the growing pains we endure pretty much on a daily basis in exchange for the great life we enjoy here. For one thing, even *before* you add the regenerative aspect, farms are a tough and unconventional business to be in. You need capital to get started, but you can't extract cash easily. The major investment you make—in your land—doesn't yield high cash flow, and all your other assets are non-liquid things like herds, and buildings, and equipment. In my case, I was fortunate enough to inherit a very nice and paid-for farm. The hard part was going to the bank and putting it at risk to have the money to put the rest of the chain together. Layer in the regenerative piece and you get into a conundrum where you are pouring money into projects that will pay off years down the line, or decades, some-times. Things like planting trees, building a breeding herd, regenerating dead land, and establishing a perennial pasture. But meanwhile, you need to generate cash, *today*, to be able to keep it all going. Plus, it can be a rude awakening to discover that regenerating land and restarting the cycles of nature works at one pace only: nature's. Making the shift from high-input farming to fully functioning cycles of nature takes longer than anyone ever anticipates, especially if the land has gotten very degraded. It can take five years to go from cash-flow negative to positive, and you have to ride through the initial destructive phase of the animal impact you introduce before it all kicks in to the positive, without losing your confidence—or your shirt—entirely. The first phase of reclaiming degraded land that we purchase, for example, involves haybombing it. We move the herd in, throw down a lot of hay for them to eat, and let them have at the fodder so they hammer the land with

impact for an entire winter feeding period of about eight weeks, dropping feces and urine all over it and working hay into the soil to restart
the cycles. It's a necessary first step in the healing, but the land looks
like a moonscape when the cattle get through with it. The meaning of
the old saying "Be sure that you have enough strength in your hands
to carry the ball the distance" becomes crystal clear as you get
underway.

Once the land starts to work the way you want it to and the abundance begins to materialize, then you've got to shape that abundance
into a marketable and monetizable product and get it sold at a price
that makes it all worthwhile. Even just getting to your newly found
customers and providing them with goods they want is a bitch to
tackle. Having to do this while also succeeding in the farming itself
turns what should be a quiet and rather glorious existence—spending
your days outdoors, stewarding the land with frolicking animals as
your companions—into something most newbies don't expect: a life
fraught with perpetual, and at times financially lethal, risk. The challenge of making our operation work financially has been so hard that
we got close to being a field casualty many, many times.

What has prevented that worst outcome from occurring is not that
we at White Oak Pastures were so much smarter than anyone else, or
that all our ideas have been unique. It's that we are fully here for the
risk and for the fight. The Harrises are lions, not sheep. We work
hard, obsessively so, it could be said. We are fiercely honest (sometimes painfully so) and we think strong enemies make you stronger
than weak enemies: iron sharpens iron, but marshmallow begets
marshmallow. I have found that generally speaking, outside the halls
of academia and corporate boardrooms, balls trump brains. That's
been the case on this farm: risk has been our constant bedfellow.

No Risk, No Reward. No Pain, No Gain.

Taking risks often helped us build what could have been a very niche, very small family business hanging on by its fingertips into a slightly niche, impressively scaled-up business that is profitable—not massively profitable by any stretch of the imagination, but just profitable enough. I'm truly not sure how we would have done it had my bloodline not imbued me with the genetic predisposition to go toward the conflicts that most others shy away from. When I wake up in the morning and drink my coffee and take my shower, I'm a bit droopy. Luckily, someone almost always pisses me off before the clock hits eight; I get ticked off, the adrenaline floods my blood, and I'm good to go for the day. Whether that's a good thing for my total health and longevity is up for debate. But it has been a good thing for running this farm.

If you are a consumer, I think it's important that you know about this stuff. The independent farmer who is producing the food you feel better about buying has likely clawed their way up a very steep and expensive learning curve, one that's studded with costly mistakes and constant threat of downslides. For every carton of pasture-raised eggs that becomes your kids' breakfast, or brisket of properly raised beef you put in your slow cooker, or quart of nutrient-packed raw milk, some farmer with mud on their boots has had sleepless nights before signing notes on land they're not sure they can afford. There are some exceptions, but all real farmers are carrying debt. Not to sound overly dramatic, but it's likely they've spent years living close to the edge personally and professionally, because in farming when you fail financially, you don't just lose a business on paper. You lose your home, your vehicles, and your retirement plans *and* very often your kids' homes, their vehicles, and their futures, too, as well as your family legacy. Everything can be taken except your health, and for many farmers the stress steals that, too. When things don't work out in the business, a complete life breakdown ensues. In short, the producer who provides you and your family with nutritious food may have paid quite a price to be radical, and not surprisingly some of that price gets passed on to you. And I'd guess that what has sustained any other unconventional farmer through their journey is very likely what's sustained me: the unflinching certainty that if you're not willing to take risks in your farming operation, then you're gonna follow the path laid out before you by someone else with their agenda—and that's never gonna be the best path for you. It's gonna be what's best for *them*.

The risks of running a resilient, holistic farm come in all kinds of sizes, shapes, and flavors. They also come in different amplitudes— sometimes they're high financial risks, other times they're less costly, but more permanent. My family has become familiar with all of them, starting with the transition from fully industrial to fully grass-fed. Being an early pioneer of the alternative methods I believed in didn't earn me quick glory. The years before I found my first grocery whole-sale customers were fiscal agony. I couldn't figure out how to get the higher prices for my cattle that they were now worth, and I ended up sending plenty of high-quality livestock, grown and fattened on lush, abundant grass and nothing else, into the commodity system I'd always been using. Some lucky folks, somewhere, were getting fully grass-fed beef for dinner for cheap, without even realizing it. It was a definite trial by fire: the cattle buyers at the commodity auctions I still had to use treated me different—though they wouldn't have admitted it. But they knew I was building a brand that went outside the commodity system, and if it worked, it would hit their business negatively. I'm pretty sure they conspired to punish me for that by paying less for my cattle than they did for cattle from the ranchers still playing by the rules. I survived the initiation, but it wasn't much fun.

The next test came in the form of the processing plant. I could have bitched and moaned about the lack of small-scale slaughter capacity locally, but that would have led me to one end: returning to being a conventional cattleman. So I turned to face the problem head-on. Once I know in my gut what I ought to do, I don't stand around kicking the tires on the idea for too long or let too many other people chime in on it. For better or worse, I don't spend months on a business plan or strategize every possible downstream consequence of my decisions. Doing that only leads to one thing: aim, aim, aim, and aim again. Having seen that happen time and time again in the corporate world, where cowardice is disguised as deliberation, I abhor that approach with every fiber of my being. Instead, I took the shot. I went to the bank and mortgaged everything I owned.

My dad used to admonish me, before dementia stole his mind, "Will, whatever you do, don't ever borrow money on the farm." That was how his generation thought. The safest way to play the game was to follow the rules as they were laid out, be modest with your improvements around the farm, and stockpile as much of what you made as you could. He used to say, when I'd tell him something needed fixing around the place, "Patch it. It'll last as long as I will." It was probably a blessing that he didn't live to see me sign the $2.2 million note the bank wrote me for the loan. If memory serves, I was equally vague with Von about just how much I'd borrowed—it's stressful enough being married to me, why add to her burden?—and as an only child, I had nobody to convince but myself.

Just like I never wanted to have almost two hundred employees, I never wanted to have a slaughterhouse. In fact, I wanted *not* to have one. I knew that if failure ensued, it would be an excellent example of utterly non-redeemable capital—a custom-built meat processing plant isn't exactly something you can hawk to the next guy or gal if the shit hits the fan. You can't get it airlifted off the farm. Plus, the minute you start doing your own processing, you enter a complex regulatory universe that ups the risk factor considerably. When you build a plant, you are not guaranteed that the USDA will even certify the plant as operable, because they won't inspect or certify it until *after* construction is complete. Assuming that part goes okay, you're now in a business where a fleeting moment of bad luck (or even a disgruntled employee with a chip on their shoulder) could shut you down with an E. coli outbreak and potentially cause your whole business to freeze or fail. Furthermore, you have to hire a squadron of employees, some of whom need highly specialized skills. You need layers of insurance beyond anything you could have ever imagined. And you've got to work with the USDA to get a full-time inspector in the plant, inspecting every carcass. It's the kind of thing that reasonable people just wouldn't get themselves into. And, frankly, it was agonizing to attempt it, knowing the little I did about what could go wrong. I quite literally was putting it all on the table—my present, our family's past, and its future—and it scared the crap out of me. Yet I kept going anyway. Maybe the early responsibility I got working for my daddy made me this way, but I don't let doubt stop me, because my instinct talks louder. I often know less about the subject than anyone in the room, but I tend to know what we ought to do about it. My daughters say that I am often wrong, but never undecided.

(Getting the USDA certificate of inspection, by the way, is a big deal; you need it in order to send your product across state lines, and if you are in distribution, you pretty much *have* to cross state lines. The regulations are onerous, but they are in place because somewhere, at some time, some bastard did something that was either stupid or greedy and that compromised the safety of meat production. So I don't begrudge the regulations. But I've observed that my meat is far *more* inspected—by the full-time inspectors who work at our plants—than the meat that moves so swiftly through the industrial plants. Industrial animals or birds move through big plants on a chain at considerable speed. The inspector has only a very brief time to look at them, checking for disease or parasites or bacteria. I don't have a chain in either my red meat or my poultry plant, so the inspector can scrutinize each carcass for a prolonged time if he wants to. (Sometimes, he wants to. I would be willing to bet that Big Meat does all they can through lobbies to make USDA inspection easy on them and hard on us little independents. I will never, however, have the means to prove that.)

Once we got the green light to start operations, it quickly became apparent that I did not know a goddamn thing about running a slaughter plant. Brian Sapp and I had roughly calculated that moving fifty cattle a week through our plant for our wholesale grocery customers would get the farm to where we needed financially. We were wrong by a factor of 100 percent. Fifty head of cattle a week was not nearly enough to keep us in business. With all the money owed to debt services, and the costs of running a highly regulated plant, we started hemorrhaging money. I felt a spike of panic, a cold rush of fear that I'd gotten in over my head. The specter of ending up like Ernie Ford had predicted, watching the bank get its hands on a then-150-year-old legacy farm and giving Von a tour of the rented mobile home we'd shortly be inhabiting, danced gruesomely before my eyes. Against the odds, we had to get our volume up, and quickly.

Luckily, we had overengineered the plant during the build. All we needed was a further investment of about $800,000 to get our volume higher; so I borrowed that, too, and made some enhancements to the facility, which pretty quickly doubled the volume of cattle we could slaughter in a week. But double the volume isn't worth a damn if you don't have them sold. Once again, I can only think that the Dead Harrises called in some favors, wrangling things invisibly for me from the afterworld. Right about that time, a Whole Foods executive named Ken Meyer, who was president of their mid-Atlantic region, came to see the plant. He was a visionary kind of guy, genuinely fascinated about the model I was building of on-farm processing and vertical integration. When I told him with unflinching honesty that what I'd built wasn't working financially, he asked what would make it work. I answered, "Moving a hundred head a week instead of fifty." On the spot, he upped his order for Whole Foods by fifty percent. The risk was redeemed; we had the break we needed. And then it was on like gangbusters. Consumer curiosity about grass-fed beef was starting to sizzle and we secured more wholesale accounts with the food distributor Sysco and grocery chain Kroger. Pretty quickly, we got to the hundred head we needed, selling at a healthy enough margin for our renegade operation to find its groove.

Expanding the farm so dramatically in 2008 should have been our downfall. The housing market was collapsing nationwide and the great recession started taking hold, commencing what would be years of economic downturn. But it was also a period of waking up. Grass-fed beef was catching traction in the marketplace and local and regional "foodie" culture was beginning to grow, too. Not down where we are in Deep South Georgia—Cherry Coke and a Little Debbie cupcake was still more like it and to some extent still is—but in Atlanta, and other cities in the Southeast, innovative chefs like Terry Koval, Steven Satterfield, Anne Quantrano, Linton Hopkins, Lis Hernandez, and Asha Gomez started sourcing prime ingredients from regional producers and showcasing the farms on their menus and chalkboards. The customers at their restaurants wanted the opposite of anonymous commodity foods; they wanted the thrill of food sourced from places they could locate on a map—the closer to home, the better. These rising-star chefs began using White Oak Pastures beef in their cooking, and our reputation started to spread. Even though logistically it was never as easy as it should have been to supply their restaurants reliably, because the restaurant supply chain is very hard to disrupt, these relationships put us on the radar. We became talked about by people who love to eat, aspirational even—and these chefs were some of our best ambassadors. (This later led me to join the Southern Foodways Alliance, an institution based at the University of Mississippi devoted to exploring and uplifting the culture of our regional food. Their support of my farm, and the short film they made about us called *Cud* was invaluable in helping us promote our regenerative program. We could *never* have made a film like that ourselves—it was another miracle moment.)

As the chefs helped foodies to hear about us, Whole Foods began to throw their weight behind their animal welfare program and began to share our story prominently, which called more consumer attention to our program. (One of their Atlanta stores even had their team wear GRASS-FED GURU T-shirts during my demos because they were so popular, which I have to admit was kind of cute. The seven-foot cardboard cutout of my likeness positioned by my demo stand was not as cute.)

As 2008 became 2009 and '10, I could feel it start to come together. Our processing system got dialed in; our wholesale grocery customers were consistent; we had kick-started a very small movement. Still a niche producer, to be sure, occupying a discrete corner of the food world, kind of like an artisan making hand-tooled leather belts versus a sweatshop churning out nylon and plastic ones. But an appreciative audience was finding us. We had established ourselves as one of the sole suppliers of locally raised, grass-fed beef in America at that time, and there wasn't much competition nipping at our heels. We entered a sweet spot for a few years in which the business became more profitable than I had ever dreamed possible.

You might think this would have delivered a phase of sweet relief. A chance to take my foot off the accelerator and relish how right I'd been. But that's not what happened. Instead, I got a little drunk on success. I got used to cash coming in at a certain rate, and got used to spending it at a certain burn rate as well. Not on anything frivolous, mind you. No Harleys or condos or boats; everything I spent on was something that needed doing for the farm. Hauling dirt, building buildings, buying pieces of land that came up for sale. Some would argue they didn't all need doing *right away*. My daddy from his resting place was surely making that case. But I have a generational view in which building wealth is more important than stockpiling cash. I need enough cash to keep my farm system alive, but having a bucket extra of it is like having a gallon of extra blood in my body—what's the good in that it? The way I see it, extra cash could be expanding my herds or building new buildings or buying another acre, building up the assets that secures the farm's perpetuity and its generational viability. If I've got so much cash I'm not worried about it running out, my theory is, I'm not taking enough risk.

It was interesting timing. My appetite for land grew as some of the neighboring farmers' appetites for non-irrigated land—which was getting desertified as hell from overfarming—began to decline.

No Risk, No Reward. No Pain, No Gain.

This presented opportunities, because I knew what to do with non-irrigated land to make it hold water. And knowing how productive it could become, it seemed dramatically underpriced. So I jumped on whatever I could to gain more acreage for my herds. My concern about future resiliency amplified, too, so I drilled wells any time I had extra cash, and sometimes when I didn't. (I figured there will be a time when a regular person won't be able to do that anymore—too expensive, or too regulated, or somehow blocked by powers that be. I wanted to make sure I had them.) All this meant taking on more debt, and increasing the burn rate to a scary degree. I guess I didn't leave behind all my love for playing hard and fast when I left the industrial system and its inputs. I just directed my perpetrator skills to banks and borrowing instead. To be clear, I never once gave myself a pay raise, even during the best of times, and I never took a dime out of the farm's operation for personal reasons (except when I built my house, way back in 1983). But expanding our assets so we had more and more control of our system was another story. It brought us very close to the brink, and it can't have been easy for those around me—Jean Turn, our financial guru, has some agonizing tales to tell of this time. Nevertheless, it got us much closer to where we are today.

I confess that in some areas, I got swept up in irrational exuberance. Once the grass-fed beef business took off, it seemed logical that there'd be an equal appetite for pasture-raised poultry. Consumers were starting to wake up to the horrors of confinement chicken operations and becoming curious about the nutritional benefits of meat raised on pasture. Besides, I needed poultry impact on my land. By that time, about 2009, I was dabbling in raising other species, not for profit but to help shape the landscape into the savannah context I wanted. Sheep came first, to help keep the fence lines clear. My daddy used to call sheep "pasture maggots"—that's how low his regard was for them. (He'd never owned a sheep, and I doubt that he ever even got close to one. Old-school cattlemen disdained sheep and shepherds. I think that came from the days when grazing was under the free-range law, and cattlemen and shepherds competed for land.) But I needed to pioneer new ways to manage this land, and since I was a good cattleman, I figured that being a good sheepman would be a cinch. It wasn't. Cattle and sheep are both ruminants, but the similarity ends there. They graze differently, move differently, have different health issues, breed and gestate differently, and handle differently. It goes on and on. Eventually, though, I got my flocks more or less under control. After that, I got goats to help clear shrubs in the timberland areas. I figured they'd surely be easier than sheep. Wrong again—being a goat man was equally hard! But I got them figured out, too. So I bought five hundred meat chickens because the soil needed nitrogen, and chicken shit is one of the best ways to get that. I couldn't get it cost effectively any other way.

I had never owned a chicken or anything else with feathers before. I was out in my fields with the flock day in and day out, figuring out how to raise them fully on pasture where they could express their natural behaviors and forage for bugs and seeds like nature intended, with chicken houses set up for protection at night. (The foraging provides deep nutritional enhancement to the feed we give them. It's not possible to raise chickens for food without providing them feed.) I grew them to full size and slaughtered them in the old-fashioned way out in the field and gave them to my employees to fill their freezers, then started over with another five hundred, and then another. Admiring the positive impact they made on the land and how much everyone enjoyed eating them, I thought, *I am one hell of a poultry guy!*

No Risk, No Reward. No Pain, No Gain.

It quickly became clear that I had to figure out how to monetize the chickens. Though their nitrogen-rich manure was precious, it could only be monetized by grazing cattle on the extra grass that it grew, and the feed still cost money to bring in. I figured that building up the poultry business the same way we'd built the beef business would be a no-brainer. Practice superb animal welfare, process the animals on-site, and offer a slightly higher-end product to enlightened consumers. We already had a red meat abattoir—Brian Sapp had that running good. Now all I had to do was replicate the model for poultry.

I know I'm not smart enough to know all there is to know about something, but I figure I know enough. My theory has always been, if you study something too much, you can end up with a bad case of analysis paralysis. I guess that was one of those times. I decided to get another loan of about a million dollars, build a poultry abattoir, hire workers for it, and since those workers deserved a forty-hour work-week, I calculated that we'd need to process about a thousand birds a day, five days per week, to make it all work. We'd have to go big.

What I hadn't fully understood was just how great the disparity would be between the cost of producing industrial chicken raised with utmost cruelty but utmost efficiency, and pasture-raised chicken raised properly and humanely. No animal has lent itself as perfectly to confinement operations as the chicken, because they're small and portable and can't hurt the laborers keeping them imprisoned. The efficiencies of scale that have been achieved as a result are mind-blowing. Put the two products side by side and it's like comparing an apple to an iPhone. Consumers have become used to the apple—astoundingly cheap poultry whose horrific backstory they'll never know. Our cost producing chickens the right way, start to finish, raising the bird on pasture, processing it in our USDA-inspected plant, and getting it wrapped and packed, was grossly beyond that—about four dollars and thirty-seven cents a pound. To make even a slight profit, I needed to sell them at close to five dollars. Then the grocery wholesaler would do their markup, and the whole chicken would end up costing the consumer twenty-eight dollars or more. Even for the most conscientious shopper in 2010, a thirty-dollar chicken was a hard sell.

It got worse. I discovered there were so many risks to raising pastured poultry that indoor confinement operations didn't face. Spurts of bad weather hobbled the flock, picking off the young and the weak. Worse, ravenous hordes of eagles appeared out of nowhere to congregate in our hardwoods, decimating our flocks so badly that guts rained down from the trees. Word must have gotten out on the eagle hotline that Will Harris had put out an all-you-can-eat buffet in Bluffton. Since nobody else in Southwest Georgia had large flocks of poultry outdoors, my farm quickly hosted every eagle in a hundred-mile radius. It was devastating.

The early push into chicken production was a dismal failure economically. Hindsight is always twenty-twenty. We were trying to build an untested and risky product category without having the right foundation in place. You see, for a holistic farm to have true resiliency, it's got to be like a sturdy stool supported by three strong legs, all of them well-built and firmly attached so it doesn't wobble or break. Production—raising the animals or crops according to regenerative methods—is the first leg. Processing, turning them into a product that can be sold for cash, is the second. And marketing and distribution those products to consumers, actually getting them from the farm to their forks, is the third. With our early chicken experiment, our production method was actually quite good, but the unpredictable arrival of apex predators threw it under the bus. The processing was on point, thanks to the facility I built. But I had completely misjudged the market and its tolerance for higher costs, and I couldn't get what proved to be an almost luxury-level food product to the people who would pay for it, at the high volume I had set up the plant to produce.

It wasn't until some time later, when I was visiting Boulder, Colorado, to speak at a conference, that the penny dropped on this. Some local friends took me to eat dinner at the Boulderama, a historic cowboy hotel in town, where a framed picture of their menu from the year 1909 caught my eye. I peered at it with interest and then drew back in horror. The clue to how I'd fucked up was right there before me in black-and-white letterpress print. The cheapest dinners on the menu back then, long before industrialized agriculture took over, were beef and mutton, at twenty-five cents a plate. Pork was next, at thirty cents. The cold chicken dinner, meanwhile, cost thirty-five cents. Chicken, contrary to what's typical today, was the *highest-priced* item on the menu. It was truly the first time I'd perceived the economic reality in such an indisputable way. Perhaps it shouldn't have been a surprise, given that my ancestors would have been extremely familiar with this logic, and I was mimicking their methods. But I just hadn't clued in to the historic truth that raising small animals like poultry the original way, on pasture and out of confinement, costs more per pound when all is said and done than raising large animals like cattle. (It was also why, when the preacher came to dinner on Sunday, you served him a chicken, because it was the family's special meal of the week. Herbert Hoover's supporters declared that he had boosted American prosperity by putting a "chicken for every pot.") I had gotten slightly complacent about the market for grass-fed beef, where a growing army of consumers would pay 30 to

40 percent extra over grain-fed prices, and had missed the fact that 300 percent extra for pasture-raised chicken was much too far a reach. I had taken a risk, and also made a big mistake, which compounded the risk.

This blind spot lost us a fortune. Over time, and after an incredible number of hiccups, we figured out how to raise and sell pasture-raised chicken without bleeding out financially. We got the poultry husbandry handled, and the large movable chicken coops out on the land that get relocated every day, and the feed and the brooding and the watering system and the guardian dogs to protect them—among many other things. We kept doing it not because it was profitable but because I still needed the poultry manure on my pasture. And because I like eating chicken, and my employees like eating chicken, and some of our customers like eating chicken. So we decided to keep raising some damn chickens. Just not five thousand a week of them.

This story sounds humbling, and it hurt financially, but I don't call it a complete failure. Taking a licking is part of the growing and my rule is that if you fuck up, you just need to be the first person to realize and go ahead and *admit* you fucked up. What it shows is that figuring out an alternative food production system can be far from pretty. You take aim and fire, and sometimes you hit the target, sometimes you miss wildly, and sometimes there's collateral damage, like chicken guts decorating your hardwoods—or hogs eating your goat babies as they are birthed. Until a person tries to establish a radical farm of their own, I don't think any of this quite lands; it can seem like it's rainbows and unicorns out there. But the reality is that when you buck the system, you discover the unicorns have got teeth. The system has a way of biting back.

I am of the opinion that struggle is just part of the human condition. Which is why it surprises some people, but never surprises me, that there is a fight here every single day. Some of them have been small-seeming ones, things I can laugh at now. Like the time when I started fertilizing my land with the remains from my processing plant before I had my composting program properly figured out. The guts got buried with a backhoe and the bones got windrowed into my pastures to dry for months in the sun. My plan was to chip them up once they were fully bleached and spread them into the soil, feeding into the mineral cycle. This would also get the farm closer to being zero waste. But someone who didn't care much for me turned me in, and soon enough a guy from the Department of Agriculture came for a look. Glancing at the bones—bones from my own animals, sitting on top of my own land as benignly as grapes turning into raisins—he ticketed me for "violating the Dead Animals Act." The ticket quarantined all live animals from leaving my land. I took the ticket from that petty bureaucrat and thumbtacked it to my office wall, where it stayed for five years as the meat left the farm as it always did, fully packaged and ready to sell—no "live animals" ever going anywhere but the plant. (Eventually, another guy from the Department of Ag noticed the fading scrap on the wall during a routine meeting and lifted the quarantine, trying hard not to laugh at the absurdity of it. By that time, I'd long since established my large-scale composting program.)

Sometimes, brief skirmishes occur, like when Whole Foods' animal welfare auditing company screwed up their auditing of a Thanksgiving's worth of pasture-raised turkeys. Whole Foods informed us, shortly before delivery was due, that they couldn't accept them because of this technical error. I let them know in no uncertain terms that the two thousand freshly slaughtered turkeys they had ordered from a regenerative family farm would soon be delivered to the sidewalk outside their headquarters in Austin. I added that the local media would be alerted to the story of turkey rot at a scale never seen before. Miraculously, the technical glitch got fixed mighty quick.

Frequently, my choices simply piss people off. Every bit of land we've acquired to increase the acreage of the farm was previously owned or leased by someone else. They weren't always happy about it trading hands, even if the landowner had made the business decision to sell the land or lease it to someone new. Out here, buying up land from your neighbors, even if it's degraded and gone to hell, is kind of like stealing away someone's spouse they haven't wanted to kiss for years. They'll get all puffed up and mad about it, even if ultimately it's doing them a favor.

Some fights are bigger ones, like the one I got into with the Department of Transportation when they expanded Highway 27. This turned what had been a sleepy, two-lane country road bifurcating one side of our property from the other (previously a dirt road in my daddy's time) into a high-speed, four-lane highway. Apparently, nobody in the DoT considered the logistics of moving a thousand head of cattle across four lanes plus a median strip, with speeding chicken trucks and Subaru Outbacks creating deadly moving obstacles. The paper pushers tried to maintain that the safe passage of my animals had nothing to do with them. I disagreed and sued to have a tunnel built under the road for our livestock to pass through at a cost of a couple of million dollars to them. A legal battle ensued that cost us dearly in legal fees, but we fought it well and when we won it, I knew we deserved the victory.

And then there's the eagle fiasco. We sued the USDA to try to recoup some of our seven-figure losses that happened to our poultry flocks under their Livestock Indemnity Program. That program decrees that if a farmer can't protect their livestock from predators that are protected by federal law—and eagles are one of those protected species, along with wolves and cougars—the USDA will help cover the financial catastrophe that ensues when those predators massacre the farmer's animals. The USDA tried to rule us ineligible, for reasons that were murky and motivated by something we could never discern. So we sued, and won, and had to sue and win again, and then got told they were appealing our win again. The lawsuit cost us over a hundred thousand dollars in legal fees, and the payout was only about two hundred grand, almost all of which is still pending at the time of this writing. My suspicion is that *not* paying us is a way for a highly placed USDA career bureaucrat to demonstrate to an industrial poultry corporation or two that he is doing his part to stick it to independent, pasture poultry producers. I hypothesize that some of these higher-level bureaucrats spend most of their careers proving their loyalty to Big Ag in the hope of getting a lavish corporate salary after retiring from government work. They think they can wear down a farm like mine until we just get tired and give up, in a war of attrition of sorts. But if they really want to take it from us like that, they're gonna have to come take it. We aren't gonna give it to them.

The biggest wars are probably the ones that try to sneak up with little fanfare or warning. A few years into our sweet spot, when the farm was making decent money and spending lots of money, but all told doing pretty well, our margins started getting crunched. This was counter to the improvement happening everywhere else, because our production methods were better, our animal welfare was better, and the land was better, too. Yet our bottom line was not. It was tanking.

The reason was that our wholesale clients were starting to procure grass-fed beef cheaper than ours and putting it out on their shelves, which hurt our sales significantly. The beef they were bringing in was not from small family farms; it was quite the opposite. The multinational meat behemoths that have gradually taken control of the industry had been watching White Oak Pastures, and a few other farms like us, build the market for grass-fed beef. Now that this market was heating up and looking profitable, they wanted a piece of it, too. To achieve that, they started importing grass-fed beef from Australia and New Zealand and parts of South America, cheaply and in high volume. They didn't sell it under the household brand names that consumers had recognized but under newly invented sub-brands their marketing teams made up to sound rootsy and straight off a rugged American ranch. (They were already importing grain-fed beef from all over the globe, so it was just another step in the same direction.) This imported grass-fed beef was different from ours; it was often of a lower standard, possibly not finished to the same levels of care or safety, and raised with unknown standards of animal welfare. There was no real way, in fact, to verify that this meat was even fully grass-fed. But thanks to a horribly misleading ruling that the USDA had made *against* a law requiring companies to list the country of origin on product labels, these multinationals could now pass imported beef through a USDA-inspected plant upon arrival and label it PRODUCT OF USA. Never mind that the animal had never drawn a breath of air in the United States and had come over already deceased on a chilled cargo container. They were selling beef that may (or may not) have come from fully grass-fed cattle but that in almost every other way was pretty close to commodity-level product, yet they were describing it very differently. (We could call this legalized fraud. It still happens every day, on a large scale in the "grass-fed" meat category, of which up to 75 percent is likely imported from overseas.) It was a perfect example of changing the message but not changing the system behind it in any meaningful or positive way, like we had. To the time-pressed shopper at the store seeking to make a better purchase, this food looked like a huge upgrade from their regular beef. It seemed, from the label, that it was helping the heritage of American family farms and ranches to survive, and even contributing to a healthier environment. But it was all corporate greenwashing: a veneer of eco and responsible messaging painted onto product that was still coming out of the industrial system with its industrial values and industrial unintended consequences. It was slick as hell and confused consumers by design. It also started to devalue our products. As a relatively small producer, we had fixed costs we couldn't manipulate downward. When other operations started undercutting us, it was extremely hard to compete in price.

We felt the crunch acutely. Having established ourselves as the main grass-fed beef supplier in three Whole Foods regions—Mid-Atlantic, South, and Florida—we got elbowed out of one of them entirely by a California outfit that was able to get grass-fed beef shipped all the way to Florida more cheaply than we could produce it in Georgia and ship it one state away. (I'll never have enough truthful information to figure out how that was possible.) I don't think we have seen the last of our product being replaced by this questionable product in wholesale grocery stores. That is one of the main reasons we have focused on selling more of our food directly to our consumers.

To be clear, when Big Meat gets in the game, they have so much money and power on reserve that they can afford to lose a little profit at first if it allows them to grab market share and dig in for the long haul. So they set prices lower than any small producer could possibly compete with. It got even harder when a few titanic forces—privately owned corporations and government-backed export groups—put their heads together. I saw that happen up close and personal several years into the wave of greenwashed, grass-fed meat when I was the president of the American Grassfed Association, which is an organization that represents family producers of American grass-fed beef. I was attending the conference of a kindred organization, the Grassfed Exchange, where independent producers meet to network and share information with each other. On the final night, I caught wind of an unpublicized meeting that had been scheduled for the morning after the independent farmers and ranchers would catch their flights home. So I stuck around to check it out. Lo and behold, it was being hosted by an Australian group focused on grass-fed meat exports. They were pitching American investor types to back a venture that would bring Australian grass-fed meat into the US. I strode into the meeting as the doors closed, coffee in hand. Everyone in the room looked at me like I was a turd in a punch bowl—an entirely unwelcome interloper who represented the very parties they were deliberately trying to crowd out. As the Aussies pitched the investors on what they were calling a "higher-quality" offering, their down-under "winter season" production promising to ensure that Americans got access to grass-fed meat year-round, the stakes were clear. It was a concerted effort, backed with government funding no less, to win Australian grass-fed beef a bigger slice of the American grocery store pie. These guys were literally touting on their slideshow presentation that "America cannot produce grass-fed beef for twelve months a year." I stood up and schooled the room that in Bluffton, Georgia, hell yes we can. That didn't go down so well. Nor did it when I wrote an article about the clandestine meeting and published it in the American Grassfed

Association's news report. But someone needed to speak truth to power. (I'm not saying that Australian grass-fed meat is bad, nor meat from other exporting countries, like Uruguay. But imported product erodes the American market, which erodes producers' opportunities to transition to regenerative models. And while American land, soil, water, and air isn't more important than Australian or Uruguayan land, soil, water, and air in the grand scheme of things, America happens to be where we wake up every morning. Building prestige and market share for other countries' products—sometimes, but not always, hidden behind a PRODUCT OF USA label—keeps American farmers from competing and gives customers no way to keep their dollars within our economy.)

The intensity of the market grab only escalated from there. By 2015, it was clear that the whole landscape was starting to change, and none of the changes were accidental. They were occurring because very powerful forces were mustering their resources to push an ever greedier agenda. The big players started forcing authentic independent producers out of the game. I watched as other grass-fed operations that had been run by independent ranching and farming families like mine got bought out by multinational meat companies that wanted them in their brand portfolios to tap the emerging consumer base. The small, authentic brands added a halo of virtue over the less-than-benevolent practices that the rest of the corporation endorsed. Then I watched as the core values of these brands, so painstakingly built and honed over years, got diluted. It was a perfect example of greenwashing in action, with the consumer never seeing what was going on behind the scenes. I had some empathy for the well-meaning folks still involved in running those small brands. Once the reductionist system gets hold of you, even if you've got every intention of sticking to your high standards, it's extremely hard to keep them. Now your production has to meet the needs of the corporate quarterly report, and efficiencies must come in. The complex system turns linear. The pieces of the whole get separated. Integrity and quality go out the window. It was like watching a hijacking of everything the pioneering grass-fed farmers had built with their blood, sweat, and tears—and the rate and intensity of it only accelerated over time.

I had zero intention of cashing out what we'd built at White Oak Pastures to enjoy my golden years in a retirement community in Buckhead, Atlanta, the suburb where you trade your pickup for a golf cart and dreams go to die. The only option I saw was to batten the hatches against these destructive forces and make our own system as bulletproof as possible. We had to fully circle back to the old ways of our predecessors and own every stage of the system ourselves. That meant taking full ownership of the third leg of the stool, marketing and distribution, and transitioning off our total dependence on wholesale grocery. We had to start getting our products to consumers directly via our own channels, and wean ourselves off using third-party distributors. Only then could we truly win back more of the food dollar and cut a clear path away from the triumvirate of Big Tech, Big Ag, and Big Food that together have a lock on farming profit. For a rural producer, this is so much harder than it sounds. For one thing, most farmers are not farming anywhere close to the places that their ideal consumers live. And if you're producing food at scale like we were, doing a circuit of farmers markets every week won't cut it. You'll never sell enough product to pay back millions of dollars of bank loans.

We had started dabbling in e-commerce and direct-to-consumer sales as a side gig around 2012. Our website was pretty janky at first.

We used it as a place to dump the parts of the animal we couldn't sell wholesale—stuff like the liver, heart, and kidneys that we had composted until we realized there was a kind of advanced consumer, educated about ancestral nutrition, who really appreciated organ meats. If there was any excess ground beef our wholesalers didn't buy each week, we'd put it up for sale online, too. It was all pretty primitive. We couldn't change anything on our website ourselves—an external company ran that—and we packed and shipped every order from the processing plant loading dock, using semitrucks as our freezer units. (We now have six refrigerated cargo containers and plan to evolve into a warehouse.) It was somewhat painful, and for several years our online channel was a nothing burger that made barely a contribution to our revenue. But we kept at it and got the wheels turning. And as our margins got tighter and grocery sales started to erode, the brutal reality came into view: we'd have to establish a proper infrastructure for nationwide, high-volume, direct-to-consumer sales.

A major e-commerce site and fulfillment center is shockingly expensive to set up and run. Getting your software right for sales at this scale, and getting it uniquely adapted to a farm model, takes lots of costly fits and starts. It's no small feat. It requires more money, ergo more debt (making this another less-than-fun time for Jean, the person who scrutinizes spreadsheets). All of a sudden, our business had to adapt to storing frozen inventory on-site rather than constantly moving fresh product through to clients. (We now hold over a million dollars in our finished product inventory.) We had to master the art of shipping perishable items across the country to thousands of individual customers instead of loading our meat on a single truck and driving it to a centralized warehouse owned by a grocery chain. We had to develop strong, iconic branding, which requires a level of sophistication we didn't have in-house. We needed more personnel along with the pricey infrastructure, which increased the cost and the risk. And there was a whole new skill set to learn that the grocery industry has dialed in perfectly: moving all the products we had in stock, the popular ones and the less popular ones alike, because a chicken doesn't come with just two breasts, it comes with thighs, and necks, and feet. We had to sell *all* the abundance our pastures produced, not just the easy sells. We also had to learn how to guide customers toward buying what we had a lot of and not picking us clean of what we had less of, and how to appreciate the fact that our steaks are a little different in size and shape from each other and not boringly consistent like factory food is. We had to teach customers to shop a lot wider, and eat the whole animal, nose to tail and everything in between. Luckily for us, a handful of dietary trends converged to make accomplishing this easier, like the Paleo diet, and ancestral nutrition, and slow food (we sell more chicken feet for making broth than chicken legs for eating, which says something), and the carnivore diet, too. Even so, mastering the flow of our inventory was a bitch to get right.

But just like a gambler putting everything he's got on red 12 every time he goes to the roulette wheel, I kept betting that the risks we took would work out in our favor eventually and that even if we were ahead of the curve by a year or two or three, enough people would be pretty close behind to make it work. In 2016, I doubled down on that bet, going full bore on building our fulfillment center, where we now pack and ship over a thousand orders each week. This meant staffing a customer service team and, very critically, a marketing team as well—because now we had to maintain and renew thousands of customer relations, not just a few big ones.

No Risk, No Reward. No Pain, No Gain.

Just like on-farm processing was not a thing in 2008, on-farm e-marketing and order fulfillment was not a thing back in 2013 and '14. People were shopping online, certainly, but not for meat. Most were still used to looking at the meat in a grocery store butcher case or shelf, picking out their steak, and then rushing home to get it in the fridge. Letting someone else do the choosing for them, putting it in a cooler with dry ice, and letting FedEx or UPS ride around with it for three days was not something most folks were comfortable with yet. Going even bigger with this distribution method a few years later was also a leap of faith. But I took these risks because my gut told me that several factors were converging to make mass-produced, questionably sourced grocery store meat feel less and less relevant to a certain kind of consumer. I was willing to let their needs start to eclipse those of our grocery wholesalers, even though from a traditional business perspective, it probably seemed ludicrous. I'm lucky that the wheel's come up red 12 a lot, so far. Red 12 has been good to me.

I wish I could say to the eager faces at our workshops that it'll all be easier for them than it has been for us. Maybe it will be. Nobody wants sterile, factory-made, and convenient food anymore, like they did when I was growing up. People want rootsy, real, and homemade food: cooked from scratch, not TV dinners; food from Somewhere, not food from Nowhere. That full-circle return certainly helps the cause. But even so, the path for a new farmer running a resilient, regenerative operation is never going to be risk free. I try to reassure them that I have never thought I made a bad decision, though I've made decisions I couldn't afford at the time. And I reassure them that when you turn toward stuff that's hard but that needs to be done, it hurts at first, but over time the blisters start to build up into a callus. Your skin gets tougher, and eventually the callus becomes a badge of honor you can look at when you need a reminder that you made it through the pain and accomplished something. You rose to the occasion.

I'm proud that very few farms start out the way we did, get to this size, and don't sell out or go out of business on the way. But the fights don't stop coming. There are plenty of entities out there that do not want us to successfully do what we're doing; it's just the way it is.

We fight to get the real message out about regenerative farming in a terrain that's getting taken over by certifications and industry standards that don't always do what they say. We fight to tell the truth with our small voice when loud voices with deep pockets don't want the truth to come out.

We get in tussles with rank-and-file cattle people who don't like that we call out the problematic methods used in industrial farming today and their negative consequences. I think they're missing the fact that my fight is not with them at all, even though our methods vary slightly; it's with the multinational companies maintaining the reductionist, resource-sucking system. But they think we are diminishing what they do.

We head-butt with bureaucrats who are accustomed to agriculture looking a certain way and are put off by the differences in what we do here. Try putting a composting toilet or two on your regenerative farm in Bluffton, Georgia, and you'll quickly see the irony; there you are trying to work directly with the cycles of nature and they wrap you in yards of suffocating red tape.

Not everyone around us has liked the changes I've made on my farm. I think some people still think I'm too big for my britches. It's okay. Maybe I'm just too big for their britches. I hope my family never worries about what people think of us in the short term. We're more interested in winning long-term respect.

No Risk, No Reward. No Pain, No Gain.

I don't see the fights ever really slowing down. I tell the directors of the farm, all of whom are a generation younger than me, not to run away from them. I have more confidence in my enemies than I have in my friends. Friends can come and go, but when you make a really good enemy, it can last for generations. That's okay, as long as *you* are the one who decides when your ass is whipped, and you don't ever give up until you make that choice. My daughters tell me the earliest memory they have of me is from their first day of preschool. I looked them in the eye and said, "Have a lot of fun. Don't be sweet, be right. And kick any mean motherf'ers in the shin." I bent down and showed them exactly where to kick. Then I told them not to kick just one time, but keep kicking and kicking until the bully turns around. I knew they'd probably inherited the gift of fight like I had, since they had 50 percent Harris DNA in their genetic makeup. I wanted them to learn to be brave and tap into the tenacity they'd inherited, something you've either got when you're born or you don't. I wanted them to be humble and respectful but not intimidated by a goddamn thing, and to never sink to the point where they judge themselves by what somebody else thinks of them. And I wanted them to always know they could protect themselves if they needed to, which they probably would need to do, because if you're gonna sail your own ship, you have to fight a few fires. Now that they're older and have kids of their own, I never fail to remind them that you have not lost the fight when you get knocked down. You have lost the fight when you don't get up.

Chapter Eight

A More Honest Accounting—the True Cost of Food

An intern once told me that I reminded her of the obedient and faithful servant from the Parable of the Talents. I never learned much about the Bible growing up, and haven't done much catching up. So I was pretty surprised by what she said, because I have never thought of myself as obedient, or faithful, or a servant. But she said it like it was a compliment, so I showed appreciation. Then I googled the hell out of it as soon as I got to my office.

Come to find out, this parable is about the virtues of taking full advantage of opportunities you are given and the sin of squandering the chances you receive. That resonated with me. I have always taught my children that the God that I worship is generous, but relentless. He—or she—gives us opportunities, but when he does, he expects us to make them work. God wants to see you push the ball as far down the field as you can before he gives you the next one. So I've learned to milk the shit out of every opportunity I've been given. My God makes you prove you are worth it, every step of the way. He is meaner than a platoon of marine drill sergeants.

In 2019, the next opportunity for White Oak Pastures presented itself. I caught wind of a land sale happening six miles south of Bluff-ton, tucked away on a dirt road at a spot called Bancroft Station, where the railroad used to stop many years ago. (Land around here doesn't change hands without me knowing.) The buyer was a com-pany called Silicon Ranch out of Nashville, Tennessee. They are one of the largest solar energy producers in the country and they planned to build a solar array on a 1,425-acre farm they had bought that, like much of the farmland around it, was in pretty rough shape. Instead of planting rows of commodity crops, however, they'd be installing rows of solar panels to harvest sunlight, capturing its energy and turning it into electricity that would go into the power grid that serves Atlanta.

I had seen solar arrays like that before—vast, glimmering seas of black panels tilted to the sun. An awesome site to behold, from an en-gineering perspective, and arguably a positive, non-polluting use of technological prowess. But I was very not awed by the idea of 355,000 photovoltaic panels installed in our ecosystem without any second thought to the land they were occupying. The fields in question were already deeply injured after decades of intensive row cropping. Re-peat planting of peanuts, cotton, and corn had left them badly de-sertified. I knew what would occur next, after years of watching the ways solar companies manage vegetation: first, a construction project to install massive amounts of industrial materials and then an ag-gressive program of vegetation control using mowers and pesticides to keep the panels clear of foliage. For the land, it would be the last straw. It would obliterate whatever biology was left in the soil, render the land sterile and unable to absorb water, rob it of biodiversity, and contribute to the breaking of every natural cycle I knew. The land's pastoral potential had been severely hobbled from years of overfarming. Ironically, this progressive and environment-friendly project of alternative energy would be its death knell.

I suspected the minds behind the project were brilliant. After all, they'd figured out how to catch the radiation from the sun, put it down a copper wire, and deliver electricity to people hundreds of miles away. But what struck me was what they *hadn't* understood: how to treat land. Apparently, their deep expertise in one specialized silo had blinded them to their impact on the balance of the whole. This stuck in my craw. I could not watch yet another land degradation project get installed, especially not one right in my own ecosystem, and especially not one that I knew didn't have to end up that way. Not informing them that I knew exactly how to do the opposite of what they were about to unwittingly allow—that I could help restore the degraded land and repair the cycles of nature using animal impact, and help their solar farm to capture greenhouse gases, retain water, and become a pocket of biodiversity—felt like being complicit in an assault. If I could show them why, and show them that managing the land the way nature wanted *and* making copious amounts of solar power could go hand in hand, it would also create an excellent expansion opportunity for White Oak Pastures.

Through some well-placed phone calls and a few financial incentives, I managed to get the company's CEO, Reagan Farr, down to Bluffton with his leadership team. A few hired guns were at my side, including my cousin Jim Knighton, who had grown up to become an electrical engineer with an MBA from Georgia Tech. We put on a real dog and pony show for these executives, taking them all over my farm to show them what we'd achieved through a holistic program of managed grazing. My goal was to convince them that there was a more economically sound way to achieve their goals—one that needn't cost any more than the technological management route they were planning to take, and that would make them better neighbors to the farms and communities they were about to move in next to. They saw the thriving pastures we had recovered from fields of hell, where life was exploding in a riot of green. I showed them how, unlike in industrial farming, with its intensive methods of tilling and row cropping, this lush, regeneratively managed terrain was locking in more carbon than was getting released into the atmosphere. They saw the places that predators lurk: the treetops dotted with eagles, the tree hollow dens recently housing sleeping bobcats and coyotes and snakes—wild animals that, inconvenient as they may be to live with as a farmer, are signs of a properly operating biome. I pointed out the biodiversity of pollinators in the pastures that ensured flora and fauna flourished not only on my farm but all over the surrounding area. I tried to help their eyes see what my eyes can glimpse in a heartbeat: the way that, once the cycles start to function again and work together as they should, everything on the land comes back to its full glory.

Then I drew their attention to land that had not been managed at all—a nearby property that had been leased by another farmer but managed without the benefit of animal impact. In contrast to our savannah, it was unruly jungle. Once land is cleared mechanically for agriculture, I told them, every natural system of balance and regulation it comes with gets changed. If you try to just take hold of that land and leave it be, without impacting it with animals, you'll have a mess on your hands. Leaving land that way is like baking a cake using your grandma's recipe, but leaving out the sugar. It's not the same cake.

Explaining further, I added that all land longs to return to the state it evolved into over eons—this state varies drastically from place to place depending on temperature, rainfall, elevation, mineral mix, microbial population, daylight length, seasonality, and more factors outside our comprehension—but the evolution always included the impact of grazing animal herds. Gesturing to the edges of the neighboring farm's chemically managed fields, and the uncultivated wetlands where crops were not planted, I pointed out the native and nonnative invasive species growing as thick as the available sunlight allowed, all competing for light, water, and root space. Shrubs, towered over by trees, were choked by vines. It was pretty, in a wild sort of way, but it was not the ecosystem that nature intended. You see, down here in the coastal plains of the Gulf of Mexico, the original state the land longs to return to is subtropical jungle. And a jungle growing over and around a solar array would be a very bad deal. So I saluted them for coming up with their first stab at a land management program, because they would certainly be helping the land by taking it out of the destructive cycle of intensive monoculturing and tillage—the process of turning the soil with heavy machinery to control for weeds and prepare for planting. And by offering an alternative, they would not be releasing stored soil carbon back into the atmosphere, contributing to warming. This was a good thing. But in choosing to control grasses and weeds around the installations through mowing and spraying, they would be throwing off some unintended consequences of their own, while losing a golden opportunity to reverse environmental damage and be a force for improving the ecosystem around them.

Mowing would throw carbon into the air (not just from the machines but also through the oxidation of the cut plant material). This was counter to their greater mission of reducing emissions through solar power. It would also rob the soil microbes of the nutrients needed to build organic matter, because mowed grass left to sit on the soil surface without any animal impact doesn't decay into microbial food effectively. It needs to be chewed and fermented in an animal's rumen for that to happen; otherwise, very little of the cut grass will ever be made available to make the soil productive. Hitting the weedy spots with broad-spectrum pesticides, meanwhile, would similarly wreak havoc, devastating the soil's microbiome and impeding the growth of healthy, diverse grassland that could over time draw down carbon from the atmosphere. If these solar gurus wanted to play a part in improving planetary health, then managing the land the way they were planning to just didn't make sense. I told them I had a better suggestion that could help them turn a good proposition—offering an antidote to extractive energy—into a great one, a business that went beyond renewable and all the way to *regenerative*. The method I'd employ would emulate nature, using the method it had evolved over eons to control vegetation. The tools I would use to execute it? Flocks of sheep.

By managing the vegetation with sheep instead of men with machines, this forward-looking company could build *up* the cycles of regeneration instead of breaking them down. The grazing herbivores would keep the grasses in check and weeds at bay, so the solar arrays could get maximum light exposure. They would also transform the grass underneath them into a precious by-product: manure. With the help of the flocks' thousands of hooves and mouths, tearing at plants and trampling on the ground, this manure would get worked into the earth and feed the soil microbes ... which would replicate and help build up organic matter ... which would contribute to greater plant growth, over time allowing perennial grasses to sink their strong roots deep into the earth ... which would improve soil aggregation and allow rainfall to be absorbed into the aquifer instead of creating flooding and erosion ... and would generate more photosynthesizing plants of different varietals ... which would draw more carbon out of the atmosphere and into the soil ... which would in turn feed the microbes so the soil was teeming with life ... which would promote more growth for the flocks to graze and generate more manure. They would not only switch on clean power near the city, they would switch on a never-ending cycle of improving the land that, especially in this rainy climate, could rapidly bring it back from the dead. And all without spewing any negative unintended consequences in their wake. Though I am not an unconditional fan of carbon credits, which is the emerging exchange market that rewards farmers for successfully re-starting the carbon cycle on their land, I knew it carries weight with forward-leaning CEOs. So I threw some cowboy arithmetic at Reagan. "Consider how much carbon you are keeping out of the atmosphere by providing people with solar power instead of coal-fired power," I mused, "then add in the carbon saving you'll achieve through grazing instead of mowing, and then factor in the carbon you'll be putting back *into* the soil through restoring a fully functioning pasture—isn't 'solar grazing' a home run for your company?"

I had steeled myself for glazed eyes and crickets from the big-city solar execs. But they were listening intently, so I bore down harder. I introduced them to the men and women bustling around our process-ing plant, slaughtering livestock on the kill floor and butchering car-casses in the cutting room and packing meat and fulfilling orders to ship out to customers. Each one of them had a life in or around Bluff-ton, I explained, and many of them a young family as well. By hiring my farm to graze their arrays with livestock that would then funnel into our plant, their sophisticated, city-based company would help create opportunities for more agricultural jobs, keep a local small food system busy and profitable, and strengthen the rural economy they were inserting themselves into. Not to mention produce some damn good grass-fed lamb in the process. They could tell anyone who cared to listen that they weren't just extracting profit out of this impoverished rural community; they were also putting opportunity back into it by making decisions for the good of the whole down here—just like we do at White Oak Pastures. They'd truly be practicing holistic management and evolving beyond siloed management models of the past. Besides, I added, you guys are called Silicon Ranch but you've got no livestock. A few thousand sheep will make honest men outta you—they laughed at that—and I'm the only sonofabitch you'll find in the Deep South who can do this for you.

For my part, I would take the risk of investing half a million dollars into the project. I'd ship in a thousand head of sheep from Texas, and add them to the thousand I already owned. I'd hire more people to manage the flocks, and hope that our customers would significantly increase their purchases of pasture-raised lamb. If this worked, we'd be able to expand our lamb production and diversify the farm's offerings, giving more types of customers a reason to buy food from us. But if it didn't work out—if the sheep didn't thrive or the market for lamb proved weak—we'd have a lot of money, labor, and effort sunk into a project that sounded better than it actually was. So even though I planned to monetize the herds that we'd graze on their land, I told the company they'd still have to pay me the same rate for managing the land with sheep that they'd pay a local landscaping company to mow and spray it every week. We Harrises may lack business diplomas, but we are not idiots.

Once the deal was made, we quickly got animals onto the land, under the care of our sheep manager Bridget Hogan, who is one of our city-gals-turned superstar farmers. A one-time successful business-woman, she arrived as a novice intern, then was hired on the spot to be our sheep program manager after completing her internship. What started to happen was beautiful to behold. The already degraded wasteland, further trashed by a year of construction, began to turn around, just as it has on countless other degraded fields we have taken on. Annual grasses like crabgrass and buffalo grass sprang forth first, big and succulent for the sheep to eagerly tear into. As a result, won-derful stands of perennial grass had a chance to establish themselves, covering the earth with a fresh head of shocking green hair aboveg-round and feeding a universe of soil organisms via their sizable root systems underneath it. Within a year we had a transforming terrain, one that was a slightly strange-looking sight, but nonetheless a satis-fying one. Clouds of mama ewes dotting a meadow, tending their ba-bies like in an Old Master oil painting, watched silently by sleek silver and black solar installations turning sunlight into usable power. The hybrid of holistic grazing and solar power is a radically traditional project that circles backward in one way while innovating forward in another. It may not be the *perfect* use of this land, but it's an improve-ment over the peanut-cotton-corn farming that used to occur on it. And the success at Bancroft Station led Silicon Ranch to expand its solar grazing program to other arrays, working with some other really good regenerative farmers like my friend Trent Hendricks in Mis-souri, and helping to forge a viable new way for other regenerative farmers to grow their businesses. (Trent became a fellow pioneer in solar grazing, but tragically we lost him far too young in 2022. My bet is that his son Reuben will continue the great legacy his dad left for him and his five younger sisters.) Our own project with Silicon Ranch will expand to nearly four thousand acres, which is larger than the total current acreage of the farm on its own. I generally try not to brag, but I can toot my own horn a bit on this one.

There's a saying in these parts: *The sun don't shine on the same dog's ass all the time.* It means if you succeed at something and get *too* cocky about it, watch out. Either the dog will move or the sun will, and it's guaranteed that the sunshine will shortly move on to the next spot. You've got to be on your toes, ready to leap, not resting on your laurels. Pivoting quickly when I learned about Silicon Ranch and winning the contract to manage their land helped me to close another loop at our farm. Closing loops means meeting your farm's needs by using the resources already available to you instead of depending on outside providers to supply them. It also means keeping as much as you can inside your system, like using waste materials to support the life cycle on the farm—not tossing them out for other entities to deal with—just as my ancestors did two, three, and four generations ago.

The reasons to strive for this may not be obvious if you weren't raised rural. So I tend to whip out a simple graphic to show people, a sketch on the back of an envelope showing an industrial farm next to a regenerative one. The industrial farm has a big arrow of inputs going into it, a big arrow of waste coming out of it, and a narrow arrow of bounty—containing only the commodity product that the farm produces—coming off it. The regenerative farm has got a very small arrow of inputs coming in from the outside, a much smaller arrow of waste going out to the world, and a broad arrow of bounty spinning off as a result. This broad arrow contains so much more than just the food product that is destined for the grocery store or farmers market or direct shipment to a consumer's home. It contains clean air, clean water, and healthy soil; it includes a biodiversity of insects and pollinators and vegetation and animals; it contains highly nutritious foods that come from well-mineralized soils, and better health in humans as a result. It contains resuscitated communities and more economic opportunities for average people doing skilled and unskilled manual labor. In an ideal world, the regenerative farm would not have *any* inputs coming in or any waste going out at all. It would have "closed the loops" so fully that it would generate its bounty solely from the sunshine, water, soil microbes, and minerals on its land working in functioning cycles. And it would reabsorb any waste by composting and making value-added products to sell as we have done, among other things. I yearn to fully close the loops at White Oak Pastures with a longing that is so deep I don't even fully understand it. We certainly aren't there yet—we buy power and utilities and way too much insurance and enormous amounts of shipping, because our customers are dispersed across many states (though I'd be happy to see our delivery radius shrink, as I'll shortly share). We buy non-GMO feed for our pigs and poultry to enjoy alongside the food they forage in the pasture, and I hope to close that loop, too, one day, by growing our own organic grains on the soil we've reclaimed and restored. (I've already told the next generation of Harrises I expect nothing less than that.) But even with these things pending, we've closed a hell of a lot more of the loops than I ever thought we would.

The Silicon Ranch deal was one of them. Gaining more land to graze—no matter if we own it, lease it, or win a contract to graze and manage it—is very important to me. It helps to wean us off a dependency I'd prefer not to have. After I built the red meat plant, I'd had to outsource the raising of a certain amount of cattle every year to nearby producers in order to have a consistent volume of animals moving through our system each week. These farmers, mainly friends or neighbors, raised livestock to our exact grass-fed specifications on their land for me, and I'm grateful for their partnership. It's helped to lift up more of the surrounding agricultural community and it's given them an opportunity to keep their farms viable in a business that gets tougher by the year. But I've always hoped to close that loop and have every animal raised under my purview, because any time a part of your business is out of your full control, you've got a vulnerability. Something bad can happen that you don't catch quick enough, and before you know it, your system is not working properly but the debt service is due on your loans, and not being able to pay the bank is what can quickly turn into a farmer losing their farm.

The first 680 acres of solar arrays that we signed on to manage increased the farm's acreage by about 20 percent at first. After the initial program's success, the next contract more than doubled the amount of land my animals graze. This brought it closer to a vision I've had for more than twenty years. It came into focus one day when, unusually for me, I was buying wine for myself in an upscale store. (I usually get my Yellow Tail Shiraz at a gas station.) Perusing all the pretty labels, I noticed a bottle that cost a lot more than the others. Its label was stamped with the words *Single Estate*. They resonated with me. I knew it meant that the winemaker grew all the grapes on one vineyard instead of amalgamating grapes from many properties into one blend. Instantly the conviction hit me that I wanted to do that, too. Running this farm as a Single Estate farm, with every animal raised on land I own myself, is a dream that started off slightly fuzzy and out of reach but is slowly coming into focus. Which is why I went after the solar grazing deal with the determination of a quarterback throwing a Hail Mary pass, even though I feared the executives on the other team might find my proposition strange.

If you've got a conventional financial perspective, it might be hard to appreciate the kinds of business decisions we make every day on this farm. Going out on a limb to start a solar grazing program, or going into debt to acquire some overfarmed land, or building a fulfillment center on the back of a steep line of credit, or installing a million dollars' worth of permanent fencing for our paddocks instead of using cheap polywire electric fencing won't show quick returns on a quarterly report. Some of those things might never positively impact our bottom line at all. But it's how we roll. The question my directors and I ask at our weekly meetings is not "What we gotta do to drive more profit?," it's "What we oughta do next—for the land or the animals or the people?" Generally, we are seeking ways to make the whole system more resilient and imbued with long-term, generational viability. The next question, once we all agree on an idea, which we typically do, is "How we gonna pay for that?" If a Harvard or Stanford MBA were judging my operation the way she'd been taught to—by its historic and expected level of profitability—she'd likely be far from impressed. In fact, she would think that I was crazy as a run-over chicken for making the investments that I make. Even though we are one of the few regenerative farms that has scaled to the point of employing a village worth of people, and have built a production model that sends $25 million of farm products out the door each year, and have almost $30 million in assets, those assets are all tied up in a business that does a little bit better than break even. Our return on investment sucks and it will consistently and forever suck because to calculate a return on investment, you divide the amount of profit you make by the amount of assets you put at risk to make that profit. Our assets include everything we own plus a boatload of debt we've taken on over the years, some of which will outlive me. Any suit-wearing accountant would quickly surmise that we take on way too much risk for not nearly enough reward. But that's okay with us. We are not trying to sell our farm to a company with accountants in suits. White Oak Pastures ain't for sale.

But if that type of person presses me on how I seem so satisfied with my farm's low ROI, and why I am not pursuing a 10 percent return per annum with bloodthirsty zeal, I explain that while it's not good for my blood pressure to ask my farm directors at our weekly meetings, as I do fifty-two times a year, "We gonna make payroll this week?" there are many other ways I measure my farm's worth and success than that. They just can't see it, because my accounting looks radically different from theirs. Mine incudes the revenue from the product we monetize, plus all the other types of abundance our system spins off in its big, broad arrow of bounty. Like the tremendous gains in water infiltration and retention we've gained by healing the split between land and livestock. It's hard to see if you're not trained to look, though nature will sometimes make it shockingly evident. We saw it after a torrential downpour, when the water running off my neighbor's two hundred acres of industrially farmed land far exceeded the water running off *two thousand* acres of my regenerated land. I captured the phenomenon on video when I was touring the farm with my friend and fellow regenerative land manager, Spencer Smith. Jenni shared the shit out of it on social media because it was so arresting that even the most head-up-their-ass among us could get the point. At the shared spillway between our two farms right on the side of Route 27, the water coming off the intensively row-cropped land was a boiling torrent the color of strawberry milkshake, filled with subsoil that the rain had bulldozed off. The water from our holistically managed pastures was a calm eddy the color of weak tea from plant tannins—much more water volume than on an average rainy day, because it was a five-and-a-half inch precipitation event, but nonetheless an indicator that our spongelike soil can handle the intense weather events coming its way. When I show the video to non-believers, I always want to do one of those mic drop moments and say, "The defense rests." I wish I had graphic evidence this vivid on the breakdown of the other cycles. The collapse is there, too. It is just less obvious. (These downpours are getting more intense with time, by the way, albeit less frequent. They show a shift in climate patterns that may only get more intense—another reason that resiliency translates to more than simply having economic security; it's about literal physical survival.)

My accounting includes other, subtler things that escape a conventional evaluation. Like the way we do *not* throw out waste products and pollutants willy-nilly but rather reabsorb them into the system by putting carcass material into a nutrient stream, not a waste stream. Getting as close to a zero-waste farm as we can is another way we emulate nature.

My tally of my farm's true value also includes things like the caliber of the closed herds I've bred for generational continuity; the resilience of the animals; the beauty and magnificence of them.

My accounting most certainly includes all the ecological indicators that the cycles of nature are working, and improving the soil and the water and air. Like the return of ibises to a flourishing savannah that is popping with insects for them to eat, and of predators and scavengers that are eating from, and contributing to, a food chain alive with birth, growth, death, and decay. Like the flourishing biodiversity of plants and insects and microorganisms that keeps nature's checks and balances in place, so that a pathogen is less able to gain a foothold and wipe out acres at a time, as can happen in a monocrop of one strain of plant. Like the busy scuttling of dung beetles, returning after decades of disappearance to play their role in reviving the soil and even metabolizing methane. One closed loop begets another.

Of course, my accounting also includes the quality of the food we produce and enjoy, too, redolent in complex flavor, built from powerfully mineralized soil and derived from animals that had as good a life and as calm a death as any domesticated livestock I've seen. Not to mention food that is shared daily by humans living and working side by side who, most of the time, enjoy each others' company immensely. Nutritionists have their technically accurate ways of talking about the benefits of nutrient-dense fodder grown on land that has not seen pesticides, herbicides, and fungicides for decades. I just think you can taste the rightness in the food from this farm, like you can kinda taste the harm in the other kind.

I love that we have brought White Oak Pastures back to a farm that measures its prosperity in the resilience and personal satisfaction and the perpetuation of family, which as far as I can tell from anecdotal evidence and stories passed down was how life on an old established family farm probably used to be.

But I've learned that all this value, as evident as it is to me, is mystifying to the person who's still stuck in the mainstream. I might as well be speaking Greek. Their understanding of worth is just so much narrower and more limited. They are looking through a slit in the fence. If my goal were to raise thousands of pigs in a space the size of a gymnasium and squeeze out as much pork as possible for the least amount of cost, I might fit better into their paradigm. Since my goal is to operate an ecosystem properly in a way that spins off abundance, there's no place in their worldview for me at all. So, I say, *Fuck 'em.* The differences are irreconcilable. From my point of view, we are deeply undervalued; from theirs, we are a losing proposition.

I've seen this mismatch play out in so many ways. Like when an appraiser came to look at a parcel of land that I was buying to add to our landholdings. It was a tired piece of cropland that had been tilled and monocropped into a hard tabletop of infertile subsoil, dusted with traces of topsoil that blew around in strong winds. I planned to hay-bomb it in order to rapidly get the microbial cycle humming so the land's natural fertility could return. I had to borrow the money to buy it, though, so the bank sent their senior appraiser over to estimate its value. The guy was experienced and sharp, and we quickly got into a good conversation, so I asked him if I could show him a very similar piece of land I already owned nearby. This land had been grazed holistically under my watch for a decade. After rotating herds onto it for short sessions of hard impact followed by long periods of rest, it had built up inches of healthy topsoil that my Ecological Verification Outcome manager, Jacquelin Deweitt, had measured at about 5 percent organic matter—a pretty impressive figure that indicates high microbial activity, effective cycling of nutrients between soil and roots, and healthy cycles of vegetative growth and decay. By contrast, the degenerated farmland I was fixing to purchase would've measured about half a percent. I pointed out how on my land, the grass was juicy, lush, and highly productive, and there was no need for fertilizer nor irrigation either, because the deeply rooted grasses had done such a good job increasing water infiltration, making the soil into a giant reserve tank. Each acre of my land could now hold twenty thousand gallons more water than the injured land. "These two parcels are the same size but one is healthy and productive and teeming with life and one is a not much more than a plot of dead mineral medium," I said. "How you gonna appraise 'em?" The appraiser answered, "For the same amount of money." Puzzled, I reiterated, "You understand the one I own already has five percent organic matter? And you understand that's at least four percent more than the other land, making it four times healthier?" The appraiser replied, "Yes, I do, and that's a god-damned shame, isn't it!"

That floored me. This highly placed individual from our local banking system knew that his appraisal of the land *should* include its biological capital—the valuable attributes we'd worked so hard to bring out that made this acreage four times more fertile and pro-ductive than its neighbors, and a much more valuable contribution to a farm and to the ecosystem at large. But he was bound to rules and principles that didn't recognize this enhanced value at all. It was like taking two identical automobiles, same model and mileage, but one badly abused and the other kept pristine, and giving them the same Blue Book value. Any fool could see it! The soil on the overfarmed land was fully inert—an orange-brown color that we call cowhide clay, just particles of ancient inactive minerals, no organic matter mixed in. Holding a fistful of it felt like holding tiny glass beads in your palm. I knew that the machines that ripped through it every spring to prepare it for sowing had deoxygenated the earth and starved its microbes and destroyed the delicate fungal networks that make nutrients available to the plants. The soil on my regenerated land was the opposite: mahogany-colored, thanks to plants and ma-nure decaying into its surface, smelling of chanterelles. If the other sell was inert—and it was—this soil was ridiculously *ert*! We both knew the regenerated land would spin off years, probably generations, of abundance if it was well managed. The unrestored farmland, meanwhile, had so many things working against a farmer. It wouldn't serve for much but to be dug out and used for dirt roads now. Yet from a financial point of view, they were both seen to be worth the same. The appraiser knew the system sucked. I knew it sucked. But neither of us could change what had been baked into it for decades.

I have a sense of why this is so. A perpetual, small food system like mine requires ownership that takes its view in generations, or maybe even centuries. (Have you ever noticed the word *regenerative* and *generation* are pretty similar?) The existing Big Food system is skewed toward enormous, publicly traded food and agricultural companies where ownership is not perpetual at all; the "owners" are the shareholders who buy in and buy out for periods of time, basing their ownership almost entirely on monetary performance over the latest quarter year, and on how well that entity performed against the competition in its singular area of specialty—its one piece of the complicated system.

But a holistic and regenerative farm like this one can't be evaluated like a piece of a linear system. My cyclical farm takes many different parts and ties them together into a whole other organism, in which one part adds value to the next. The farm is not just a plot of land you can appraise with a calculation of dimensions and dollars per acre; the land is the first layer in a complex system that turns everything we raise into something with a more advanced value. The herds are not just a bunch of assets worth X-many dollars per animal, they are adding value to the first layer, and improving it exponentially because of what they do to it. The processing plant is not just a useful building valued at the cost it took to build it; it's the next layer of the system that adds value to the previous layers, because it helps us monetize what we raise. The online marketing and distribution system that moves our food from farm to customers, allowing us to sell much of it for full retail price, is another economic layer that adds more value to everything underneath. The hospitality offerings, including the farm-to-table restaurant, don't just generate revenue per guest or meal, they generate intangible benefits like visitors' memorable experiences, and their sharing about White Oak Pastures to friends and followers afterward, and the loyalty and goodwill that makes them keep coming back as customers.

There's more: all of those parts, working together in a thriving small food system, gives the Bluffton homes we've purchased to house interns and farm-stay guests and employees more value than most real estate agents would understand. The administrative umbrella that sits over the top, managing 180-something employees and keeping daily operations on track, adds tremendous value to all the layers underneath. All of this, by the way, feeds into one bank account, which is a powerful incentive to not let any one part of the farm struggle or fail, and to try our darnedest to make decisions that benefit the whole. Surrounding the farm itself are the ecosystem benefits that have accrued by doing the right things for years: the drastically improved organic matter of the soil reflecting its drastically improved health, the renewed biodiversity, the significant drought tolerance, and the carbon captured in the soil, among many other things. Factor in the benefits to the human ecosystem and count the meaningful jobs offered and the benefits of keeping wages in the rural economy, and the positive ripple effects of building a fully functional small food system are almost too many to count. (Especially not by conventional business's siloed valuation method, which is like valuing your kidneys, and adding their value to that of your heart, plus your legs, plus your testicles plus plus plus . . . that total can't ever capture the true value that you are worth to your family and your community.)

I'm only just starting to wrap my head around how to account for the full reckoning of what this farm and business really is, a quarter of a century into the project of returning White Oak Pastures to its roots. But what's clear is that there is so much value that doesn't get attributed to us, and that is to our detriment. If the mainstream is going to fully understand what we're doing as regenerative and resilient farmers, and if consumers—as well as progressive entities with the power to improve our food system—are going to throw their weight behind it, we need an entirely different economic model from the kind the current finance system has in place. We need a better kind of scorecard, one that tells the truth about the economics instead of hiding it.

I do the work, I don't do the math. And I can't say I know how to best design this scorecard. But I know that it should help the person buying the abhorrently cheap food to understand the food's bigger-picture cost, in the form of pollution falling on the environment, and chronic ill-health caused by the chemicals, not to mention the unrelenting tsunami of processed foods in our system made possible by cheap corn and soy and other commodity subsidies. It should include the steep health costs of lethal antibiotic resistance from the overuse of subtherapeutic antibiotics, and the devastating weather events caused by desertifying land and greenhouse gas emissions, and the extinction of countless plant and animal species. It should include the diminishment of minerals that are mined to make fertilizer, and the injury to soil that is so robbed of fertility that it poses a tremendous threat to our food supply, and the reliance on resources that are not only finite but often controlled by overseas interests such as Brazil and China, who can cut the supply of them any time they want. The scorecard, to be honest, would have to include the whole gamut of things that anyone who's drawn to better food is likely already talking about but that anyone who's not is sadly oblivious to. Like the cost to society of millions of workers making paltry wages with no health care, while being hurt by the chemicals they spray and the packing-plant lines they run. And of kids exposed to terrible toxicity from the massive industrial hog facilities operating in their town or the pesticides and herbicides in the air and water of their agricultural community. And of the financial ruin of rural America. It should help them to realize that from a holistic and generational perspective, the cheap food constantly pumped their way is actually much more expensive—but most people aren't talking about it because they aren't paying those costs at the grocery store checkout. They do pay the full costs later, however, as a taxpayer who foots the bill for environmental cleanup and health care for chronic diseases and subsidies that keep the system the way it is.

The scorecard should also help the consumer who is stretching their budget and going the extra mile to buy more expensive food that has been raised the right way, to understand all the benefits they are paying for, and what greater costs they are saving themselves, as well as the environment and society, down the line. It's not easy to communicate this information. The entities making the most money are not interested in letting the truth about the harms they are well aware of, nor the benefits of alternatives like us, be known. They have big platforms and loud voices and myriad ways to ensure they dominate the conversation. But if we don't try to remedy this, we'll be stuck with a system that rewards and incentivizes the wrong things in the ceaseless quest to make ever more abhorrently cheap food. This side of the scorecard, the true value of food produced right, is what my farm can best contribute to, because we are doing it right. So it's on us to tell what we have done.

My claim to fame, if I have one, is that I can implement the return of things working the way they should on the land and on the farm. But I need other people to help figure out how to demonstrate that on paper. I'd rather not have to do it, but linear minds sometimes demand it—the old "If you don't write it down, it didn't happen" thing. Becoming a regional hub for the Savory Institute in 2017, which Allan Savory founded to encourage the growth of regenerative farming around the globe, helped us to start tracking and showing our ecological gains. When you're a Savory hub, you share what you've learned about managing land holistically in your specific regional context with other farmers, ecologists, and stakeholders. One way you do this is by measuring one-year and five-year improvements in your farm's ecosystem health—a process called Ecological Outcome Verification (EOV). By measuring ten factors including biodiversity, water infiltration and retention, ground cover, and soil health, we get a read on our total land health that we can monitor over time, and we can demonstrate the results to the public. Having this data in hand let me confidently proclaim to the land appraiser that my soil organic matter was five times richer than surrounding industrial farms, and four times better at holding water. It's like giving the land a voice to report how the cycles of nature are working. (This is different from what is tracked by most third-party certifications for animal welfare or even certified organic food. Those things track that a farm is following certain processes or achieving standards in their methods. They don't actually track whether the results of those processes are better for the land or the animals, or, frankly, for the consumer either.)

The methodology we already had in place got a boost when one of our customers, the Paleo snack company Epic Provisions, was bought by General Mills. Epic had been started by a husband-and-wife team, Katie Forrest and Taylor Collins, who are passionate proponents of grass-fed meat and regenerative agriculture. When they started buying beef from us, they didn't hesitate to tout the ecological benefits of their products in their marketing, making their wildcat operation one of the first popular food brands to assertively tell a regenerative story. I assumed that General Mills would drop us like a hot rock when they acquired the company. They didn't, but they did want third-party proof of our ecological results to satisfy their legal team, and they had the budget to hire an environmental engineering firm named Quantis to do a life cycle assessment (LCA) of our farm. I'd never heard of an LCA, but General Mills' VP of Sustainability, Jerry Lynch, explained that it was a methodology of evaluating the environmental impact of food production on our farm. It would focus primarily on our overall greenhouse gas footprint—the amounts of carbon dioxide, methane, and nitrous oxide our livestock and production activities emit into the atmosphere as well as the amount of carbon our soil sequestered out of the atmosphere. The researchers would use soil sampling from fields at seven different stages of regeneration—from recently purchased degraded soil to pastures that had been holistically managed for twenty years—as well as modeled data.

I can tell with a shovel alone that the carbon footprint on my farm is pretty damn good. A few big scoops of soil that looks like chocolate cake, because it's so rich in carbon-based organic matter, tells me all I need to know. But I understood why an upstart "good meat" brand with a solid mission needed hard numbers in their pocket; knives are drawn and claws are sharpened these days when it comes to telling a better story about meat and the environment. The anti-meat brigade are so relentless in their crusade to make cows the villains of climate change that if you're presenting a truth they don't like, you'd better be ready on the draw yourself with a bunch of countermoves. You have to be able to show that what *they're* touting—a message more aggressively and well coordinated and funded by the year, as far as I can see—is bullshit. It's based on junk science. (Literally, as my friend the nutritionist Diana Rogers carefully points out in her book *Sacred Cow*, cowritten with Robb Wolf.)

The anti-meat militants will tell you that cattle are adding ungodly amounts of methane into the legacy load of greenhouse gases that are tipping our planet toward runaway warming—worse culprits than cars, planes, and power plants. But they're wrong in so many ways. First off, the old and problematic statistics most of these blowhards are using have been radically downgraded by the EPA, as Diana describes. Second, their argument villainizes the animal when it should be villainizing the industrial production systems. Industrial meat production does indeed contribute several percentage points of the US's total greenhouse gas production, primarily methane, with a lot of that coming from the hog, dairy, and egg industry and the manure lagoons they use. Fertilizer-enhanced feed production for confinement animals and transportation from point to point most certainly contributes. (Of the emissions attributed to livestock, about half of that comes from cattle.) But it is not fair to include pasture-raised livestock in this tally. As the Silicon Ranch executives learned when they toured our farm, the environmental impact of grazing cattle is incomparable to that of industrial cattle production, and it is incomparable to the impact of burning fossil fuels. When we humans extract ancient carbon from the earth in the form of oil, coal, and gas, and burn it to power our activities, we're taking carbon that should have stayed permanently buried and ejecting it in the form of greenhouse gases into the atmosphere, where we now know it stays for hundreds and thousands of years, causing warming. Cattle and other ruminants do the opposite of this when holistically grazed: they take carbon (and hydrogen, oxygen, and nitrogen) that has been photosynthesized out of the atmosphere and turned into physical plant matter, and they transform it, cycling it onward through the earth's natural carbon cycle. After eating the carbon-based plants in the field, they turn some of that carbon into their own carbon-based flesh (which we will later eat, feeding and building up our own carbon-based bodies), and then they turn some of it into manure and urine—which the soil microbes turn into humus/organic matter—and release some of it into the atmosphere by belching and farting methane (made up of carbon and hydrogen molecules). Over the course of about ten years, the methane is converted into carbon dioxide and water that finds its way back into the plants through photosynthesis. Most importantly, a lot of carbon is stored in the roots of grasses and plants, where millions of pounds of it accrue, thanks to the miracles of photosynthesis and ruminant fermentation digestion and microbial magic. This carbon stays locked in the earth for a very long time, slowly converting into organic matter that makes the land infinitely more productive. That's what makes healthy grasslands a carbon sink. (In a functioning ecosystem, manure gets dropped all over the land and it doesn't emit methane like the manure lagoons at factory hog and dairy farms do. Dung beetles tunnel through the cow patties, bringing oxygen in, countering the production of methane.) After twenty-five years of practicing land regeneration, I can tell you that the lies about cattle as planet Earth enemies serve nothing but to make a few rich entities even richer. The truth is the opposite: land that has been degraded by industrial farming practices cannot cost-effectively be healed *without* animal impact.

I'm pretty familiar with the anti-meat militants. A certain subgroup of angry vegans like to take me to task when they can. So I'm well aware that they will espouse, based on their questionable interpretation of science, a diet of plant-based everything. I have no problem with whatever diet anybody chooses to consume, but I wish they would be aware that the plant-based food products that dominate grocery store shelves and fill restaurants rarely come from a regenerative operation. They come from conventional row-cropping farms that douse land in nitrogen-based fertilizer (a primary driver of climate-warming nitrous oxide in the atmosphere), till it frequently (releasing sequestered soil carbon into the atmosphere), cause an apocalypse of the cruelest kind of death across the animal kingdom (birds, rodents, reptiles, insects, and amphibians), and contribute to tons of carbon in the atmosphere from machinery and transportation at every stage of the industrial food system. (Not to mention causing impoverishment of rural communities.) Biodiversity and healthy wildlife are rarely a feature of such systems as they are at this farm. I also have another wish for militant vegans (who are different from vegans, by the way—a vegan is someone who's made the personal choice not to eat meat, while a militant vegan has made the universal choice that *no* person will eat meat). I wish they might pause for a moment and realize that we have an enemy in common: Big Meat.

Quantis's LCA confirmed what our EOV was showing and what I

knew intuitively about our ecological benefits. When it comes to cycling carbon into the soil and locking it down, this farm does an unbelievably good job. So much so that the researchers called in a team of academic experts led by Dr. Jason Rowntree of Michigan State University to confirm they'd done their job right. They had. They proved that our regenerative farm stores enough carbon in its soil to offset at least 100 percent of greenhouse gas emissions from the entire life cycle of our cattle and production of beef and as much as 85 percent of our total emissions, when you factor in all our other species. Jason then took his team's data and published a peer-reviewed paper that irked the hell out of the meat haters and the fake-meat crowd. It highlighted some startling figures from the Quantis report: where conventional beef production emits thirty-three pounds of carbon per pound of meat to produce, and pork emits nine, and chicken emits six, the fully grass-fed beef from White Oak Pastures actually "saved more than it spent"—our production methods actually *sequestered* three and a half pounds of carbon per pound of meat produced. The part that pissed off a whole bunch of folks with a stake in plant-based dietary domination was when Jason compared these numbers to the LCA from Impossible Foods, the mega company backed by millions of dollars of investor capital that has made a huge play to disrupt the protein market with its plant-based Impossible Burger. They tout this fake meat as a solution to environmental ills and as far superior to animal protein. But the company's own LCA showed that the production of its "burgers," made from industrially raised GMO soy and peas, *emits* three and a half pounds of carbon per pound of fake meat produced. The irony was not lost on us. A person would have to eat almost exactly one pound of our grass-fed beef to offset the carbon emitted from a pound of their highly processed stuff made from industrial, monocultural commodity crops. Fake-meat proponents did not like us pointing it out. It led to a lot of bickering between different factions over the scientific methods used to measure the carbon levels and what the final figures should be. The fake-meat corporations hire scientists to create confusion about which scientific method is proper for measuring stored carbon in the soil. All of these methods seem less than perfect to me. But I ain't in the business of *measuring stored carbon*. I am in the business of *storing carbon*. And no one who looked at our LCA could argue with the fact that we are doing exactly that.

I was proud that we demonstrated that we walk the walk on this farm. Though I think the myopic focus that's currently happening with soil carbon measurement and carbon credits is too reductionist. It's not all about the damn carbon. Yes, carbon is important—and it's one of the easier things to measure, so it gets the conversation started about all the ways farms like mine are building unacknowledged value. It starts to sketch the edges of a new scorecard. You just can't expect that getting one cycle going better, and ignoring the rest, fixes the whole.

If there's a way to capture the fullest value of what we're creating here, it'll take a person with a brain vastly different from mine to figure it out. Fortunately, that person appeared in 2021 in the form of a young financial analyst named Cole Allen. Cole found White Oak Pastures, like many people do, while on a quest to restore his health. He'd started researching better foods in order to resolve a medical condition that doctors couldn't fix. That led him to research better soils and the numerous downstream effects of soil health on people, the environment, and society at large. Inspired, he dug deeper and arrived at regenerative agriculture and then at our gate, where after twenty-four hours on our farm he felt convinced that the financial world was dismally failing to evaluate what we do. He offered to use his decade of experience in finance and valuation to do a holistic evaluation of our business.

I'll be honest: I normally think that a consultant is a man who knows ten thousand ways to satisfy a woman but doesn't have a wife or girlfriend. (That's after hosting many a Big Ag consultant on my farm with more swagger than real-life skills.) But Cole was a rare gem. He began to dig into our financials and all the data from our EOV and LCA to discern the positive side effects of our farm's methods—all the intangible stuff that fits inside our big arrow of bounty alongside the tangible, monetizable products we generate, from ecological benefits to social ones to better animal welfare and more. Then he looked at the latest scientific studies and research to ascribe a dollar amount to these benefits. It's a uniquely tricky exercise, because the new economic model he proposed includes the value of the positive side effects we spin off, like cleaner water and air, and healthier food, as well as the savings from the negative things we *don't* spin off, like cancer-causing chemicals and volumes of waste sent to landfill. It's the kind of project that could go on and on, but Cole narrowed it down to the key areas of improvement that were supported by scientific research.

The results of his initial analysis took my breath away. Cole, being an inspired yet prudent kind of person, ran the numbers a few ways to give a range of possible values. Using the traditional valuation methods as a baseline—just evaluating our farm according to our cash flows, the way a conventional lender would—he then added in the value of some uncontroversial unacknowledged benefits, the ones he could reliably calculate without pushing the envelope. Things like the increase in land resiliency due to our heightened water-carrying capacity. This makes our land, most of which qualifies as nonirrigated, more comparable to irrigated land, which sells for a premium. This greater water resilience conservatively upped our land value by $439 an acre, for a total $1.3 million increased evaluation of the entire farm. Next, he added the savings in costly health impacts to society from agricultural nitrogen runoff. Compared to industrial agriculture, our fertilizer-free pastures leach far less nitrogen into the environment, which reduces the incidence of cancer and respiratory disease risk in downstream communities and marine habitat destruction. (Some nitrogen does enter waterways from grazing livestock.) This societal savings theoretically adds $1.8 million savings per year or about $14 million of value for our farm.

Cole also looked at the value our farm adds to the economy by employing far more people than average, thanks to our layers of production, processing, marketing and sales, and hospitality. Our 180-plus employees far exceeds the 60 employees one would expect on a farm or ranch this size, combined with a small processing facility, and they are paid significantly higher than average for our area. (Almost double the average wage for our rural county, as it happens.) The contribution this job creation makes to the local economy via earnings circulation and taxes paid is about $3.8 million per year. He added in more benefits like carbon credits, which, while generating a lot of buzz, don't yet add up to a lot financially for the farmer, and the value of being zero waste, and a conservative valuation for increased well-being and sense of purpose for the individuals working here. He even looked at how happy our customers are about buying from us, because their satisfaction can either add tremendous value to a company or impede it significantly. By running surveys, he found that our net promoter score, which evaluates customer satisfaction and loyalty, is significantly higher than for all major retail grocery chains. (He is still working on a value for restoring biodiversity to our land, the effects of enhanced nutrient density on consumer health, and improved animal welfare, which one day we may be able to add in.) All told, the sum of these benefits increased the valuation of our farm sixfold—a very impressive amount. This was the low-end result, a number Cole felt he could reasonably defend to stick-in-the-muds with little imagination. But he also ran the numbers another way, looking at the high end. This included calculating what carbon credits could net if they reach the potential that experts and researchers project they will eventually—significantly higher than what they are in their nascent state—as well as factoring in how bad chemical runoff in industrial systems can actually be. In this model, which is speculative yet inspiring, the value of my regenerative, holistic farm is *ten to thirty times* the total that a tight-assed, constipated, suit-wearing bank executive with a limited viewpoint would give it today.

This holistic evaluation is very much a work in progress. I wouldn't try to defend the high-end numbers to the MBA crowd. They're not up for defense—they represent a possibility, a new way of thinking. They force the acknowledgment, at least, that we've improved things profoundly through our small food system. How *much* we've improved things may be subject to debate, but the fact that we've done it is not. What may be more important than arriving at a definitive final number for the whole is that, taken individually, the metrics show possibilities for finally tipping the scale in favor of farmers like us. Acknowledging the value of higher land resilience can help decrease insurance premiums (because of resistance to drought). Demonstrating the long-term paybacks and additional income streams available—

through carbon credits or other ecosystem benefits that might come next—can show the industrial farmers at our county Rotary club that there is another viable way to farm, one that might just be appealing enough to attract their kids back to the family business. Showing the benefits to the soil and biodiversity, and demonstrating the true savings to society of avoiding negative downstream consequences, can attract much-needed capital to what is still a horribly niche and undercapitalized sector, helping farmers who want to farm regeneratively to acquire land, livestock, and the significant start-up needs for a farm that no loans will cover. We're already seeing that happen with the emergence of alternative lenders that exist to give regenerative farmers better terms on loans. A new sort of lender is beginning to evolve. These leading-edge firms working in agricultural finance aim to give regenerative farmers much kinder access to capital by tying loan terms to soil health. We worked with one of them on the very first loan they made: they refinanced our good ol' boy cowboy debts, which were shackled to ridiculously high monthly payments, with much better terms for a savings of about half a million dollars per year. In exchange, we committed to showing them the data on our ecological improvements. I always knew we were doing farming right. This new economic model, evolving as it is, affirms my instincts were on point.

Let's be clear. None of this innovative thinking makes the day-to-day effort to stay cash-flow positive any less treacherous around here. I've lately come to realize that only someone who is willing to operate with a generational perspective and without an exit strategy should choose this route. By spending millions of dollars on nonliquid assets like grazing infrastructure, herds and flocks and droves of many species, and long-term land renovations, I have knowingly put us in an extremely nonliquid position—it'll take generations to recover these investments.

So there's no easy out. But I've done it to remove the temptation to reverse course, like the way early explorers arriving at their destination burned their boats so they wouldn't be tempted to go back. I found a weird kind of freedom on the other side: When you put yourself in a position in which there ain't but one way out, you are free to quit worrying about future decision-making. You also change your idea of what winning even is. Usually in business, every success has a cost somewhere along the line. That's as true in commodity farming as in any other endeavor; you play a zero-sum game; my gain is your loss—if I make one hundred dollars, some sonofabitch somewhere lost a hundred, or a hundred people lost a dollar apiece. That was exactly how I used to think and I was good at it, too. But that's not how we do things now. There's a lot less losing going on when it comes to the land, and the animals, and the people and places around Bluffton. I'd venture to say that, save Big Tech, Big Ag, and Big Food, who lost the land I took out of their system, just about everybody wins. I know I did. I went from being a farmer with high capital outlay, low risk, low financial return, and low quality of life to a farmer with high capital outlay, high risk, and low financial return, but a high quality of life instead. It's a trade I would never reverse.

Many around me might argue life would be easier if I'd only put the shovel down and quit digging for a spell. But I tell them that's one of the few things that puts the fear of God in me. I don't want Him judging me lazy or lacking in determination to succeed in what I start on. I don't want Him thinking I'm a quitter. Because I'm pretty sure that if you rise to the occasion and give it your all, the next step will be presented. Then the choice is yours: bust your ass to make it work, or risk such wrath that you get made to sit the next few out. That's why my most ardent prayer, the one I say most often, is a short one I can remember: "Put me in the game, Coach."

Chapter Nine

Ten Thousand Unicorns

I was pulling on my boots one morning when the TV news told me the food system was breaking. It was May 2020 and the CEO of Tyson Foods was on one of the cable news networks. Tyson is one of the Big Four meat corporations that control the majority of America's meat supply and is the world's second-largest processor of chicken, beef, and pork. In the meat business, this guy is one of the four most powerful people on the planet. He was describing the bottlenecks that were occurring in our nation's massive centralized meatpacking plants, where the rapid spread of the SARS-CoV-2 virus between workers had shut down the lines. It was the height of pandemic panic, and in the food industry as in every other huge institution, the powers that be were wrestling with what was fast becoming a global state of chaos. The processing bottlenecks had a horrific unintended consequence: Farmers were forced to euthanize millions of hogs and chickens on their farms. Their next—and vitally important—link in the supply chain had been forcibly shut down. The animals that were ready for the processing plants had reached maximum weight—and now they had nowhere to go. Keeping obese, sedentary creatures in confinement after a certain point is not an option; it leads only to a slow and gruesome death.

The collateral damage of that stoppage was devastating to farmers—economically, emotionally, and environmentally. The farmers not only lost a lot of money, they each had to kill tens of thousands of animals (or many, many more) and dispose of horrifying amounts of their carcasses, cruelly aware that raising these creatures had been in vain. For consumers already gripped by anxiety about getting sick, the possibility of serious food shortages in the stores loomed large. I'd never taken a picture of a TV screen before, but I took one then.

I've lived through many other moments of food system fragility. Hurricanes and floods, riots and power outages, pandemics of livestock disease, product recalls due to contamination at the plant—all kinds of natural and man-made disasters have temporarily impeded food production. They've made it obvious that the food chain that feeds us is not nearly as strong as it seems. So what occurred that spring wasn't a surprise to me, or to most of us in the regenerative farming world. But the scale of the COVID food supply shock showed society at large something new—how dependent we are on an undependable essential service. Undependable and essential are two adjectives that should never be used to describe the same noun, especially when it comes to food. But because the linear system is so consolidated and is scaled up so massively to achieve great economies of scale, with excess piled upon excess in the name of profitability, it has become very vulnerable to collapse. The taller you build a tower, the less it can resist stress without tumbling down. And the taller it's built, the greater the disaster when it inevitably falls. Likewise, one unexpected choke point on the food supply chain can take the whole system down, a victim of its own weight. It has become too big *not* to fail.

On our cyclical farm we didn't miss a beat. That's not said from a place of arrogance. But the pandemic impacted us a lot less than it impacted the Big Food system, because we are not as dependent on external sources for the things we need done, and we don't rely on other entities to take our products to market. Building a system in which we have control over production, processing, and marketing made it easier for us to pivot under duress. When the pandemic put a crunch on grocery and restaurant sales, we were well positioned to sell straight to consumers' doors, and sell we did. As the big plants shut down, our e-commerce sales tripled almost overnight. New customers found White Oak Pastures and they were eager to stock their freezers in case of further stoppages. It was a wild fucking ride. Our sales skyrocketed and it was all-hands-on-deck, with cowboys packing orders after dark and the fulfillment center staff working way overtime. We had our best year of sales ever at a time when so much struggle and suffering was occurring worldwide. I'll admit I thought our time in the sun had come.

I hated seeing what had happened to other farmers. But I felt gratified to know the catastrophe wasn't happening on my farm. Sure, the situation could have gotten even more knife-edge. FedEx could have shut down, making shipping impossible. Or my staff could have gotten sick, causing our plants to shut down. But even then, we wouldn't have been forced to euthanize any animals; the cattle, hogs, and poultry would have stayed out on pasture, getting a few months older and a few pounds heavier. The pork chops or chicken breasts we eventually harvested might be bigger than average, but they'd get priced accordingly. Losing weeks of cash flow would have hurt—but in comparison to the grotesque waste occurring in the industrial farming system, there'd be zero waste of life or food occurring here.

The national panic ended before things got truly hairy. The meat-packing industry's production lines started up again and food got back on the shelves. No consumers in America went hungry as a result of the processing bottlenecks, as far as I know. For most people, it was like they got scared by a rubber snake; they got a fright but never got a bite, so they soon forgot about the issue of food security. But a certain percentage of Americans *did* get the memo. Some started to see, maybe for the very first time, how our nation's food security is not as bulletproof as they always thought. They'd glimpsed how a failure in any one link of our hyperefficient, hyperconsolidated food supply chain could have devastating effects across the whole system and all the way to their kids' hungry stomachs, and it could happen fast. They saw how we are one shock away—one virus or one hurricane or one power grid failure or one cyberattack or one finger on a button—from not being able to eat. And these people started talking about this vulnerability in a way they hadn't before. I always thought God would have to slap the shit out of humanity before we started to realize we should do things differently. I was pessimistic enough to think the only way change would happen was through direct personal pain, because as far as I can tell, there's never been much change without pain. But the events of that time in 2020, and the additional destabilizing events that occurred afterward—threats of fertilizer shortages and agricultural droughts, invasions of major food-producing nations and the failure to plant crops, a devastating bird flu hitting the poultry industry, skyrocketing inflation and surging fuel costs—hard as they have been, are changing my mind a little bit. These multiple challenges, one after the next, are making the truth hit home. A greater percentage of people than ever are waking up to why a resilient food system matters. We might still have an opportunity to make things better before the pain gets too bad to bear.

The change just isn't gonna happen the way I always thought it would, like a tsunami, fast and devastating, taking down everything old to rebuild the new. There will be industrial food as long as people want to eat it. I don't think it's ever gonna be outlawed or made so undesirable it disappears. But the balance can shift away from the industrialized, commoditized, centralized system that dominates our food supply. Even a born skeptic like me has to admit that the fact that our food system has been moving toward that for seventy-five years does not mean that it always will. Pendulums do swing, and then they swing back again.

But I've had to make peace with this more realistic pace of change. Banking on an overnight reversal of our food system is self-defeating. Big ships are hard to turn and our food system, which is interwoven with every part of our lives—the environment, our economy, our health, our resources—is a very, very big ship, powered by a helluva lot of money. Think about how many powerful forces keep that damn ship on its current trajectory day in and day out! You've got the way the average middle-class American thinks (outside of some of the more enlightened population centers). They believe the food brands they've always enjoyed, and the stores they've always shopped at, must be doing things *just fine*, or "they" wouldn't let the food be sold. (That same overexuberant confidence my mama's generation had with medicine and Big Pharma, where she took every pill the doctor told her to take because doctor knew best, is at play with people and their food. I think we're a at least generation from getting past that.

The fact that *some* consumers have gained insight does not mean that *most* consumers have gained insight.) You've got the fact that the old guard in corporate food and agriculture haven't made way yet for the new generation of leaders, and these old geezers damn well won't ever admit the way they've run things for years might have been fucked up. And the fact that almost all politicians lack the courage to address the real cost of cheap food, no matter how bad the downsides may be— and that what shapes the legislation to keep it that way are lobbyists working for corporate interests, armed with overflowing pails of money. The anti-meat crusaders and fake-meat purveyors are the cherry on top; they can't afford to acknowledge that well-managed grazing animals are an essential element in a healthy biome. This, too, distorts public understanding.

Then there's the reality that most farmers working today cannot simply "choose another system" just like that. They are invested in, educated in, and believe in the current system, and even when the motivation to change to a regenerative land management model strikes, it's not a quick switch to do it. The linear system might be able to add production lines to a factory and blow up their model at speed when demand goes up. We can't do that. Establishing holistic, self-reliant food systems that work with the complex cycles of nature, not against them, means working on nature's time. It takes longer.

At some point we need to reconcile that it's not about changing *their* system. It's about strengthening and growing ours. My directors and I still chuckle about seeing the two systems clash colorfully when we had a visit from the upper management team of Chick-fil-A, the Georgia-based fast food chain whose business is basically built on fried chicken sandwiches sourced from industrial poultry farms. Six middle-aged white men, clad in shirts buttoned up to the chin, came down from the Atlanta corporate offices to see us, shepherded by one eager millennial whose job was to launch sustainability initiatives for the corporation. This extremely well-meaning young lady wanted the executives to learn the possibilities of an anti-factory farm, and to start to think about steering their big ship on a new, better course. I welcomed their visit, but I saw from the get-go that it was gonna get awkward. With our higher costs of production and lower volume, we were as poor a fit for them as a size 32 pair of Wranglers would be on me. The executives knew it too. They were so tightly wound that if they'd been spinning tops, they'd just about have flown away. So as we sat around a table making small talk, I disarmed them. I said, "Don't worry. I'm not gonna try to sell you my chicken. In fact, I wouldn't *want* you to buy my chicken. Not only do we all know that you can't afford it, and we don't have the volume you need, but our customers would die if they found out we were selling to a fast food operation." With a few startled harumphs, all the hot air went out of the room. The guys loosened their ties and checked themselves for a second. We went on to have a great time touring our farm, showing these fast-food execs how differently we do things here. By the end of the day, they were trying to calculate if their company could at the very least use some pasture-raised chicken backs for soup stock and tell a small regenerative story to their consumers. (They couldn't; the cost and volume equation still didn't pencil out for a company that size.)

I've come to understand that meaningful change will result not from tidal waves but from bubbles—individual examples of independent and resilient food systems dotting the rural fabric of our country. Right now, I pretty much know who all the bubbles are. In addition to my farm, there's my good friend Gabe Brown in North Dakota, who raises grain and livestock at his farm, Nourished by

Nature; and Greg Gunthorp in Indiana of Gunthorp Farms, who produces lamb and pork; and Carrie Richards in California, who produces grass-fed beef at her farm, Richards Ranch; and Blake Alexandre in Northern California, who produces milk and eggs at Alexandre Family Farm. (There are some others, but they are few and far between.) These are all producers who have successfully established regenerative and resilient farms that offer a highly nutritious, whole-food alternative to the increasingly unnatural calorie stream of the standard American diet. They are different sizes, with different outlets for their products, but they have all found ways to operate with autonomy outside of, or skirting the edges of, the industrialized system. Though each of these farms is quite different in our goals and what we produce, we have all been at it a long time and all found success—no *Lifestyles of the Rich & Famous*, to be sure, but enough profit, and renown, and customer support to keep us successfully in business.

Independent, resilient food systems also include the small processing facilities operating on their own terms—not just slaughterhouses, but butcher shops, bakeries, creameries, and all kinds of small-batch food producers and craft food efforts such as breweries and distilleries and farm-to-table restaurants and cooperative food hubs that together start to make up an alternative food web. Farming has been so consuming for me that I was always a little oblivious to the number of "bubbles" that small food businesses like these have contributed to the movement. Maybe I still bear the traces of my upbringing, when we thought there was no better cheese than Velveeta, and *craft* was spelled with a *K*. I didn't at first see the similarities between what I do and what the folks making local beer or sourdough donuts or sauerkraut and kimchi do. But now the affinity is unmissable, and I have immense appreciation for these other revolutionaries.

What none of us resilient farms have done is grow to a titanic size. Far from it. You see, bubbles don't operate according to the linear growth mindset; they are circular, and they don't exist to scale up and up. My volume of business is probably the maximum of what I'd ever want it to be. When you run a circular farm, your priority is closing the loops and building the health and wealth inside your own system, not achieving infinite growth. (Which is why I can safely say there will *never* be a truly regenerative, humane, fair farm that will scale to a national level—much less multinational.) The upside is that they are inherently more resilient as a result. Farms that follow nature's life cycle of birth, growth, death, and decay over and over are used to crashing and renewing. They have the qualities of adaptability to challenge built in.

Right now, the few dozen of us bubbles in the US—the regenerative farms producing food at a significant scale, employing a significant workforce beyond immediate family members or a very small crew— are like unicorns: it's a rarity to find us. (If people in Washington State want to see a unicorn, the closest one they can find may still be here in Bluffton, Georgia—we're just that sparsely distributed.) But the interesting thing about circular systems is that while we aren't predisposed to scaling up, or franchising ourselves to make a buck, we are set up to replicate. A good crew of us leaders have figured out how to build them. We've done the heavy lifting and got them worked out over ten, twenty, or, in my case, twenty-five years of trial and error. And we can teach others to do it. The templates we've ended up with can be applied to different contexts, and markets, and to the production of different foods and fibers. Every ecosystem and every economy are different, and the farm must evolve to accommodate these different circumstances. At our farm alone, we've trained a few dozen interns in regenerative methods over the last ten years. Some of them are well on their way to becoming the next bubbles. John and Mary Pederson of Verdant Acres Farm in Virginia are just one great example of this. They met as interns at White Oak Pastures, got married, and then went on to produce cattle, hogs, poultry, eggs, and vegetables on their own farm in the Shenandoah Valley. Helping more bubbles to start appearing on the map is where I think we have to go now. We want more of them in number, not size—we want to get to where you have to look only to the next town or the next village to see a real live unicorn up close. That's a lot closer to the way it used to be. The problem is that we pretty much annihilated these unicorns in the last half of the twentieth century, in almost the same way that we did the buffalo a hundred years earlier.

I know I wouldn't fear the existence of nearby regenerative producers or see them as competition; on the contrary, the more farms acting as food hubs for their areas, the more each of us can reduce our customer radius, helping to reduce our reliance on shipping long distances, reducing our carbon footprint and increasing the connection of communities to their farmers. I once tried to calculate how many local-ish families my farm would require in order to support our current volume of business. Based on the published per capita consumption of protein in our country, and assuming each household bought all their meat, poultry, and eggs from us, I ended up needing sixteen thousand households to do it. Our nearest big city, Atlanta, has *five million* residents—and granted, these are just back-of-the-napkin numbers that assume a certain income level and diet. But they show what could be done.

I can't say that helping local resilient farms to pop up nationwide gives all the answers to the dilemma of food system fragility. But it's a damn big piece of it—and it's been a lifetime achievement to figure it out. I can attest, at the very least, that three good things would happen if there were one or two or three or more White Oak Pastures in every agricultural county in the nation. We'd save the rural from going the same way as the wilderness—a half-forgotten artifact of an earlier time. The money would come back to rural villages and towns, the businesses would come back, and the young people would come back—it would offer meaningful jobs to a workforce displaced by automation and digitization. We would see a reversal of what has been occurring since the Second World War ended. (Farming may be complex, but it is not complicated—a person who is dedicated can get proficient at it without a degree or years of study at a desk.) To be sure, the welfare of millions and millions and millions of animals would be dramatically improved to a near utopian kind of existence. We would be cleaning up the earth and pulling greenhouse gases out of the atmosphere, where they do harm, and putting them in the ground, where they do good (while the technocrats are still scratching their heads wondering how to do it with machines). I don't care where you are on the political spectrum, or whether you are a die-hard carnivore or vegetarian, you can't argue that these aren't all very good results.

Having more bubbles on the map would also help to develop resilient networks that would help holistic farms like ours to keep producing even when catastrophes hit. Because even with all the things regenerative farmers do to buffer our farms against adversity, sometimes bad shit happens. Like in 2018 when Hurricane Michael ripped through our farm. The storm hit us as a category 4—we were ground zero for the hurricane's landfall. The 115 mph winds showed us no mercy, tearing up miles of fence line and downing scores of massive oaks. We lost more than half our poultry—small animals are the most vulnerable to hurricanes—plus several dozen pigs and a few pregnant cattle. All told, Michael left us with over a million dollars in damage (which insurance, being the fickle beast it is, did not cover). White Oak Pastures survived, and recovered, but at quite a cost. And it showed us how vital it will be in the future to have other nearby operations able to keep food production running when one farm gets slammed by Mother Nature, or by some other unforeseen force wreaking havoc. This, too, is how we emulate nature: natural systems evolved to have redundancies built in so if one part of the system gets compromised, another part catches the slack. We need to be thinking about how to set up our small food systems to run the same way.

I've spent enough time around the aforementioned bubbles to know that all of them were born of fairly humble financial and intellectual origins. This oughta be encouraging news. The handful of us who got it figured out are not Fulbright Scholars, we didn't come out of government think tanks, and while most of us did already have some equity in land, which is an inarguable advantage, we are pretty average types of people. I, for one, created my bubble in the poorest county in the nation, where admittedly, my labor costs are lower than in, say, Connecticut or California. But there are downsides to this upside: the pool we draw from also has a shallower skill set—not many folks around here have extensive inventory or machine maintenance experience—and unlike those more sophisticated states, we're pretty far from zip codes where high-income consumers reside. Every economy has its own advantages and disadvantages, just like every ecosystem, and the farmer who wants to operate outside the mainstream has to figure out how to navigate them. But it's far from impossible; and with all the interest and passion and labor available, other similar farms can be up and running and making their contribution in five years. Some will make it and some will not, but anyone who makes it will inspire the next bubbles, and so this movement will grow. Hopefully, our existence will save the next ones twenty-five years of experimenting, and help them push the ball a lot farther down the field.

My bet is that if, as a society, we steadily help this replication to happen, rather than overly focusing on abandoning the current system, we will create a playing field where resilient agriculture can start to take hold. We don't need to concern ourselves so much with breaking down the industrialized, commoditized, centralized system. It is already breaking—and it's showing us every day how many ways it can, or will, fail. We can run out of some of the extractive products that are required to farm industrially, like potassium and phosphate that are dug out of the ground for fertilizer, or nitrogen made from natural gas. We can run out of petroleum required for powering the farm and even the topsoil that the plants grow in (this part is inevitable; in fact it's already happening). We can put so many toxins into the soil that it loses all its life force, or use so many GMOs that we are overtaken by superweeds no chemicals can kill. We can kill all aquatic life with our polluted runoff and create unstoppable epidemics in our confinement livestock populations because pathogens outsmart our overused antibiotics. There are just so many ways that our disruption of the natural order might play out. So let it break. But meanwhile, we can build the alternative, starting immediately.

Now for the humbling news: helping the movement to grow will take significant effort. Two big obstacles stand in the way. The first is a lack of education—there aren't currently enough places for farmers to learn how to farm this way, quickly and directly. I'm pretty sure we in the first wave of regenerative farming can help solve this part.

Pioneers like Gabe Brown as well as non-farming experts like Dr. Jason Rowntree have become educators of the first order, and thanks to their work, hundreds of farmers have gotten started with regeneratively managing land without enduring the worst hardships of being the first ones up the learning curve. We also have to educate the people who purchase food and fiber at much larger scale to supply their business needs. They need to understand why regenerative producers matter. At White Oak Pastures, we founded a leadership organization called the Center for Agricultural Resilience (CFAR). It brings farmers and thought leaders from businesses as well as non-profit groups and policy makers together for several-day sessions to learn what has worked here for twenty-five years, and figure out how to get this knowledge widely understood. It's like a Davos forum except with the good guys and gals. The goal is to disseminate real-world experience in regenerative agriculture from accomplished experts, as widely and quickly as we can. I believe that between us leaders, we can figure out ways how to teach what we have learned.

The second obstacle, however, is a bigger one: lack of capital. Even if impassioned individuals and groups can fund the education piece, farmers need capital to transition their land from the conventional system to this one (if they already have land) or to fund them to acquire land (if they don't have it). Young people wanting to take over the family farm need to pay sky-high inheritance taxes. Insurance costs are going way up. And there are little to no subsidies or support for this type of production. Most of the land in America is owned by people who do not live on it, do not understand it, and have no idea how to manage it. But through some innovation and smart financial strategizing, we could get enthusiastic, smart people onto the land who will do all three of those things competently. It will take financiers and government entities stretching their thinking to do this, no doubt. It will require institutions breaking out of all the conventional, linear ways they've become accustomed to evaluating worthiness and success. Fortunately, as we have experienced at White Oak Pastures, there are individuals and investors starting to figure it out. The flip side of this new era, however, is that some of those stretching their thinking and figuring it out are not playing on this team. Some of the people who've become deeply interested in owning agricultural land are so unfathomably wealthy that they are buying vast acreages of farmable land, setting prices higher than anybody else can compete with. I suspect they've cottoned on to something I've long believed: that despite the market valuation of rural land being historically low until recently, the truth is very different. I've spoken and written many times about the moment I saw that an acre of land was worth less than an ounce of gold, and how fucked up I thought that was. They're both nondepreciating assets, and places to park your currency, but one is good for putting in your sock drawer till you need the cash or showing your mother-in-law that you're more of a baller than she thinks you are. The other one can be improved, and used to grow things, and spin off abundance, and hunted on and fished on and used to get water—and sure, it's a little less liquid than the gold, but nobody can steal it and make off with it. The unfathomably wealthy people and companies buying up land have realized this, too. Though they are almost certainly not planning to convert the land the way we have done. Their technology-backed plans for it are different. You don't need to be a rocket scientist to question what they know about what's coming down the pipeline that the rest of us don't.

There are a lot of moving parts to growing a resilient food system larger. I can't claim to know exactly how it will unfold. But I do know that what will drive it happening, at the rate required to avoid the worst of the pains of change, is simple: consumers deciding they want it. When enough people decide they want a resilient food system over an efficient one, and when enough people become tired or disgusted with consuming utterly bland, overly caloric, boringly consistent Food from Nowhere and decide they want to experience Food from Somewhere—a place they can name, or speak with, or visit, with taste and nutrition and a story that excites them—and when enough people decide to believe that treating the land and the animals and the rural workers right is worth investing in with their purchases, the first bubbles can spawn new bubbles and those can spawn the next ones.

This may sound overly simplistic, and it is not the complete solution by any means. But farmers will innovate in response to what consumers show they want, because fundamentally they are entrepreneurs who have to keep their businesses going. For White Oak Pastures, consumer support was the spark that lit the fire. Without interested consumers appreciating and purchasing our products, I would still be an industrial monocultural cattleman, Bluffton would still be a ghost town, and the ecological improvements around here would be... nonexistent. And the movement of resilient, regenerative food as a whole would be extremely niche. I hope that Big Food might even evolve their system in meaningful ways—not just paying lip service to regenerative practices with token projects—if consumers' shifting desires force a competition to the top instead of a race to the bottom. (This may be too big a swing for them to make; time will tell.) Even changes at the public policy level will be driven by how much you ask for it and want it—by how hungry you are for this kind of food.

The question is, what will it take for you, the person buying the food that farmers like me raise, to make the decision that you want resilient food over efficient food, and that you want to support the growth of a system that regenerates and renews rather than degenerates and degrades? Simply having the insight that there are consequences to how your food is produced is a start. Then, the awareness that a lot of effort goes into keeping consumers like you from understanding the consequences is next. And then, a choice: Are you willing to rip the curtain back and see the impact of your food choices? Can you look at it and still continue to empower these destructive forces?

If your answer is no, or even maybe not, then start exploring where your food comes from, who raises it, and how. If you eat meat and poultry or consume dairy products or enjoy eggs, educate yourself about what happens on the farms of origin to fill cooler after cooler in stores across the nation with these foods, at prices far below what it actually costs to produce them right. Next, learn where the animal goes after it leaves the farm and what consequences ripple off each step it takes to get to your plate. That exploration has likely started by reading this book. Maybe it started way before doing even that, and if it has, you might already know that this isn't armchair exploring. It requires some legwork. Because unfortunately, there's no single word on a package, and no single certifying seal or stamp, that will reliably tell you whether food is truly being raised a better way or not. I'm often asked to break down the marketing terms used today to make shopping for properly raised food easier to do. *Grass-fed, pastured, free range, free roaming, humane this, sustainable that* . . . people think if they can just decode the lexicon, their work will be done. I won't do it. Because every word or phrase that good farmers have come up with over the years to describe their better methods has gotten hijacked or abused by bigger parties for their own benefit, and most all of the words have gotten distorted as a result. My farm was one of the very first to use the word *grassfed* on our beef; that soon got coopted and diluted by Big Meat and Big Grocery. We were pioneers in using the word *pastured*—ditto the above. It's just a matter of time before the word *regenerative* is taken away from us, too. (Which is partly why we use the word *resilient* around here more than any other word these days when describing how we farm; that one is hard to greenwash—you either break under pressure or you don't—but make no mistake, if *resilient* catches traction with consumers, Big Ag and Big Food will eventually hijack that word, too.)

Similarly, I'm a skeptic about certifications and seals that prove certain farming standards. I was there when the certification industry was birthed. White Oak Pastures has certification number 0001 from the American Grassfed Association. I was the first farm east of the Mississippi to be "Certified Humane." I was at the very first producer meeting of the Global Animal Partnership (GAP) in the early 2000s, a body that Whole Foods created to let farmers demonstrate five possible levels of humane animal welfare to consumers in their stores. The goal of GAP was worthy—to motivate farmers to improve their welfare standards by educating consumers about the possibilities of improvement; from less cruel, to somewhat fair, to pretty good, to better, to best. Having a range of steps was supposed to give industrial farmers an achievable entry point and start them on a path of improvement. But that upward mobility never happened. Harried shoppers didn't have the bandwidth to distinguish between the lowest score and the highest. They just saw GAP CERTIFIED on the label and made their purchase, which meant the market stayed full of Step 1 and Step 2 product with very little of Step 4 and Step 5 available even today, twentysomething years later. The whole thing got diluted.

There are some really good certifications and some not-good ones, and the problem is the consumer gets so confused that they cannot tell the difference. I decided long ago that becoming our own kind of gold standard is more meaningful than any of that. Tell and show the world the truth about what we do, and let other farmers and producers strive to meet our bar.

Which brings me to my not exactly politically correct theory of where things might be going. I think we may be heading to a place where if a "good" animal protein product is on a grocery store's shelves, it probably hasn't been raised in the way you think it has, based on your quick read of the label. I say that from lived experience. After Whole Foods championed us as exemplars of the local food movement, we grew from being a very small provider to them in one region to a very large one—for us, at least—in three regions. At one time, Whole Foods Market accounted for more than half of our business. But as the grass-fed category got saturated with foreign meat products, our orders got smaller and smaller. It was incredible to me to see our product—the same product with no changes in how we produced, processed, or marketed it—move from prestige position, with our name and story given top billing, to less prominent and barely calling out our name, to basically nonexistent marketing and minimal shelf space. Let me be clear: we were not being replaced by other American family farms, offering the same level transparency we do. It was the greenwashed "grass-fed" beef of uncertain origin. I feel sure that the reason for these changes in Whole Foods were made because our already highly priced products didn't provide as high a margin as imported products. This narrow focus on quarterly returns above all else has displaced the few intentional and responsible brands. I'll forever be grateful to the first wave of Whole Foods visionaries who helped us bring our better food to market. Now that those first wavers have gone, I'll put it as tactfully as I can: I'd love to show your current executives how to get back to the ethos that your corporation was founded on.

This is not to say that all grocery stores have this same mentality, and I hope other grocery outlets do not follow suit. Farms like ours desperately need secure outlets for our products; but because corporate-owned competitor brands can achieve efficiencies of scale and cheaper prices and can create deliberate confusion among consumers with slick marketing on top, it feels like there's less room every year in that system for us. This is one of the greatest disappointments I have felt in this entire lifelong campaign.

Which means that as a consumer, you might have to get radical along with us. You might have to break your dependency on Big Grocery in order to support better food production systems. It's just too entwined with Big Food and Big Ag. The three of those have long since formed a triumvirate that's got less and less to do with my farm and those operating like mine. The truth is that if you seek humane and regenerative products through the industrial system's retail channels—the big supermarkets, the big-box membership clubs, the online superstores—you won't fully be contributing to the change we need. (Not to put too fine a point on it, but you will be feeding the industrial competitors of the farmers and producers who are doing it right.) Anything the big retailers have got is a poor substitute for what we've got, designed to take you halfway to better in some cases—like grass-fed but nothing regenerative about it, or organic but woefully inhumane—or absolutely nowhere in others, like any number of highly greenwashed meat and poultry brands that are little better than industrial. Some of those have pastoral farmyards in the foreground you can photograph, and industrial facilities in the background that you cannot.

I could list examples of all of these by name, if I didn't have tact and a fear of litigation. (It's mostly the fear of litigation—I could get past the tact part.) But I have seen "pasture-raised" egg operations that have simply cut a hole in the wall of the industrial chicken house to give the birds access to outdoors—they don't go outside much when you do it like that, by the way—and when the chickens do go out, it's into man-made pens where their droppings pile up on the same spot and cause polluting runoff into nearby waterways and soils. The worst animal welfare I've ever seen in my life was on a USDA-certified organic cow feedlot; the worst land abuse I've ever seen in my life was on a certified organic vegetable farm. (I understand that the farmers and ranchers running these operations are earning a hard-won living and are evaluating success through a different lens from mine, one still based on yield, profit, and quarterly reports. But to me, industrial organic farming is "death by cultivation" because their ridiculously intensive, monocultural methods destroy the soil microbes and leave the soil laid bare to the elements.) It's not just the raw meat, or milk, or carton of eggs you need to think about: today there's an endless stream of processed food products made out of those things. They, too, often tell an origin story many miles away from the truth. Brand names evoke green fields and meadow-this and farm-fresh-that and everything has a polish of "wellness" on the top. You can't turn around in a grocery store without one of those charlatans smacking you in the eye. With a little digging, it's typically not that hard to discover which megacorporation actually owns these bucolic-sounding brands. The wordsmiths on Madison Avenue (or wherever advertising copywriters work today) have done a terrific job putting veils between that truth and you. Big Food today reminds me of Big Tobacco in the 1960s—masterfully invested in keeping the truth covered up, even truths that they have hard evidence cause harm and degradation.

These days, Jenni and Jodi and I are watching a wannabe category wheedling its way into the grass-fed beef market—something that some smart person, probably in some kind of branding think tank, named "pasture-fed" beef. Sounds much the same as ours, doesn't it? Except it means the cattle got fattened on monocultured corn and soy-based feed while being out in a field. If you buy that beef expecting your purchase to support a regenerative system that helps the environment, or hoping to avoid industrial inputs and chemicals in your or your kids' meals, you'll be paddling up the wrong creek. I don't want to pick a fight with producers of "pasture-fed" beef. Different strokes for different folks. Some of the producers that send cattle into that category are likely people I know and like, running a small-time calf cow operation with every bit as much determination to succeed as me. I just think the marketers might play fairer if they called that beef "feedlot free."

We're also watching the so-called vegetable protein market expand, offering pretend meat made from industrially grown legumes and grains, raised in massive monocultures. There, too, the virtuous words pour forth suggesting more sustainable, healthier alternatives, for the planet and our future. I'm not in the business of taking down that Goliath. Our customers tend not to be their customers; people who want the nutrition of grass-fed and pasture-raised meat and poultry tend not to be especially hungry for highly processed, chemically raised, soy, pea-and-potato-based fake food. But I understand why it can be hard to resist what they offer. Animal-free burgers and hot dogs are made to sound benign and benevolent for the environ-ment, so much better than real meat. I beseech you to be discerning. Depleting the earth, pillaging resources, squelching biodiversity, and cutting down the wilderness in the name of meat-like processed foods is another iteration of a decades-long paradox that skews our food supply: for every problem that technology has caused, another tech-nology has been brought in to solve it—which makes the tech com-pany kinda like the same store selling you bullets and bandages, scooping profit off all of it, and invariably causing another set of prob-lems. None of these expertly marketed foods make things better for the land where the food is grown, or the animals, including the wild-life and tiny soil microorganisms that live on that land. Most of them make things better for entities that have nothing to do with our rural economies. These patented systems of foodlike products are central-ized around technology and I don't believe they are the answer to the fragile modern food system; they're like answering a question with another question—the answer is just not there.

The bittersweet truth is that you've got to go all the way if you want to participate in a better food system. Find producers who are aligned with the higher values you hold dearest, which might be different val-ues from mine or from your neighbor's. Perhaps your personal pri-ority is supporting a producer that follows the highest possible animal welfare, even and above an adherence to strictly organic feed. (Turns out a lot of our customers think that high-level animal welfare and strict organic standards are the same thing and always go hand in hand; they're not and they don't.) Maybe ultrapure standards of feed—not a lick of non-GMO feed ever used on the farm, no excuses—is the hill you die on, more so than the animals expressing instinctive be-havior or being slaughtered in an on-site abattoir overseen by the farmer. Every farmer has made different choices of how they raise their livestock or food, depending on the context they are working toward and what they can realistically pull off, physically and financially. Until you understand the thinking behind their choices, you can't make good ones yourself.

I'm sure there are other ways to earn this understanding, but I just can't think of a better one than getting to know your farmer again, like your forefathers and mothers almost certainly did. That involves taking back the know-your-farmer movement, which also, sadly, has gotten as co-opted by the monopolistic forces as any of the other parts of agriculture. With all the storytelling being done on brand websites about family farms and American ranches, you can still *feel* you've got a connection to your farmer when you shop for better food. I'll tell you that, unless you can make actual contact with the people who've got their boots on the ground and their hands in the dirt—and that can look a lot of ways, including following them on social media if you can't visit where they farm—you probably don't. A prime example of this is some of the venture-capital-backed subscription services for grass-fed meat that give the impression of being devoted to supporting the American rancher—but that import most of their meat from overseas.

The reality is we're at a tipping point. The farmer is getting squeezed out of the food system a little more each year. It was hard enough for commodity farmers: in their (highly subsidized) system, the farmer purchases retail-priced inputs from the monopoly corporations . . . to provide cheap commodity products to the monopoly corporations . . . to make highly processed, value-added brand-name products to sell to consumers . . . all of which benefit the monopolistic corporations, who want more and more and more. The farmer who is not taking the shortcut has been pushed and squeezed until all ability to make profit disappears, and I fear that the farmers who are doing it right can, and probably will, be taken out of the equation when his usefulness is gone.

It's already happening. We've got a $120 million indoor farm opening a few hours from us in Georgia, closer to the urban metropolis of Atlanta. It will grow food without soil or sunlight, on top of itself instead of rooted in the ground, and it boasts that it doesn't need the annoyance of "favorable weather" or actual humans to do the inconvenient task of "heavy lifting." (Robots do that part.) It claims it will produce over three hundred times more food than an ordinary farm—which means a resource-intensive monoculture farm—using 97 percent less water. Patented seeds will surely be used, enhanced through genome modifying and editing to have attributes better than any nature could come up with. Sure, humans will be on hand at the facility. Their job is to "focus" on extracting the most yield possible from the system. But there's no mention of a farmer at this so-called farm at all. That's because this is not a farm. It is a factory where technicians replace the farmer, just as technology replaces nature. The Georgia indoor farm is not an anomaly. As the tech and agriculture elite who start these operations make a bid for more and more control of the food supply, I can't help but wonder what the opposite approach could generate: Imagine putting the same amount of money into purchasing fifty thousand acres of nondepreciating land. The farms this spawned would employ legions of local people eager to work and learn to steward nature in all her biodiversity and resilience, and produce nutritious fresh food immediately available for people who live nearby, and be somewhere children could visit to get their hands dirty in the earth. What better future might that achieve? We could repeat the same mistakes of the past through our hubris, believing that science and technology can and should improve on nature (and even if that turns out not to be true, we'd still see all the money flow away from real rural communities to Silicon Valley and Wall Street nonetheless). We can sit by, in awe of the titans and their promises, as the climate, the rural economy, and consumer health turn out to be the big losers in this game. Or we can sit up and pay attention and do something different this time. Something radically traditional.

If a rural America full of factories generating food with robotic assistance is as unappealing to you as it is to me, then it's time to flex your power to help that from occurring. You do it by throwing your hat in the ring with the opposite team. Be the kind of person who is connected to their food and knows much more than your parents did about where it's sourced. You wouldn't buy a house without checking it out in person—why would the building blocks of your and your family's health be different? Get to know the people involved in raising your food. If farmers come to a market or co-op or food hub near you, that's a good way to start connecting. Start asking your friends who you know care about this where they buy their better food. Use a website like the ones listed in the Resources section of this book to find producers in your area who practice better methods. Or you can get acquainted with some regenerative producers online, read what they write themselves on their websites, and follow them on social media.

What I'd most like you to do is show up in person. Go visit the farms you want to buy from. Be involved. Make the effort. Look for places with open-door policies and run from those that don't. My motto at White Oak Pastures when it comes to production methods has always been "Don't do it if you're not willing to talk about it." So go ahead and ask your local farmer every question you've got. Ask to walk through closed gates and see behind closed doors. They might not be as ready as we are for an instant tour—we've got hosting visitors dialed in—but if you're genuinely interested, a farm with no secrets will bring you into the fold. We have never turned anybody away from White Oak Pastures, whether it was PETA or a writer with a strong opinion different from ours. We tried to invite Pat Brown, the CEO of Impossible Foods; we invited Bill Gates; we told Elon Musk on Instagram to come see how to capture carbon. None have come yet, but our offer still stands if Pat, Bill, or Elon want to take us up on it.

Here's an easy way to get the knowledge you need: task yourself with discovering what happens at each stage of the cycle of life on the farm—birth, growth, death, decay. Just going over those four, having the producer share what they do, will tell you much of what you need to know. Don't be shy. Curious and engaged consumers not only support the farmer, they incentivize him or her to hold to her side of the better-farming bargain. If you can't go visit the operation yourself—and don't be so quick to write that off; we get visitors from all over the country—then piggyback on the efforts of someone else. Look for hashtags on social media with the name of your farm. Other people may already be sharing their own findings. Pretty much any day of the year, we've got visitors doing their own due diligence here, touring our fields and facilities, including the kill floor and our cutting room. Or go ahead and make a phone call or ask your questions in an email. Farmers and producers aren't known for spending time at the desk, but many of them do want to communicate with customers and will respond.

Going all the way like this isn't convenient. I discovered that when I started switching our system. Giving up the glitz and the ease that seduced my daddy's generation and returning to a cyclical system was a helluva lot harder than staying in the status quo or than improving things "just enough." It certainly cost more to do it. But, ultimately, it was immensely more satisfying than doing things half-assed. It reconnected broken threads—to my heritage, to my land, to my livestock, and to other people. Should you, too, have the gumption to give up a little convenience, and a little of the fight in you to try for better food, I think you might find that reconnection, too.

If you are a farmer and producer wanting to change your farming method to regenerative, the reality is that you simply have to find a way. You can't just say, as I've been hearing said lately, that you just don't have the "bandwidth" to try new things. Admittedly, it takes three things to get a project off the ground: money, management, and time. And it's not the best two out of three. You need all three. So maybe that's the bandwidth people are talking about. But I'm hearing about too many bandwidth shortages these days. I think not having enough of it is analogous to *I don't have the ambition*. Or *I'm too lazy*. Or *I don't want to fuck with it*. This is not okay. Somehow you just have to get started, because the time to start figuring this all out is not in the midst of a crisis. That's too late. You don't go to the fight with what you want. You go to the fight with what you got. And you have to start developing experiential wisdom seasons, or years, before the shit hits the fan. (This applies whether you are starting a small garden at your home or an actual farm.) As you get started, find the people who've done it and are willing to share what they have learned with you. Connecting to our educational arm, CFAR, at White Oak Pastures, could be a way in. We can't tell you exactly *what to do*, step by step, on your land in your ecosystem. But we can teach you how to *think* about it in a new way and how to be that experiential scientist who discovers, through trial and error, what your land and farm truly need.

All of this inevitably brings up the question: What about the higher price of food from farms like mine? I don't have an easy answer to that one. I can't change the fact that when a farmer gives up the inputs and methods that take cost out of production, he or she adds cost back to their production. There's no way to avoid the reality that food from a resilient system costs more to the consumer than food from an efficient one. Truly grass-fed beef raised with good animal welfare might cost 30 percent more than industrial beef. Chicken raised the right way, currently, will have a much higher differential than that. Heritage pork from a regenerative and high-welfare operation like ours can be anything from 30 percent higher in cost than the so-called natural pork that gets sold in bulk at the average grocery store, which comes from animals raised in hellish, unnatural conditions, to significantly more than that if you're shopping for premium cuts or bacon and charcuterie. Only you can decide which types of foods you will prioritize in your weekly shopping, or how much higher-quality animal protein you choose to put in your daily menu alongside vegetables, fruits, and grains. In the longer term, and from a collective perspective, that money comes back in savings of preventing the high health costs from agricultural chemicals and from pollution, and in avoiding the catastrophic recovery costs from weather disasters, and saving the exorbitant cleanup costs from environmental destruction and the loss of productivity of the soils. But even that sound logic might not make it any easier on the pocketbook today. I can't fix economic disparity. I have figured out one part of the food production problem. Fixing these two gargantuan problems requires very different skill sets. What I do know is that if consumers stop mindlessly supporting a bad system and are educated enough to demand something better, it stands to reason that it could begin to shift the big ship's trajectory. But first, consumers have to decide.

In the meantime, let it be known that ordinary people can find ways to support small food systems. We certainly don't cater to the elite. We frequently get to meet the moms and dads, and the athletes and cops and teachers, and the students, nurses, and the like who buy our food. We also get to see inside *their* kitchens on social media, just as they see inside our farm. We've noticed a few commonalities in how they feed themselves and their families. Number one, they prioritize nutritious food as a core value in their lives, and save money for it by cutting out other more superficial lifestyle expenditures that don't deliver health. Almost all of them cook meals from scratch, a lot, saving on eating out, take-out, and processed foods. They have often returned to their roots, mastering the kind of old-school cooking my mama and grandmama did—stews, braises, broths, and soups—the kind that uses the cheaper cuts of meat and stretches that protein further. They eat proportionally, meaning they eat nose to tail—some days with highly affordable offal or a chicken soup loaded with vegetables and rice on the menu, then occasionally a higher-priced splurge of steak or duck.

There are other options to make eating from farms you know more cost effective, too. You can buy a share of a whole animal, which comes butchered and ready to store in the freezer. We sell a tremendous amount of what we call "cow kits"—an eighth of a cow, or a quarter, or a half. It helps us to move inventory in a balanced way, and helps the customer because it gives them a variety of cuts to enjoy at a cost savings from buying à la carte. Plenty of farmers across the country offer this service.

Sometimes, showing up in support of better food systems will require you to find the gift of fight in yourself. It's just so much easier to roll over and go back to autopilot. The temptation is all around you to comply with what's on offer. It takes more time, more effort, and more commitment to procure food this way than a weekly stop at the store. But as I said, struggle is part of the human condition. Without a little of it, we get weaker. Without challenge, we don't have enough stimulus to survive. We shrink as a species. So let your clarion call be the Harris family's best fighting words: *If you do what you've always done, you'll get what you've always got.* If you want to make a difference, see a difference, or feel a difference, does it make any sense that you can continue to operate in the same way you always have? Do it different. Get out of the armchair, get out on the land. Touch the dirt. Connect.

I don't know which way this thing is gonna go. We are hanging in the balance, wondering if the pendulum that has swung so far to the technological, industrial side is swinging back, or if it'll just keep swinging further to the side of more technology, more consolidation, and more transfer of land from families who know what to do with it to billionaires who, I am certain, do not. Of these two options, we have bet everything that it's not the latter one. I am not saying we have reached the ultimate regenerative and resilient model at White Oak Pastures. We are still evolving. It was a big flex to get from überindustrial to this, and it's a good start. I hope when I've gone, my children continue to evolve what I started, returning to the more natural way.

I am goddamned tired of hearing "You can't feed the world with your regenerative system." It's flawed logic. For one thing, we aren't trying to feed the whole world; we are trying to feed our communities and in so doing show how an alternative system to the extractive model can exist. This alternative can exist, and replicate, and grow only if people participate in it. I'm not trying to save the world. But I'm damn sure saving White Oak Pastures. Maybe the folks who are trying to save the world can pick up some hints and clues.

Should you make it to Bluffton one day, there are a few things you should know. You will have to prepare to embrace the bounty because you might get a few things you didn't expect, like reptiles, rodents, and insects, and relentless humidity and unbelievably drenching rain. And there are a few phrases you might want to jot down to help communications with us natives run smoother. For example, "Hey, y'all" means "You are very welcome here." "How y'all?" means "I am really glad that you are here." "Help y'all?" means "Can I do anything at all for you while you are here?" And "Who y'all" means "You need to leave here. Right now." As long as you are cordial and gracious, and not too fussy about heat, humidity, and a slower pace of life, I'm sure we won't need to exchange but the first three.

What I hope you take away from your visit is not just knowing me, your farmer, and those who make White Oak Pastures the holistic organism it is. I hope you also get to know a part of yourself you might have gotten separated from, too. Being in a place where the cycles of nature are really rocking, full tilt, has a profound effect. It switches on the part of you that's a little wilder, a little more atavistic. *Atavistic* is one of those words I like to use a lot, without realizing that almost no one actually knows what it means. I looked it up in the dictionary. The definition reads, "The reappearance in an individual of characteristics of some remote ancestor that have been absent in intervening generations." Being a throwback, in other words, to a type of person who used their senses to be connected to their surroundings. Who isn't all up in their head. I know I'm designed that way—my cowboys will ask me how I can see what's about to go awry in a pasture hours or days before anyone else. I tell them it's not a special sixth sense; it's just that I've spent so long in the fields and forests, I am deeply grounded in the normal. When the slightest thing changes, it stands out to me with a crudeness that is unmissable, like a dime-size spot of mustard on a fashion model's face. I believe the people who have, or who cultivate, this sensitivity, who are more feral and less bookish, will be the ones to lead us out of this mess. And when you come to my farm, or Gabe's farm, or any one of those who are working with nature, not against it, the more feral side of you will come out. That's a very good thing, because you'll quickly develop the capacity to recognize what good food production looks like—it will start to attract you, while the damaging farming will repel you. It might also remind that ancestral part of you why it matters so much to preserve the rural. We screwed up when we destroyed the wilderness. We still got some time on the rural.

There's an old saying that goes "Good things happen to good people." I'm not sure I believe that. But I do think that good things happen when you do what's good for your farm. Because the truth is I don't do any of this for our customers, though I'm very grateful for their support. I don't even do it for the greater movement of regenerative farming, though I'm glad it is coming up. I do what I do here because I love the land and the animals, just like some people love music or art. They are my passion; I'd steward them whether it paid me or not. Which is good because everything here is a work in progress. The to-do list is freaking incredible. Sometimes, I just have to say, "We've been doing this 157 years; if we can't get on it today, we'll probably get on it tomorrow."

Acknowledgments

For conceiving the idea for this book, I am grateful to Tess Callero and Marc Gerald of Europa Content. Who the hell would have ever dreamt that anyone would want to read a book about an irreverent and profane family of farmers in South Georgia who are known to drink too much, talk too loud, and play to win? Tess and Marc did.

For writing this book, I am grateful to Amely Greeven. It took the patience of a saint to listen to many hours of my rambling recollections, opinions, and observations. It took incredible organizational skills to transform my never-ending, cyclical, random thoughts into a linear story that was tellable. And I don't know what it took for an English-raised, California-residing, forty-something-year-old woman to learn and interpret the language of a sixty-something-year-old profoundly southern cowboy.

For getting this book over the finish line, I am grateful to Emily Wunderlich. I don't think that there are many editors who could find a way to market a book that is based on experiential wisdom in a time when the greater public worships at the altar of reductive science.

For putting up with my other shortcomings, which are too many to list, I am grateful to the cowboys, butchers, and farmers of White Oak Pastures. My friends, we have worked hard and risked much to build something unique here. There ain't another one like it right now. There's no damn doubt about that. I know that y'all are just as proud of it as I am. We all hope that there will be many others in the future.

Resources

If what you have read has inspired you to seek food from farms and ranches like ours, there's a world of ways to get started.

Our Farm

You can buy food from our farm—if you live in the parts of the continental US to which we currently ship. Please visit our website, white oakpastures.com to discover more. We would love you to visit us in Bluffton and buy directly from our store—we have plenty of farm-stay cabins if you want to stay a night or three. Signing up for our newsletter is a great way to stay in the loop of special products and offers, and following us on social media will keep you apprised of all the latest happenings here in Bluffton.

Our Friends

We are proud of the relationships we have with the producers who raise livestock similar to ours. Their production systems mirror their environment and ecosystem, and so may be distinct from ours, but we have visited them and have seen firsthand the care they put into their production systems. There are too many good folks to name, but you should consider getting to know Gabe Brown of Brown's Ranch (https://brownsranch.us), Greg Gunthorp of Gunthorp Farms (https://gunthorpfarms.com), Carrie Richards of Richards Grassfed Beef (https://richardsgrassfedbeef.com), and the Alexandres of Alexandre Family Farms (https://alexandrefamilyfarm.com). All these folks not only raise livestock and sell meat and poultry but also do a tremendous amount of education that they openly share with their customers and followers.

In the Stores

The packaging you might see at your local grocery store—even the high-end stores—or online retailers does not always guide you right. Many of the most widely used marketing terms lack clear standards, verification processes, or independent oversight, allowing farm conditions to vary widely across producers. Take the term *grass-fed*. The USDA used to have a definition of this term, but it does not legally stand now, so producers can put it on their meat without anyone checking up on them about the practices they follow.

Marketing terminology can be woefully unhelpful, or even deliberately confounding, on other animal food products as well. On egg cartons, the words *cage free* do not connote that anything good has occurred—the poultry are typically still raised in crowded indoor warehouses—and *free range* may mean they had access to a concrete outdoor patch through small, rarely used doors, not the meadows a consumer may expect. Even the term *pasture raised* can be misused, as it is not regulated. On pork products, the words *natural, vegetarian fed, humane/humanely raised,* or *no antibiotics* tend to mean little. These are unregulated terms, and federal regulations prohibit the use of hormones in raising pork or chicken anyway—so using them on pork products simply adds a halo effect of virtue.

Do not conflate the USDA ORGANIC stamp with good welfare or regenerative practices that heal the cycles of nature. While there are some very good practitioners of organic farming, the vast majority of USDA Organic products come from the industrial organic system... and industrial is industrial. Organic milk, for example, typically comes from mama cows confined indoors for most of their lives, and cruelly stripped of their calves. *Grass-fed milk* is supposed to signal that cows live fully outside unless inclement weather drives them inside. Some new certification seals exist to help consumers know what they are getting. The word *regenerative* is also becoming used more widely today. There is no legal standard for that word either.

As for the large online retailers of better meats and products, even the flashiest websites and brands require coolheaded review. Greenwashing is rampant and there are no penalties for misrepresenting what they sell.

Certifications

Some people are fans of using certification seals to guide their shopping. If you are one of those people, our friends at the American Grassfed Association (AGA) (https://www.americangrassfed.org) have a good program certifying ruminants, pork, and dairy producers who meet higher standards. AGA performs audits every fifteen months to ensure that the farms they certify really do what they say they do. The various certifications from the group A Greener World (https://agreenerworld.org), including their Animal Welfare Approved label, also require inspections of a farm's practices. The Certified Humane seal involves similar on-site inspections of welfare practices (https://certifiedhumane.org). So does the Global Animal

Partnership, which I recommend looking at only for farms that reach Step 4, 5, and above (https://globalanimalpartnership.org). The Savory Institute's Land to Market Verification Initiative label requires providers to show scientific outcome verification of regenerative farming processes (https://www.landtomarket.com).

Give some of these websites a thorough read to educate yourself about standards and certifications. But please be aware that certifications are not the holy grail—good practices in one area (animal welfare for example) do not mean good practices in all of them (like land management), so you still have to use your own discernment. Many, many good farmers choose not to become members of certification projects because of cost or other factors. Some have them one year, then not the next, because circumstances and financial factors have changed on their farm.

Finding Your Farmer

Terms and standards will constantly evolve. Certifications will work for some producers and not others. To our mind, there is no substitute for knowing your farmer. Nothing can take the place of a relationship. So how do you create that relationship? With a little time and effort.

Finding local farmers, ranchers, and food producers who practice methods you feel good about supporting might require some digging—this is the opposite of the centralized system, after all. Remember that locating a farm is just the start of the fun: you want to get a look inside the operation. Talking with the farmers directly is a good start—ask questions about their practices, and how they treat the land, the animals, and the people who work for them—and you can start to decide if their values line up with yours. (This is not about seeking perfection; it's about aligning with what you decide matters most.)

Start with the obvious: your local farmers markets. Vegetable/fruit producers will far outnumber meat, poultry, and dairy producers, but someone from all the food groups will likely be represented. Search Local Harvest (https://localharvest.org) to find farmers markets near you, as well as other options like CSA programs that let you subscribe to a local farm's seasonal offerings. This supports them to keep going. The National Farmers Market Directory (https://nfmd.org) will also help you find options near you. The farmers themselves may not be the ones working the booths, but you can find out a lot by just asking questions.

Ask your friends whether they already have leads on local producers who follow better methods. Post a question on online community forums, parenting groups, and the like. Ask your local food co-op or independent grocery or health food store, or even healthy café or restaurant, who they order from. Chances are they will already be carrying products from nearby producers that they know a lot about. Talk to the people responsible for stocking the shelves.

There are growing numbers of online databases and platforms for connecting consumers to independent farms, genuine pasture-raised producers, and specialty butchers. Note, these websites typically *do not check* if what a farm or producer is telling them is true. They may include all kinds of farms following different practices, some of which you may not want to support. The farms can describe themselves as they wish. Consider them a resource to start your search. Use them to get to know what's local to you, then use what you've learned in this book to dive deeper into asking about and understanding the producer's methods.

Eatwild (https://eatwild.com)

American Grassfed Association database of Certified producers (https://www.americangrassfed.org/aga-membership/producer-members)

Organic Consumers Association (https://organicconsumers.org/regenerative-farm-map/)

Good Meat Breakdown (https://www.goodmeatbreakdown.org) includes a switchboard run by the Good Meat Project to connect consumers to small farmers and butchers as well as to post jobs and ask for help in production. The site shares multiple ways for consumers to procure meat outside the industrial system. Their website has gathered a group of online databases to help you on your search. Just please remember to use this as a jumping-off point, then dive in with your curiosity and questions. Here are a few of the databases it lists:

Near Home by Ground Work
(https://nearhome.groundworkcollective.com)

Get Real Chicken
(https://www.getrealchicken.com/find-a-farmer)

Niche Meat Processor Assistance Network
(https://www.nichemeatprocessing.org/consumer-resources)

Local Catch Network (seafood)
(https://localcatch.org)

American Indian Foods
(https://www.indianagfoods.org/producers)

Food Animal Concerns Trust (FACT)
(https://www.foodanimalconcernstrust.org)

American Society for the Prevention of Cruelty to Animals
(ASPCA)
(https://www.aspca.org/shopwithyourheart/consumer
-resources/certified-farms-state)

SoilCentric
(https://www.soilcentric.org)

Other Regenerative Resources:

The Savory Institute
(https://savory.global)

American Council on Rural Special Education (ACRES)
(https://www.acresusa.com)

Farmer's Footprint
(https://farmersfootprint.us)